A Handbook of Legal Education in Nigeria

A Handbook of Legal Education in Nigeria

Professor Festus Emiri

malthouse MP

Malthouse Press Limited

Lagos, Benin, Ibadan, Jos, Port-Harcourt, Zaria

Malthouse Press Limited
43 Onitana Street, Off Stadium Hotel Road,
Surulere, Lagos, Lagos State
E-mail: malthouselagos@gmail.com
Tel: +234 (0)802 600 3203

Distributors:

African Books Collective Ltd
Email: abc@africanbookscollective.com
Website: http://www.africanbookscollective.com

Dedication

This book is dedicated to all my colleagues teaching Law as an academic subject, as well as my students over the years.

Acknowledgements

I should like to acknowledge the direct and indirect contributions of my teachers, colleagues and students to my intellectual development.

Preface

This book is on the nature and practice of legal education in Nigeria, with comparative material sometimes deployed to shed light on current local situation. The primary goal of legal education is to prepare students for the profession. To do this, a faculty will need to pay attention to a theory of learning to guide it in implementing a programme that will serve the mission. It is hoped that the basic information here provided on the basic structure and content of legal education and ensuing challenges should point in more fruitful directions to all in the legal profession in Nigeria.

Contents

Chapter 1

Politics of Teaching and Learning

Introduction

It is likely that the reader of this book is a law teacher, or someone interested in legal education. If you are we congratulate you because you are one of the few that take interest in how teaching and learning in our faculties of law and law schools can be effective in delivering educational goals. Sadly, the majority of law teachers are anti-intellectual about their primary professional concern, namely interrogating the content and method of legal education.[1] This unsatisfactory situation is described by Jay Feinman and Marc Feldman this way:

> "Most legal educators are anti-intellectual about the area of their primary professional concern: the content and method of legal education. This anti-intellectualism is characterized by an unwillingness to reflect on the goals of legal education, the content of the curriculum, the methods of teaching, and the ability of law school graduates to practice law competently. At most law schools, the purposes and methods of teaching are regarded as unfruitful, if not unfit, topics for conversation. Of almost 200 journals of legal scholarship, only one regularly addresses legal education itself. The little discussion and sparse literature that does exist is mostly anecdotal or platitudinous."[2]

If that describes the position in America thirty years ago, the situation is not any better in Nigeria. Law teachers have exhibited lack of interest in their primary professional calling. The umbrella body of law teachers, the Nigerian Association of Law Teachers (NALT) has not for once interrogated teaching pedagogy since its existence in 1963. Rather its annual themes have centred on economy, rule of law, national unrest, anti-corruption, etc., topics more congruent for the Bar to interrogate.[3] May be this is attributable partly to the fact that many in the

---

[1] Jay Feinman & Marc Feldman, Pedagogy and Politics (1984-1985) 73 *Geo. L. J.* 876.

[2] Ibid.

[3] Only the 2013 NALT Conference in Ado-Ekiti, Ekiti State, interrogated in a limited way the question of effective teaching and law in legal education.

academia take more concern in legal practice than in the business of teaching. It is thus possible to be infested with the practitioners' mindset.[4] No journal interrogates teaching pedagogy in law, not even the Nigerian Law Journal (NLJ) published by NALT.[5] The faculties' journals are no better. Not even the Journal of the Council of Legal Education addresses issues of pedagogy.[6]

This posture is not surprising. The "publish or perish" mantra of law teaching diverts attention from teachers' primary professional responsibility. It is suggested that this orientation by the academia is heightened by fear of confrontation of its belief structure that questioning teaching pedagogy would resurrect a flood gate for interrogating the entire edifice of legal education with adverse consequences for status quo. A conspiracy of unreflective silence is imagined to better settle the inquiry. What mistake. Concerns about legal education can no longer be met with apathy by the academia. Not only are people increasingly questioning the competence and character of the practitioner, laying the blame at the doorsteps of educators, even members of the legal profession are showing dissatisfaction with how faculties train would be members of the profession.[7] Growing dissatisfaction with legal education is widespread. All of this must be turned around.

The primary goal of legal education is to prepare students for the profession. To do this, a faculty will need a pay attention to a theory of learning to guide it in implementing a programme that will serve the mission. This theory must be systematic, conceptual, and rigorous.[8] Unfortunately, law teachers' think that educational researchers and theorists are a bunch of charlatans that can contribute little or nothing to legal education. They are therefore content and comfortable with their pedagogy, measuring their success against the backdrop of students they graduate year after year. Typically, the law teacher is satisfied if on graduation a few students excel, others fumble and wobble through, and some fail. Such

---

[4] There is ongoing debate about the desirability of law teacher practicing law. See however, Nuno Garoupa & Thomas S. Ulen, The Market for Legal Innovative: Law and Economics in Europe and the United States, Illinois Law and Economics Working Papers Series Research Paper No. LE07-009, available at http://papers.ssrn.com/paper.tar/abstract, accessed on 12 May 2015 ("A very important aspect of the legal academic market in the U.S. that differentiate it from . . other countries has to do with salary and the terms and conditions of employment. . . . By custom, university statute, and legislation, U.S. professors are typically supposed to limit their outside consulting activity to one day per week during the academic year, which usually run from early September through early May. For law professors in the U.S. the upshot of this restriction is that there is a relatively strong wall separating the practice of law from the practice of being a legal scholar. . . (they) are expected to be researchers, teachers, and colleagues first and foremost, and to keep their outside business interests at a minimum.)" see also my Ado-Ekiti lecture.

[5] Recently a few tangential articles show a legal education bent. See for example, the Proceeding of Annual Retreat of the Nigerian Law School, 2014

[6] Mention attempts at annual teachers' retreat and some concern expressed by the NBA Section on legal education.

[7] Refer to Carnegie and the like. NBA needs assessment.

[8] Jay Feinman & Marc Feldman, Pedagogy and Politics (1984-1985) 73 Geo. L. J. 876 at 895.

satisfaction is dangerous for education because it set the threshold too low and fossilize students' capacity for optimal performance. It assumes that natural abilities of students cannot change by adopting even effective teaching and learning techniques. It is commonplace to hear teachers attribute failure of law students to students' disinterest in learning. While not wanting to trade the blame-game here, we must state that with a little more investment of time and resources than is now expended, a learning environment would be created where virtually all students can and will learn well and possibly pass well also.

According to Feinman and Feldman, the concept of achievable, widespread excellence is known as "mastery learning".[9] The theory debunks the customary belief that students' different capacities is the reason for sorting of large numbers of students according to their ability, and that it is not the fault of the faculty that some just don't learn and do well. The Darwinian theory of immutable ability is simply false assumption made prevailing by society and its infrastructure for supporting hierarchy. The immutable ability concept is evil because it supports social institutions that prevent the full development of human potentials and conscript freedom of excelling. It is further false because mastery learning and several studies show that widely distributed learning outcomes are more a bye-product of ineffective teaching than of the abilities of the students.[10] The essence of mastery learning is that faculties must move away from the idea of providing students equal opportunity for their natural ability will result in natural stratified outcome. Rather it suggests that faculties can achieve substantial equality of educational outcomes by providing an educational environment that provides students with the resources and the situations with which they can best learn. When done, nearly all students can achieve mastery, not minimum competence. After all, in law, most of our students are well motivated. That was why they chose the course in the first place. It is the not so good grades and the learning environment that turns their energy away from law into extracurricular and non-curricular activities in the midstream of their legal education.

This is a modest goal for any good faculty interested in training students with mastery of the law. The task isn't that daunting as some may imagine, neither does it require a foundational makeover and overthrow of traditional teaching pedagogy. Mastery learning employs a large percentage of traditional teaching

---

[9] Mastery learning is a philosophy of schooling and instructional strategy rooted in the concept that the majority of students can be trained to be competent performers. Benjamin Bloom mastery learning standard is that learning is effective only if eighty percent of the learners learn eighty percent of the material. See, Benjamin Bloom, *Human Characteristics and School Learning,* 1976; Benjamin Bloom, Mastery Learning: Theory and Practice, in J. Block, ed. 1971; J. Block & L. Anderson, *Mastery Learning in Classroom Instruction,* 1975; B. Bloom, *Our Children Learning,* 1981, all cited in Feinman & Feldman, at 896.
[10] Feinman & Feldman, above n. 8 at 897

methodology. But it goes beyond it. It requires that the teacher be more explicit and systematic about what is learned and assert more control over how it is learned.

Four steps of implementation are recommended, namely: defined objectives and formulation of learning units; formative evaluation; development of alternative learning resources; and final evaluation and grading.

This book sets out to discuss how teaching and learning in faculties of law and law schools can be improved and effective in training students. Many of its suggestion may appear not doable by traditionalists. That is understandable. Confronting as this book does dominant orthodoxy and consciousness is itself a threat to law curriculum and the way some teachers constitute their self-identities, consciousness. Professional identity and the circumstances in which people operate create social hierarchy. Law teachers interact with colleagues, students, and other under the dominant ideology of correctness, so a challenge to that ideology would invariably translate to challenging the very essence of her social hierarchy. Strong reaction and resistance is change is to be expected. The good thing however is that the academy can no longer resist change. Change is here for good. The sooner the academy pays attention to educational theories and studies for effective teaching and learning, the better it will be for all stakeholders in the business of legal education.

In addition to this change may be resisted because the law academy encourages implicit sticking to the old method. The "publish or perish" mantra for law teachers is itself an academic policy that discounts innovation. Promotion and hire depends not on how effective a teacher is, but on number and quality of publications. Ranking of faculties rarely consider teaching skills or effectiveness. What counts more is faculty publication. Thus, law teachers have incentive to be minimally competent teachers and excellent scholars.[11] Also, the pressures to conform instructional format with laid down faculty or institutional regulations could constrain a teacher exploring innovative teaching techniques.[12]

Despite the present lockdown in law instructional pedagogy of dubious merit, we must congratulate the few teachers and faculties that are developing insightful experimental instructions and sound andragogy scholarship in the field of learning theory and instructional design to improve our teaching education.

As this chapter was concluding I received a message from my dear friend on WhatsApp worth sharing as it emphasizes the role teachers play in society.[13] It is said to be a quote by Dr. Ben Carson. It states:

---

[11] Michael H. Schwartz, Teaching Law by Design: How Learning Theory and Instructional Design Can Inform and Reform Law Teaching (2001) 38 *San Diego L. Rev* 347 at 360.

[12] Ibid.

[13] Message from Dr. Ayuba Giwa, received August 15, 2017.

"When the ancient Chinese decided to live in peace, they made the Great Wall of China. They thought no one can climb it due to its height. During the first 100 years of its existence, the Chinese were invaded thrice. ... And every time, the hordes had no need of penetrating or climbing over the wall...because each time they bribed the guards and came through the doors. The Chinese built the wall but forgot the character-building of wall-guards. Thus, the building of human character comes before building of anything else...That's what our children (students) need today. Like one of the Orientalists said: if you want to destroy the civilization of a nation there are three ways. Destroy family structure. Destroy education. Lower their role models and reference. In order to destroy the family, undermine the role of the mother, so that she feels ashamed of being a housewife. To destroy education, you should give no importance to teacher, and lower his place in society so as that the students despise him. To lower the role model, you should undermine the scholars, doubt them until no one listens to them or follow them. For when a conscious mother disappears, a dedicated teacher disappears and there's a downfall of role models, who will teach the youngsters value?"[14]

Contextualized to legal education, it demands of us teachers to pay due attention to our primary professional responsibility by striving to do the hundred and one things necessary to effectively teach and enhance learning of our students.

---

[14] Dr. Ben Carson

Chapter 2

Cognition and Learning Theories

Introduction

Legal education has largely been introspective. Law teachers have ever doubted that legal education pedagogy can benefit from advances from other discipline. This is understandable. Lawyers for decades have striven to protect the majesty of law from all invading army of knowledge. Talk like 'law is an autonomous discipline,' 'it is the only learned profession' are commonplace among lawyers. That probably explains why legal education over the years have not thought it fit to interrogate and examine the ontological security of law, rather the profession has sought to run away from it by turning to epistemological security for refuge in answering fundamental questions of ontology.[1] This strategy for securing the laws' empire heightens the resistance of legal education to learning from theories of learning that are beneficial to training of its professionals. Generally, law teachers with the traditional-autonomous mindset are comfortable with their curriculum design and teaching methodology not minding emerging cognitive developments in science, education and learning. It is therefore not surprising if legal education pedagogy has not benefited much from the cognitive science. For many lawyers and legal educators', it is not easily conceivable how cognitive science interacts with law, talk more of legal education in ways that can improve the teaching pedagogy of law.[2]

The history of education teaches one basic fact: education, and invariably, learning has long suffered from the resistance of education to advance and changes. For example, when printing was invented in the fifteenth century, medieval universities were skeptical of mechanical printing fearing it would degrade monastic education and possibly destroy academic tutelage with the then

---

[1] Pierre Schlag, Hiding the Ball (1996) 71 *New York U. L. Rev.* 1681 ("in truth, this question about the identity of the authoritative legal sources-this ontological question-is rarely posed. It is one that resists inquiry. If we were to answer this ontological question, we must first try to understand the nature of the resistance that the inquiry confronts. If the question confronts resistance, it is because legal actors and legal thinkers have been trained to refrain from pursuing that inquiry.") at 1683.

[2] Goerge Lakoff, Cognitive Science and the Law (article showing that since law is committed to the use of human reason and human language it cannot afford to dispense with development of the cognitive science where language and thought are empirically studied. For legal analysis see, Steven Winter, The Metaphor of Standing and the Problem of Self-Governance (1988) 10 (6) *Stanford L. Rev.* 1371; Steven Winter, Transcendental Nonsense; Steven Winter, The Cognitive Dimension of the Agon.

Socratic independent inquiry associated with it.[3] You may think that is over 600 years ago. Things are not that bad today. That is mistaken. [Give example from the Montessori type of learning]

Even today, despite the significant advances in theories of learning, law teachers still teach much as their own teachers did decades ago. Law faculties are dominated by teachers who continue to depend on rigorous lectures and instruction in doctrine, legal concepts, and the like with little teaching on skills and professional responsibility, thereby turning out students that are not client-ready for the profession. At the end of the lecture exercise, the teacher is tired and her students are fatigued, having learnt only a little.[4] What is more, law teachers have remained largely oblivious of the cognitive science and its usefulness in unveiling emerging techniques of harnessing brainpower.[5] Traditional law school pedagogy is acknowledge to create barriers to learning because it is not responsive to law students' learning processes, so its pedagogy may be a major reason for the lack of correlation between student effort and performance because it does not explicitly provide a context for understanding, analyzing, and applying legal concepts.[6]

The profession however has no choice but advance in learning. Like a commentator put it, since law teachers are thinkers and communicators who train students expected to succeed in the new, highly competitive global economy by their ability to analyze and articulate better than other professionals, law faculties come under an obligation not to neglect how new forms of gathering, organizing and disseminating information which will improve legal education.[7] This chapter sets out to examine how law teaching, and in fact the legal profession can benefit from insights to how the brain works to better capture human learning. The concern here is to provide teachers a basic understanding of these theories of

---

[3] Deborah J. Merritt, Legal Education in the Age of Cognitive Science and Advanced Classroom Technology, [2007] Public Law & Legal Theory Working Paper Series No. 94; Centre for Interdisciplinary Law & Policy Studies Series No. 63, Ohio State University. See also Bernard J. Hibbets, Yesterday Once More: Skeptics, Scribes, and the Demise of Law Review (1996) 30 *Akron L. Rev.* 267 at 268-272, cited by Merritt.

[4] Lakoff, *op. cit.,* above n.2.

[5] For example, Maureen Fitzgerald noted of American law schools that "the use of theories about teaching and learning is seriously lacking in law school...Law faculty tends to gravitate toward the case-method and large-group forum, only rarely introducing innovative teaching methods. Although several universities acknowledge that different teaching methodologies should be used, in practice, the introduction of new teaching methodologies has been extremely slow." See Maureen F. Fitzgerald, What's Wrong with Legal Research and Writing? Problems and Solution (1996) 88 *Law Lib. J.* 247 at 259.

[6] Paula Lustbader, Construction Sites, Building Types, and Building Gaps: A Cognitive Theory of the Learning Progression of Law Students (1997) 33 *Willamette L. Rev.* 317.

[7] Deborah J. Merritt, Legal Education in the Age of Cognitive Science and Advanced Classroom Technology, [2007] Public Law & Legal Theory Working Paper Series No. 94; Centre for Interdisciplinary Law & Policy Studies Series No. 63, Ohio State University.

teaching and learning so that they can make informed choices about how best to proceed with the business of teaching. It therefore sets out both theories of learning and models for effective teaching.[8]

A. Learning Component
1. Theories of Learning
There is no question about it. The primary goal of legal education is to train students to enter the profession of law, with the requisite knowledge of law, professional skills and values to be effective and ethical practitioners. Researchers identify four key theories that can enhance learning. They are (i) cognitive psychology, (ii) intellectual development. (iii) learning styles, and (iv) character of adult learners.[9]

Cognitive Psychology
Cognitive scientists using brain mapping have made vital contribution to learning theory.[10] Cognitive psychology is concerned with explaining the mental process, especially how it works in connection with memory, decision-making, and problem-solving. The goal of the science being to illuminate comprehension and knowledge to enhance meaningful learning. In pursuing the goals, the science has focused primarily on how the brain processes information, the structure of knowledge, the process of thinking about thinking itself, often referred to as metacognition, and how social interaction affect the cognitive process.

How the Brain Processes Information
Teachers need to learn new methods of harnessing the brain to work harder and smarter, such as the synergy between the two-brain hemisphere, the limitations on working memory and the importance of personal interaction between teacher and student.

---

[8] For general concerns about how the legal academy ignores learning theories and so adversely affects students with individual or group peculiarities see, Carrie Menkel-Meadow, Feminist Legal Theory, Critical Legal Studies, and Legal Education or The Fem-Crits Go to Law School (1988) 38 *J. Leg. Educ.* 61; Deborah L. Rhodes, Missing Questions: Feminist Perspectives on Legal Education (1993) 45 *Stan. L. Rev.* 1547; Kiberl C. Williams Crenshaw, Foreword. Toward a Race-Conscious Pedagogy in Legal Education (1989) 11*Nat'l. Black L.J.* 1(discussing the problems created by a pedagogy that assuming an objective perspective which is often white, middle-class coloured).

[9] Gerald F. Hess & Steven Friedland, *Techniques for Teaching Law,* North Carolina: Durham: Carolina Academic Press, 1999, 3.

[10] Deborah J. Merritt, Legal Education in the Age of Cognitive Science and Advanced Classroom Technology, (2008) 14 *B.U.J. Sci. & Tech. L.* 40. [2007] Public Law & Legal Theory Working Paper Series No. 94; Centre for Interdisciplinary Law & Policy Studies Series No. 63, Ohio State University. See also Bernard J. Hibbets, Yesterday Once More: Skeptics, Scribes, and the Demise of Law Review (1996) 30 *Akron L. Rev.* 267 at 268-272, cited by Merritt.

Brain two divisions: The human brain has two halves, the left and right brain parts. The left hemisphere generally processes linear, sequential information while the right concentrates on patterns and connections. The left hemisphere for example, helps a person to predict that the numbers after 1 are 2 and 3, etc. In like manner, the right enables a person to correlate the connection between concepts. That being so, the left analyses the piece (e.g. the particular class topic, say consideration as an element of contract), while the right synthesizes the big picture (how consideration could shade into promissory estoppel etc.). So, in a subject like mathematics, the left side does all the data transmission and statistics, while the right part interprets that linear information in context of its applicability. That being so, total learning must draw on both parts of the brain.

Unfortunately, much of legal education transmitted through the prevalent lecture or seminar style, or the Socratic interrogation method simply concentrates on doctrinal exposition which only engages the left-brain hemisphere. The absence of skills and values components leaves untapped the right brain potentials, which comes with the benefits of integrating concepts, perceiving connections and other sophisticated forms of analysis and performance.[11] . Because of the right brain penchant and ability to draw meaning from pictures and diagrams in interpreting context and patterns, it helps deepen learning and understanding. It is therefore mistaken to associate pictures with elementary education.[12]

Left-brain education dominance comes with heavy costs to the profession. Recent quarrels with pedagogy emphasising doctrinal learning to the exclusion of skills and values have created a situation where would-be-lawyers are not client-ready, necessitating call for the infusion of professionalism in legal education.[13]

Legal education must strive to engage both hemispheres in the learning process. Recognizing the vital role both hemispheres play in legal education holds a key insight for law teaching. It must cover the gamut of lecture, solo reading, student-participation, performance, law clinic and simulation. It requires the integration of linear left brain thinking with the integrative thinking that the right

---

[11] Jack A. Hiller & Bernhard Grossfeld, Comparative Legal Semiotics and the Divided Brain: Are We Producing Half-Brained Lawyers? (2002) 50 *Am. J. Comp. L.* 175.

[12] Michael Macaulay & Ioanna Pantazi, Material Difficulty and the Effectiveness of Multimedia in Learning (2006) *33 Int'l. J. Instructional Media* 187 (states that multimedia presentation helps student learn difficult materials and boost long-term memory recollection). See also, Peter B. Bensinger, Jr., Magazine Briefs, A-Z Consultants at peter.bensinger@bartlit-beck.com ("when you learn something complicated, it is a lot easier to look at pictures. Often the most persuasive evidence in any jury trial is the demonstrative-the photo, the diagram, the blow up of the document with the key phrases highlighted. Yet when it comes to time to persuade a judge, the traditional legal brief is just words, no pictures. A picture is worth a thousand words. Even with a judge.)" this is said to be the "show, don't tell" approach to briefs.

[13] Carnegie Report.

brain controls. Sadly, as the legal academy continually expands law curricula and doctrinal components of learning,[14] it drifts further away from harnessing right brain training. This challenge should be met head-on by refocusing not in content expansion but by tilting legal training away from liberal studies to training in professionalism.[15]

Memory Components: Cognitivist tell us that most humans can only pay attention to one thing at a time and that memory capacity for holding new information is fragile. Memory can only accommodate few new concepts in a short time span. Memory becomes stable when the information is stored in the long memory store. This explains why rote memorizing learning will not likely reach long term memory and be meaningful in learning, especially if new concepts are linked to a framework. Some young one learning the alphabets can memorize A-Z, but when called upon to even identify say alphabet K they would simply not know it. Since lawyers must be trained to not only know concepts but also know how to use them in problem-solving, legal educators must pay attention to how to link the short-term (working memory) and long-term memory for effective and meaningful transmission of knowledge, skills and values.

The human brain is like desktop computer with two types of memory: working memory and long-term memory. Sadly, the former is not only fragile, but is small. It can only hold about seven pieces of information simultaneously.[16] But it is the gatekeeper. All information must pass through it to reach the long-term memory. It is the computer RAM that can only retain information for twenty seconds. That explains why as children we constantly do rehearsal aloud when sent on errands to prevent us from forgetting details of errands. Adult also use it as technique to master new telephone number. On the other hand, the latter (long-term memory) which holds recollection and accumulated knowledge is vast.

This being the case, the limitation of working memory can pose challenges to legal education. Its limitation demands that novel information should be transmitted in small bits. Here is the challenge for law. The subject is not only novel to our students, it is sometimes complex and voluminous. Transmitting information in structure that is minute is not a characteristic of law teachers. In

---

[14] In recent years NUC BMAS has added many humanities subjects. See Ado how it can be made sensible. Increased content in legal education comes from many sources. Law itself grows. Globalization. Regulatory bodies. Fancies of teachers. The combination of these trends creates unmanageable amount of information that teachers attempt to transmit for absolution by students.

[15] P.A. Jones, Theory and Practice in Professional Education (2000), 7 *Int. J. Legal Profession*, 239

[16] Merritt, above n. 8, 45, citing as authority John Sweller, Implications of Cognitive Load Theory for Multimedia Learning in Richard E. Mayer, ed., *Cambridge Handbook of Multimedia Learning*, 2005.

fact, teachers rarely contemplate the constraints posed by working memory, even though this an inherent brain structure.

Effective learning demands that teachers work within the constrain of human memory by learning to keep teaching within the narrow capacity in the following ways: (i) when complex and difficult materials are to be presented, the teacher should use both verbal and visual communication techniques synergistically,[17] (ii) reduce class distraction if complex materials are to be discussed. Class distraction in this respect include even benign distractions such as jokes, tangential information, stories and the like. While these embellishments have their place,[18] they attract attention from the complex and overtask the working memory if a teacher is to transmit difficult material; (iii) the bridge between working and long-term memory can be narrowed if new information is related to information already in stored long-term memory. This works well because studies suggest that the ability of the working memory to recall information from long-term memory is much larger than its capacity to hold same. This is so because long term memory organises information into schemas (a group of information clusters), which working memory treats as single information that can be manipulated or examined. For example, once the teacher completes teaching the ingredients of an express trust: (analogical to the essential of a contract: offer, acceptance, consideration and evidence of seriousness) it becomes easy for the student to build these cluster into a schema, essentials for an express trust, that their working memory can now treat as single information to understand (with less confusion) why similar rules do not apply to implied trust. That is how it works. So, the teacher can make her students progressive and effective learners by helping them to draw new information into working memory as they organize data stored in long-memory as schema to be recalled to supplement new information. As schema grow and combine into larger clusters, working memory can handle increased information within the narrow confines of working memory. The simple law teacher's key is relating new concepts to ideas previously learned.[19]

Discoveries about the capacity of human memory offers several lessons for legal education. Legal concepts are highly complex, requiring simultaneous attention to the facts of controversy, the legal procedure underlying resolution of the controversy, the substantive law governing it, distillation of ratio and obiter and several other nuances, which are by no means easy to grasp in one go. What

---

[17] Macaulay & Pantazi, above n. 12, 47.

[18] They could recreate classroom environment and make it conducive for learning. See discussion on classroom environment at.

[19] Above n.12 at 46.

this invariable mean is that law school instruction probably exceeds students' memory capacity, a challenge heightened by the fact that teachers rarely recognize the constraint. They are accustomed to combining the complexities into larger schema over the years which they draw up into working memory with ease, a thing their students will gradually learn over time. The invisibility of the challenge deserves attention of legal educators.[20] Thus, improving legal education requires that teachers recognize the constraints of working memory and make conscious effort to work within its narrow channel in ways that enhances its capacity to draw on long-term memory.

Structure of Knowledge

Effective learning is constructive, rather than a receptive process. So, teachers recognizing this would tilt professional learning in a way and manner that would help their students navigate the three-basic structure of knowledge in the course of the student professional life.[21] Knowledge often begins with what cognitivists term encoding. Encoded knowledge is basic knowledge of fact.[22] It is what is referred to as knowing "what," such as knowing what ingredients a plaintiff ought to raise to prove negligence: duty of care, breach of the duty, and resultant damage, all generally governed by the test of neighbour, reasonableness and remoteness respectively. This is simply knowledge of basic concepts.

Thereafter, knowledge progresses to proceduralization. Students integrate their knowledge of basic concepts with new sets of knowledge by performance and application to solve problems. For example, at this stage of knowledge, they can draw up pleadings on negligence claim, do a list of documents needed for interrogatories, argue motions and the like.

Composition is the final step in transforming and using knowledge. Students continue to improve in their performance ability over time by repeated performance. For example, experience gathered through the nuances of the practice of law, which is a process they learn throughout their professional careers.

Law teaching must help student develop through the structure of encoding, proceduralization and composition if it must be constructive. The legal academy can only help students traverse the ladder by integrated legal education that minimizes present lecture/seminar methodology.[23]

---

[20] Merritt, above n. 8, 48.

[21] See above, n.6

[22] Festus Emiri & Felicia Eimunjeze, Legal Reasoning, Epistemology and Comparative Law: Some Reflections on the Law of Obligations (2012) *Univ. Ibadan L. J.* 63

[23] Hess & Friedland, above n.7, 4.

Important to brain processing is the mode of transmitting information. Two basic mode exist for human information: verbal and visual information. A combination of both enhances legal education.[24]

Metacognation

Thinking about thinking is referred as metacognition by psychologist. It connects two interrelated learning concepts: student awareness about *how* they learn and student *control* of their learning strategies.[25] The how and control are central in the learning process. The how entails that each student identify the most effective strategy she needs to learn a particular content or skill, such as whether reading, discussion, performance or writing is most effective to learn. Having identified the how, the student is required to control the learning strategies, such as plan, monitor, and alter the strategies for the applicable subject-matter or teaching style. Here is where the teacher steps in. Students' learning is enhanced when they are conscious of how they learn and how they modify or control the strategies to accommodate the subject and teaching style.

The teacher contributes to metacognition of student by drawing attention to the process of learning, modelling different ways to approach a problem, and providing feedback to the students on the effectiveness of their learning strategies.[26] One way this can be done in performance evaluation is for the teacher after receiving assignments from her students in say a legal writing class, is to give feedback on the writings, provide samples of what is considered good writing, and thereafter ask the students to evaluate whether their writing is effective.

Social Process

The cognitive process of articulating thinking and effective performance grows with social interaction over time. That being so, students thinking and problem-solving capacities are enhanced when they work together, as in group activities, connect with the real world, as in clinical and externship and activities connected with teacher and peer mentoring.[27]

---

[24] See discussion on visuals and technology in Chapter 9. See also, Macaulay & Pantazi, above n. 12 on how visual when combined with verbal human communication can enhance learning of difficult materials.

[25] Hess & Steven Friedland, above n. 7, 5. See also, Alfred G. Smith, *Cognitive Styles in Law School,* 1979

[26] Hess & Steven Friedland, above n. 7, 5.

[27] Francis McGlone, Student Peer Mentors: A Teaching and Learning Strategy Designed to Promote Cooperative Approaches to Learning and Development of Lifelong Learning Skills (1996) 12 *Queensland U. Tech. L.J.* 201; See Felicia Eimunjeze, Mentoring in Yenagoa Campus. Since the beginning of history, human beings have formed communities that share cultural practices reflecting their collective learning: from a tribe around a cave fire, to a medieval guild, to a group of nurses in a ward, to a street gang, to a community of engineers interested in brake design. Participating in these 'communities of practice' is essential to our learning. It is at the very core of what makes us human beings capable of meaningful knowing." Cristina D. Lockwood, Improving Learning in the Law School Classroom by Encouraging

1. Intellectual Development

Theorist over the years have formulated several models about adult mental development, most of which apply with equal force to legal education.[28] By our modest count, the most applicable to legal education is that on construction site analogy used by Lustbader.[29] The construction site theory on learning progression identifies a preconstruction site and four construction sites (the technician, drafter, designer and creator sites), while the gaps between the sites represent the learning challenge that the students must conquer before they can move to the next site. The theory is very apt in the context of legal education because it is situated in research based on legal education. The learning progression hypothesis is useful for the academy for many reasons, it is a diagnostic instrument, it more particularly identifies areas where students experience learning challenges, and it proffers modest solutions. The stages are as follows:

Preconstruction Stage

This describes the transition of new law student from non-law student to law student. Students have to confront law from their non-law perspective. One opening course available in this respect is legal methods. From that point, they are required to establish a foundation of knowledge about law school teaching pedagogy, the legal system and its mainstream values. At the preconstruction stage, they cannot reason or think like lawyers. Their arguments are either

---

Students to Form Communities of Practice (2013) 20 *Clin. L. Rev.* 95 at 98 (quoting Etienne Wenger, *Communities of Practice and Social Learning Systems*, 2000 Organization, 2000, 225, 229).

[28] See Jean Piaget cognitive theory (the researcher is reputed to be the first psychologist to make a systematic study of children's cognitive development. His theory proposes four stages of cognitive development: the sensorimotor, preoperational, concrete operational and formal operational periods.) See Kayle Lane, et al., *Jean Piaget's Theory of Cognitive Development*; Erik Erickson model of psychosocial development (the theory articulated in collaboration with Joan Erickson, is a psychoanalytical theory that identifies eight crisis stages of development from infancy to adulthood) See Lauren M. Stephens, Melissa Dieppa & Patrice LeBlanc, Erickson Model of Psychosocial Development with Autistic Children and Connections to Evidence-Based Practices for No Child Left Behind, paper presented at August 2006 meeting of the Association of Teacher Education, Philadelphia, PA, USA, accessed www.eric.ed.gov.; Lawrence Kohlberg theory of moral development. (expanding on the earlier work of Jean Piaget, Kohlberg defined three stages of moral development: pre-conventional, conventional and post-conventional), William Perry theory of intellectual and ethical development (he posits that adult students go through four stages of development, further divided into nine positions: dualism, multiplicity, relativism and committed relativism). Some legal educators consider Perry's theory more related to legal education because it is framed from research on adult education, studies of cognitive and ethical development of undergraduate students, to which mould legal education fits. At dualism, student believe every problem is solvable by dual categorization of good or bad. They simply learn right answers and obey authority. Multiplicity is where there are two types of problems, solvable and those for which answer is not known. At relativism, all solutions to problems must have reasons and be viewed within certain context. At committed relativism is the stage where there is an acceptance of uncertainty as part of life. So, personal experience and evidence learned from outside source is used to arrive at conclusions. See Hess & Steven Friedland, above n. 7, 6. See also Festus Emiri & Isa Chiroma, .

[29] Paula Lustbader, Construction Sites, Building Types, and Building Gaps: A Cognitive Theory of the Learning Progression of Law Students (1997) 33 *Willamette L. Rev.* 317.

characterized by what lawyers term irrelevances. When required to solve controversies they could simply include in problem-solving techniques irrelevant matters, such as paying attention to details about people or events etc. Not surprising, they could even argue with class hypotheticals, create facts and reach conclusions without disciplined analysis. To overcome all of these barriers one of the first primers in legal method teaches them how to organize legal writing and argumentation, such as the IRAC rule.[30]

Technician Stage

With the foundation from a course such as legal methods, or legal writing and research, the students are armed with foundational understanding of the legal system, its values and how to organize thinking, writing, and research. They learn basic syntactical and substantive schemata for studying law. At this point, like a technician, they can understand substantive information, identify elements of concepts and categorize facts into legal compartments. Like technicians, they can carry out simply legal analysis, dogmatically applying (P)IRAC as the only paradigm of analysis, hardly considering wider policy and ethical issues.[31]

The technical stage demands that students master metacognition, syntactical schemata the legal system, factual application, and concrete policy application.[32] Metacognition requires that students to master the when, what and how to study and modify them to approached that work best for them. They must master the basic skills of note writing, listening so that they can develop the sophisticated skills of understanding, synthesizing and analyzing because if the basics are not quickly mastered it would distract and compete with their study tasks.

Mastering syntactical schemata demands that they become familiar with the legal system connections, how the (P)IRAC rule connects the social world from where controversies are generated, distinguish between ratio and obiter, significant facts of a case, articulate arguments, etc. The developed schemata are thereafter used as guide to analyses hypos and state what issues are implicated by the facts of given cases. They could at this stage move on to consider concrete policy application to hypos in very simplistic ways as they arrive at broad policy conclusion, like the rule in the case appears unfair, unethical etc. without proffering sophisticated grounding.

The technician stage appears to be most challenging of all the stages because of the volume of new information and varied skills required for the students to stay afloat and earn good grades in the faculty. No wonder, studies suggested that

---

[30] Festus Emiri & Ayuba Giwa, Revisiting the Traditional *IRAC* Organisational Structure for Legal Analysis: Towards a Multidisciplinary Approach [2016] *Nig. Law Journal* 23.

[31] Ibid.

[32] Lustbader, above n. 29 at 333.

much of students' dissatisfaction and frustration with legal education is experienced in the beginning of law school education.[33]

Law teachers can help make less challenging this stage of learning progression by teaching their students effective study strategies, by explicitly explaining to students what is expected of them, expressly constructing syntactical schemata and model for reasoning, and by providing necessary feedback on students' performance. This is why the practice of assigning foundational courses like legal methods and writing, and first law courses like contract, Nigerian legal system and constitutional law courses to new law teachers is unhelpful. If anything, these are courses that should be taught by older, more experienced faculty.

Lustbader provides a useful checklist for knowing whether our students' have mastered the technician stage and are ready for the drafter stage. They are as follows: (i) whether the student has clear structure and organization to her analysis; (ii) is able to articulate rules; (iii) at times is able to be explicit in her analysis; (iv) identifies most of the issues; (v) is aware that policy implications are relevant; (vi) strictly adheres to the (P)IRAC structure, which often leads to form-over-substance analysis; (vii) discusses all parts of the rule, even those that are not relevant, or is imprecise in articulating the rule; (viii) includes counter-arguments even when there are no arguments to be made; (ix) cannot tell when an area of law is in issue, when to raise and dismiss an issue, and when to discuss an issue at length, and will add facts to discuss nonissues; (x) fails to discuss most of the facts provided; (xi) analyzes at a very superficial level; (xii) adds policy in a meaningless way; and (xiii) is typically inefficient.[34]

Drafter Stage

This is the stage that students begin as it were to doubt the iconoclastic sanctity of blackletter law, viewing it more of grey-lettering. Policy underlying doctrinal concepts comes unto the centre stage of legal analysis. As drafters, students begin to use policy to justify rule-choices, results and conclusions. For example, using the *Speluncean Explorers* case,[35] they reason that the law of murder could hardly be intended to have extra-territorial application to be the governing law regulating the affairs of the explorers underground.[36] They could even extend

---

[33] Refer to Carnegie Report.
[34] Lustbader, above n. 29, 340.
[35] Lon L. Fuller, The Case of the Speluncean Explorers (1949) 62 Harv. L. Rev."
[36] Ibid. see judgment of

their policy consideration to navigate the connection between state prohibition of murder and the place of contract and personal autonomy in the jurisprudence.[37]

The stage could pose challenge for students who have difficulty developing policy arguments, a situation likely to be exacerbated for disempowered persons who have never experienced position of authority. Teachers can make the challenge less prevailing by providing contextual understanding to concepts using class simulation and legal storytelling to recreate empowering consciousness.[38]

Lustbader again provides a useful checklist for knowing whether our students' have mastered the drafter stage and are ready for the next, designer stage. They are as follows: (i) a drafter still follows the (P)IRAC structure, but does not label every sentence; (ii) narrows the discussion of the rules to those parts that are most relevant; (ii) includes an argument only where there is one to be made; (iv) begins to understand when to raise and dismiss an issue and when to discuss it in depth, but still tends to raise nonissues; (v) uses more of the facts than a technician, but still needs to use more of them; (vi) includes policy in a meaningful way, and (vii) develops more in-depth analysis.[39]

Designer Stage

This the stage all teachers want to bring their student to enable them join the profession with requisite skills. It is characterized by sophistry in legal analysis, problem-solving and persuasive writing. Students see and make the subtle connections between doctrines and policy, deviating from the (P)IRAC reasoning and writing style and are able to weave more facts to analysis. They become masters of law and policy, employing the tools of classical and modern rhetoric in persuasion confidently.[40]

Unfortunately, many students and lawyers get caught up between the drafter and designer stages, because they have developed a mechanical orientation to law and legal analysis that they cannot remove themselves from the Procrustean mold of (P)IRAC reasoning.[41] They can only see controversies through the lens of

---

[37] Ibid., see judgment of.

[38] Festus Emiri, Mainstreaming an Interdisciplinary Approach to Legal Education: Imperatives for Nigeria's Development (Keynote Address) 2015 Proceedings of the National Association of Law Teachers Conference 1.

[39] Lustbader, above n. 29, 346.

[40] Emiri *et al.* above n. 30

[41] The Procrustean bed symbolizes a standard that is enforced uniformly without regard to individuality. It derives from the Greek mythical giant Procrustes or the mode of torture practiced by him. According to George Gopen, Procrustean lived off the road from Athens to Eleusis. Each evening he offered hospitality to travellers on the road. While the food and wine he offered his guest were fine, the sleeping arrangement was not. The guest was required to fit perfectly to the iron bed he constructed. If the guest was taller than the bed, he would cut off the guest feet and legs to fit into the bed. The obvious effect is that the guest will die. See George G. Gopen, Keynote Address at the Capital Area Legal Writing Conference, Feb. 26, 2011,

parties, rules of court, applicable ratio and the like, that they lose sight of the human nature that trigger controversies in the social world. That keeps them operating as building masons when they ought to be building architects.[42] Having accustomed to the (P)IRACian style that many teachers use as primer (some even teaching it as paradigmatic of legal analysis, despite its recognized shortcomings), many simply resist change to more sophisticated ways of analysis and so remain where they are comfortable, the mundane of (P)IRAC analysis, no more.[43]

Students master the designer stage if they develop the following knowledge, skills and values: (i) are able as established designers to take the developed analysis of the beginner designer and integrates it, including the rule and the arguments; (ii) does not use the (P)IRAC structure because it is not needed, although it is implicit in the discussion; (iii) organizes her analysis around concepts instead of parties; and (iv) is more efficient in her analysis.[44]

Simulation, storytelling and teaching the Brandies brief style or the flexible (P)IRACian style as continuous legal writing exercises throughout the five years of legal education can help address the challenge.

---

in IRAC, REA, Where We Are Now, and Where We Should Be Going in the Teaching of Legal Writing (2011) 17 *J. Legal Writing Inst.* xix

[42] See Emiri, *et al.* above n. 30

[43] Emiri, *et al.* above n. 30. For general reading on a critique of the IRAC paradigm for legal writing, see, Terri LeClercq, The Success-And Failure-of IRAC (1987) 50 *Tex. B.J.* 222; Jane K. Gionfriddo, Dangerous! Our Focus Should Be Analysis, Not Formulas Like IRAC, The Second Draft Nov. 1995 of the Legal Writing Institute, Tacoma, Wash, at 2; Wilson R. Huhn, Teaching Legal Analysis Using a Pluralistic Model of Law (2000-2001) 36 *Gonz. L. Rev.* 433; Helen A. Anderson, Changing Fashion in Advocacy: 100 Years of Brief-Writing Advice (2010) 11 *J. App. Prac. & Process* 1 (judges expect legal analysis to go beyond atomistic logic); Christine M. Venter, Analyze This: Using Taxonomies to "Scaffold" Students' Legal Thinking and Writing Skills (2006) 57 *Mercer L. Rev.* 621; Jennifer Sheppard, Once Upon a Time, Happily Ever After, and in a Galaxy Far, Far Away: Using Narrative to Fill the Cognitive Gap Left by Overreliance on Pure Logic in Appellate Briefs and Motion Memoranda (2009) 46 *Willamette L. Rev.* 255;; Kristen K. Robbins-Tiscione, A Call to Combine Rhetorical Theory and Practice in the Legal Writing Classroom (2011) 50 *Washburn L.J.* 319; Soma R. Kedia, Redirecting the Scope of First-Year Writing Courses: Towards a New Paradigm of Teaching Legal Writing (2010) 87 *U. Det. Mercy L. Rev.* 147; George D. Gopen, IRAC, REA, Where We Are Now, and Where We Should Be Going in the Teaching of Legal Writing (2011) 17 *J. Legal Writing Inst.* xvii (keynote address at Capital Area Legal Writing Conference, Feb. 26, 2011- "there is not and cannot be a single structure that is the right answer to the question of how argumentative thought is best conveyed from the mind of a writer to the mind of a reader. ... These organizational structures [CRAC, CREAC, MIRAT, IDAR, ILAC, TREACC, CruPAC, ISAAC, CRRACC, BARAC etc.] are both necessary and dangerous, both supporting and defeating. As with any good idea or good invention, they can all be used for harm as well as good," id xviii); Laura P. Graham, Why-RAC? Revisiting the Traditional Paradigm for Writing About Legal Analysis (2015) 63 *Kansas L. Rev.* 681. But cf. generally, Lurene Contento, Demystifying IRAC and Its Kin: Giving Students the Basic to Write "Like a Lawyer," *The Second Draft*, Nov. 1995 of the Legal Writing Institute, Tacoma, Wash; Tracy Turner, Flexible IRAC: A Best Practice Guide (2015) 20 *J. Legal Writing Inst.* 233 (recommends the syllogistic IRAC reasoning, while suggesting the best guide for teachers use of the rule, such as the one-sequence IRAC; the alternating IRAC; IRAC by paragraph; the IRAC sentence; and the narrative add-ons which mixes facts into the "I" of IRAC).

[44] Lustbader, above n. 29, 351.

Creators Stage

This is the expert stage in learning law. It is perhaps the most difficult stage to attain for students and lawyers. A percentage of lawyers never reach this stage even after years of long practice. Like any inventor, the creator does not feel conscripted to rules but operates them in wider context to achieve value specific goals. Operating more from the position of intuition the creator is able to stretch principles to recreate lawyering and achieve desired outcomes. It could involve challenging established mindset and received legal knowledge. An expert is a risk-taker, who does not fear her actions as risky because she is confident that the desired goals will be realized even within the structure of legal analysis. Innovative scholarship, like law and economics, feminists' jurisprudence, critical legal studies, etc., are examples of reaching the creators stage for the legal academy.[45]

Students that have failed to internalize all preceding learning stages cannot grow into this stage. Teachers should therefore ground their students in the design stage as vital to training legal architects. A very helpful way to train students to grow into the creator stage would be to make available to students' risk-free opportunities to try new approaches to law that are creative in legal writing assignments, with accompanying feedbacks. Teachers would say they have done so if their students exhibit the following in thinking and performance: (i) if the creator implicitly follows an (P)IRAC structure, but organizes more around concepts; (ii) approach the subject from policy perspective and develop more creative arguments in regard to facts; (iii) considers the practical and future implications of the court decision; (iv) focuses more creative arguments on facts; (v) demonstrate doctrinal knowledge but argues for a change in standards where

---

[45] Nuno Garoupa & Thomas S. Ulen, Market for Legal Innovation: Law and Economics in Europe, and the United States (discussion on what legal innovation means, as is any new technique of scholarship, a new subject area to the study of law, such as legal realism, public choice theory, literary techniques etc.) For examples of expert lawyering, especially those recreating new consciousness, see, For illustrative examples see, Cunningham, above n.4; Lucie E. White, Subordination, Rhetorical Survival Skills, and Sunday Shoes: Notes on the Hearing of Mrs. G (1990) 38 *Buffalo L. Rev.* 1 (where the commentators using the story of Mrs. G welfare hearing application reveals that cultural images and long-established legal norms construct the subjectivity and speech of socially subordinate groups, like women, blacks etc., as inherently inferior to those of dominant groups). See also Binny Miller, Give Them Back Their Lives: Recognising Client Narrative in Case Theory (1994) 93 *Mich. L. Rev.* 485 (showing how the practice of lawyering should be reconstructed to embrace a greater role for clients in constructing case theories). See also the interesting read, W. Lance Bennett & Martha S. Feldman, *Reconstructing Reality in the Courtroom: Justice and Judgment in American Culture*, Rutgers Univ. Press, 1981 (the social science researchers state that American criminal trial is organized around storytelling). Martin Jay, Must Justice Be Blind? The Challenges of Images to the Law, in Costas Douzinas & Lynda Neads, eds., *Law and Image*, Univ. Chicago Press, 1999, 21. See generally, James P. Eyster, Lawyer as Artist: Using Significant Moments and Obtuse Objects to Enhance Advocacy (2008) 14 *J. Legal Writing Inst.* 87 (a discussion of how to apply key techniques of the visual artists-the obtuse objet and significant moments to legal advocacy and their persuasive sting according to art history scholars, aestheticians, psychologists, and psycholinguists). For a discussion on the mental structures (rationality) that raise human cognition, see George Lakoff, *Women, Fire, and Dangerous Things: What Categories Reveal about the Mind*, Univ. Chicago Press, 1987. Kenneth D. Chestek, The Plot Thickens: The Appellate Brief as Story (2008) 14 *J. Legal Writing Inst.* 127

appropriate; (vi) has the confidence and experience to eliminate discussion of unnecessary issues or she can concentrate on salient issues only.[46]

As a theory of intellectual development, the learning progression hypothesis is helpful because it helps teachers and students to identify what point in progression the student is working through, thereby helping the teacher to focus specifically on the knowledge, skills and values the student ought to master before making progress into another stage. Knowing the stage in progression of student provides teachers with a common vocabulary to explain student's error or deficiency in performance. Gaps between each stage alert teachers to understand learning challenges that they should address. It also helps create the necessary emphatic environment for the teacher to understand the learning challenges of the student and to reassure them that progression will result if they pay attention to stage expectations. Very importantly, the theory is theraphatic. It offers specific teaching strategies to help students master the sites and build bridges between them. The checklist is a good gauge for the medicine. It further serves as a dialogue stimulant for teachers to interrogate reasons for the gaps between sites so that they can develop effective teaching strategies to address less than competent performance. The learning progression theory has significant implications for legal educators. It speaks essentially to the *transformation* of the learner, not the *transmission* of knowledge. In effect, teachers must pay attention not only to how they transfer knowledge but also how the transferred knowledge is able to transform a novice to become an expert. The transformative nature of legal education is consistent with the dominate conceptualization of legal education, which speaks to the identity of "thinking like a lawyer." Gaps between sites explains why some students may write poor exams not because of their study habits but because of their stage of intellectual development. It further demonstrates that teaching methods can affect students' progression and students can develop analytical and lawyering skills through an conducive learning environment, variety of teaching methods and evaluation, clear course and class objectives, active learning techniques, such as externship, role-play, simulation, group activities, with frequent and timely feedback.[47]

2. Learning Styles

It is now time to pay attention to the characteristics way a person acquires and uses knowledge. Generally, there are four learning characteristics: personality models (basic characteristics of learner); information processing models (how information is acquired and processed); social interaction models (behaviour of

---

[46] Lustbader, above n. 29, 353.
[47] Hess & Friedland, above n. 7, 8.

learner in class); and instructional preference models (preferred teaching and learning styles).[48]

The learning style models of Myers-Briggs Type Indicator (MBTI) of personality inventory is a theory of psychology is used widely in the humanities and law.[49] It is designed to assess the way people to receive information and make decisions. It classifies individual based on four preferences: extroversion or introversion; sensing or intuitive; thinking or feeling; and judgment or perception. It is expected that a law class should have students with these preferences. Teachers are therefore obligated to learn how best to effective teach students with their different preferences, none being obstacle to learning.[50]

The tables below set out the basic characteristics of each preference and the considered effective teaching/learning style appropriate.[51]

3. Character of Adult Learner

Law students are characteristically adult or at worse mature minors.[52] Thus, leg educators and improve teaching and students learning if they understand the bas characteristics of adult learning and then shape teaching methods to align with t characteristics.

Voluntary Learners

Most law students are persons who participate voluntary in learning. They most like choose to study law on their own volition. It therefore must be that they choose la because they are interested in acquiring new knowledge, in learning new skills, ar gaining insight into the world of law. They are thus expected to be generally we motivated to learn and willing to participate in the process. That being so, they wou be willing to join in group activities, simulation, role-play and the like. They will on withdraw from learning if they feel legal education does not meet their expectation, or the learning environment is not conducive.

Mutual Respect

Mutual respect underlies adult learning. Teachers must show that every student valuable as an individual. That is the way they grow from one site to another.

---

[48] Hess & Friedland, above n. 7, 8.

[49] MBTI explains that the much seeming random variation in behaviour is actually quite orderly and consistent, being due to basic differences in the ways individuals prefer to use their perception and judgment.

[50] Vernellia R. Randall, The Myers-Briggs Type Indicator, First-Year Law Students and Performance (1995) 26 *Cumb. L. Rev.* 63.

[51] Hess & Friedland, above n. 7, 9-10.

[52] Gillick competence.

Collaborative Learning

Collaborating teaching/learning demands that both teacher and student dialogue in choosing course objectives, teaching methodology and evaluative criteria. Once students feel that they are part of teaching and learning, it creates a synergy of eagerness to learn on the part of students.

Contextual Learning

When adult learn new concepts, skills and values, they would often relate them to their experience to ground meaning, thereby redefining how they might apply them to other settings and situation. This is what makes legal storytelling a veritable tool for adult education.

B. Teaching Component

The legal academy is concerned about how to enhance teaching skills of faculty. Faculties, institutions and group continual make huge investment and make available many resources for promoting effective teaching and teaching excellence.[53] It is said that the components effective teaching is a myth because researchers are still exploring its components. This notwithstanding, to the extent that teaching majorly takes the form of communication, some verbal, visual and demonstrative components can be distilled as common components for effective verbal communication.

1. Components of Effective Teaching

Proper Communication: To communicate effectively the teacher must speak clearly. Students will not be motivated to learn if they do not understand what is being spoken. Slurred words must be avoided because they do not motivate the hearer. Teachers should identify what makes verbal communication indistinct. Failure to open the mouth sufficiently, lips that rarely move and rigid jaw muscles. Unless the teacher suffers from structural defect in the speech organ, she should project the voice to be clearly heard by the class. For a teacher who suffers from initial audience fear it could be helpful to release tension by controlling breathing. Deep breathing and release can calm release the tension.

Learning to pronounce words correctly add to the teacher's dignity as a responsible professional. A teacher should take time to consult a dictionary for familiarize herself with pronunciation she is not familiar with.

---

[53] Refer to Carnegie, Journal of Legal Education, quarterly journal published by the Association of American Law Schools, to promote rich interchange of ideas about legal education and related matters of the legal profession, legal theory and legal scholarship. At present, it has a readership of over 10,000 law teachers, with ovrr526papers published.

Fluent delivery has a way of keeping the attention of the class, preventing the minds of the students from wandering. Teachers should avoid speech mannerism of inserting such expressions as "you know" on to whatever they say in class. Even in fluency, a teacher must learn to appropriately pause in speaking so that her speech is clear. Generally, pausing is appropriate to signify change of thought, for purposes of emphasis, and also when classroom environment so demand, e.g. to get response from the class, or to allow passing noise or distraction subside.

In speaking, proper sense stress can be useful to emphasis key words and thoughts. For example, in teaching the tort of negligence, the teacher can sense stress the phrases "neighbour," "reasonable-man," and "remoteness," to emphasis what controls the notion of a duty of care, breach of duty of care, and resulting damage. By the greater volume, or intensity of feeling in mentioning them they stand out as signpost of knowledge. Though sense stress helps student understand what is said, the teacher still needs to make good use of volume, pace and pitch to make listening enjoyable t the audience.

Very importantly, delivery should be animated, giving the class the teacher's strong feeling about the value of the course and the content being taught. Speaking with feeling is contagious. If a teacher uses good audience contact and is enthusiastic, the class will pick up the enthusiasm and be eager to learn. Teacher can heighten animated delivery by ensuring that her facial expression reflects the enthusiasm as she speaks with strength and vigour. Enthusiasm is not warrant for been nervous, stiff, or awkward in speech because of being self-conscious. Rather teacher should be natural in delivery.

If the class is large with basic technological appliances like a microphone, it should be kept at between four to six inches from the mouth to prevent word distortion. Even when in use the teacher should keep a level of eye contact with her class.

Up-building and positive comments about students' performance builds confidence a requisite for growing student on the learning progression sites.

Every lecture must have a theme developed for it. It unifies the presentation and helps students to understand what the teacher says and to remember it. Even at that main points in the theme should be made to stand out because they serve as memory aid, thus contributing to reflection on what students learn.

Without much ado, every lecture should end with an effective conclusion, some summary showing the connection of what is learned to the social world or previously learned concepts, designed to move the students to deepen understanding and application. Teachers do well to be mindful that what is said in the conclusion is often remembered the longest.

Use of stories or real-life experience and visual aids contributes to learning and so teachers should recognize their place in contributing to learning. For example, stories often command attention with remarkable effectiveness. They stimulate the thinking faculties in ways difficult for abstract concept to do.[54] When visual aids are coupled with spoken words, information is received through two senses. This may help to hold attention of the class. Note however that the purpose of visual is not to entertain but to effectively teach.

Legal educators who want to enhance their teaching skills can use a variety of the techniques listed above with a variety of resources and models of teaching excellence available in learned writings and those developed by their institution for the purpose.[55]

Implications of Learning Theory for Legal Education

Three concepts are at the crux of learning theory. They are learning, instruction, and transfer.[56] Learning is a change in human disposition or capability, which persists over a period of time, not ascribable to growth. That being so, the duration of change is long term; the locus of change is the content and structure of knowledge in the memory or behaviour of the learner; and the cause of change is the learner's experience in the environment. Instruction is the deliberate arrangement of learning conditions to promote the attainment of the desired goal. While, transfer or transmission is the application of learned knowledge in new ways or situation.[57]

---

[54] Power of stories. See Factory Closure case in Ado lecture.

[55] See generally, Gerald F. Hess & Steven Friedland, *Techniques for Teaching Law*, North Carolina: Durham: Carolina Academic Press, 1999, 12; *Benefit from Theocratic Ministry Education,* 2001, published by the Watch Tower Bible & Tract Society of Pennsylvania, available at www.jw.org.

[56] Michael H. Schwartz, Teaching Law by Design: How Learning Theory and Instructional Design Can Inform and Reform Law Teaching (2001) 38 *San Diego L. Rev* 347 at 366

[57] Tonta Kowalski, True North: Navigating for the Transfer of Learning in Legal Education (2010) 51 *Seattle Univ. L. Rev.* 51 (discussion examining transfer theory as a method to integrate the larger law curriculum. It proposes that law schools should employ mental maps based on schema theory to help students encode knowledge for future transfer and conceptually integrate their courses); Michael H. Schwartz, Teaching Law by Design: How Learning Theory and Instructional Design Can Inform and Reform Law Teaching (2001) 38 *San Diego L. Rev* 347 at 366. On how to transfer knowledge and skills in specific course areas see, Laurel C. Oates, I Know That I Taught Them How to Do That (2001) 7 Leg. Writing 1; David A. Binder, Albert J. Moore & Paul Bergman, A Depositions Course: Tackling the Challenge of Teaching for Professional Skills Transfer (2007) 13 *Clinical L. Rev.* 871); Susan E. Provenzano & Lesley S. Kagan, Teaching in Re- verse: A Positive Approach to Analytical Errors in 1L Writing (2007) 39 *Loy. U. Chi. L.J.* 123; Sandra R. Daffron, Lessons Learned from Palestinian Professors about Transfer of Learning (2005) J. Leg. Educ. 571. Robin A. Boyle, Employing Active-Learning Techniques and Metacognition in Law School: Shifting Energy from Professor to Student (2003) 81 *Univ. Det. Mercy L. Rev.* 1 (discussion that because human beings tie their learning to very specific patterns, any solution to the transfer problem in law school must involve the search for highly inclusive meta-schematics that can span multiple contexts, as well as stimulate students to access those cognitive maps through learner motivation and metacognitive strategies).

There are three major learning theories: behaviourism, cognitivism, and constructivism, each with implications for informing and reforming law teaching.

Behaviourism

Behaviourism is rooted in Aristotle's empiricist philosophy. The central theme of behaviorism is that learning occurs when the learner exhibits the proper response to specific environmental stimulus. So, learning occurs when the connection between stimulus and response is developed and strengthened. For example, for behaviourists the ability of a say a person to choose healthy from unhealthy food is evidence of learning the difference between both.

Behaviourism pervades legal education. When for instance, a student can issue-spot from facts of a hypo, articulate and evaluate arguments and predict likely resolution, the student is said to have learned to respond (answer) to the stimulus (the hypo).

Behaviourism is relevant for law teaching. The approach developed the idea assessing learners to determine the point at which instruction should begin. So, following the Lustbader construction site analogy, it provides the teacher insight to be mindful of gaps between sites and how to determine what skills student must master before progressing to the next site.

Interestingly, the mastery learning concept of Bloom's 80-80 effective test of learning was created by the behaviourist, Benjamin Bloom.[58] The approach also developed the idea of sequencing teaching to student capacity. In this respect, it encourages teachers to be mindful of the limitations of working memory, and introduce complex topics in ways that are easily understandable.

Behaviourists developed the idea that learning can be enhanced by developing non-human and non-classroom instruction. Teachers should therefore explore non-human and non-classroom mediation in instruction such as course webpage, listservs, computer labs, etc., to enhance learning.[59]

Behaviourists have posited that instructional materials should be reviewed by empirical testing the effects of materials on student performance and satisfaction. The continuous improvement of instructional material is reformatory of teaching and learning strategies and techniques. But as a learning theory it suffers limitation of explaining the acquisition of higher skills or those connected with deeper processing, such development of critical thinking, inference generation, problem-solving, etc. As in our construction site analogy it is useful at the preconstruction and technical sites.[60]

---

[58] Benjamin Bloom, Mastery Learning: Theory and Practice.
[59]
[60] Michael H. Schwartz

Advances beyond require the application of cognitivism and constructivism learning theories. Cognitivism developed in the 1950s (though suggested to be rooted in Plato's rationalism) uses a set of theories based on how the brain processes information- how knowledge arises through the mind.

Implications of cognitivism for legal education generally follow the many instructional principles subscribed to by behaviorism, but it goes further. Since it learner-centred it encourages students to connect between new and previously learned material. Recognizing the constrain of working memory it emphasizes structuring, organizing and sequencing of teacher information to facilitate processing. It also encourages integration of learning material that allow active student participation in learning-metacognition. It further encourages multiple representation of material for clear understandable. To this extent it encourages the use of visual and technology in instruction.

Constructivism like postmodernism, view learning and knowledge as being constructed by each individual from her experience. They generally don't agree that there are absolute truths because as a theory rooted in the philosophy of Jean Piaget, knowledge comes from the relationship between the mind and environment. So, by this thinking a teacher does not necessarily transmit knowledge of the real world, rather each learner continually constructs and reconstructs her own images of what the world is like from experience and its interpretation. Invariably, learning is a product of experience, construction of the meaning of the experience and negotiating the meaning of the experience.[61]

For legal education constructivism encourage experiential learning as through clinic, externship programmes. Because it encourages learners to construct their own understanding and validation, it is a call to grow student intellect and reasoning to the creator site of learning progression.

Together the theories suggest that teaching should grow students' skills from the simple (behaviorism) to the intermediate (cognitivism) and then to complex (constructivism). All three learning theories are relevant to legal education, yet they remain largely ignored by the legal academy.

---

[61] Michael H. Schwartz

Chapter 3

Teaching Guide for Beginners

Introduction

No doubt it can be exciting to join the legal academy as a law teacher. It is a status with influence and prestige in our society.[1] Intriguing as this can be for the new entrant to the business of teaching law, it is not without a level of apprehension as to how best to fit into the profession. Anxiety could relate to what subject to teach, how teaching should proceed, what to expect and do on first day in class, what text to recommend to the students and a host others. This chapter is design to address the likely challenges of a new and not so new law teacher. All teachers can however benefit from it by using it as an evaluative material to improve on their techniques and strategies for teaching law.[2]

Preparing for First Day in Class

Once assigned a course, the teacher should make out a list of broad range of objectives she desires her students to master and perform. The range should take cognizance of the faculty's mission and learning outcomes. These goals should be manageable in number to enhance proper implementation.[3]

Even if the new teacher is familiar with the subject of the new course, it would still be beneficial to do some deep reflective thinking to see how the course contributes as a building block to the edifice of law and the competence of the faculty. This requires the teacher to see the big picture, which can throw further

---

[1] That was not how it was back in the day. Relate challenge of making law a profession and the attitude to law teaching-appointment of Professor Amos Andrew in the university. Refer to English Legal History book and articles.

[2] Howard E. Katz & Kevin F. O'Neil, *Strategies and Techniques of Law School Teaching*, New York: Aspen Pub. 2009. Susan Baker recommends the following articles as helpful to the beginner law teacher on the art of teaching law: Paul G. Haskell, Teaching Moral Analysis in Law School (1991) 66 *Notre Dame L. Rev.* 1025; Marin Roger Scordato, The Dualist Model of Legal Teaching and Scholarship (1990) 40 *Am. U. L. Rev.* 367; Clark Byse, Fifty Years of Legal Education (1986) 71 *Iowa L. Rev.* 1063; Michael L. Closen, Teaching with Recent Decisions: A Survey of Past and Present Practices (1983) 11 Fla. St. L. Rev. 289; Lon L. Fuller, On Teaching Law (1950) 3 *Stan. L. Rev.* 35. See, Susan Baker, Advice for the New Professor: A View from the Trenches (1992) 42 *J. Leg. Educ.* 432.

[3] See generally, Kent Syverud, Taking Students Seriously: A Guide for New Teachers (1993) 43 *J. Leg. Educ.* 247; Susan Baker, Advice for the New Professor: A View from the Trenches (1992) 42 *J. Leg. Educ.* 432; Douglas Whatley, Teaching Law: Advice for the New Professor (1982) 43 *Ohio St. L.J.* 125.

insight as to how teaching and learning is enhanced. For example, if a faculty's competence tilts to say law and economics, a teacher of administrative law should be conscious to connect the individual course topics to an analysis of cost-benefit administrative law, its connection with regulation law and the economic and social justification for administrative intervention; while for torts it would be by plotting the economic essence of tort law in using liability to internalize externalities created by high transaction costs. Looking at the big picture in the context of interrelationship between subject for example, a teacher of equity can reason on how the defence of estoppel shades into . All of these are possibilities open by gaining mastery of the subject.

It will then be time to settle down to form a teaching manual or outline for the subject. The teacher should then *choose a book* that fits the goal of the course.

The new teacher should then settle to *design a syllabus* for the course. In designing the syllabus, it would be necessary to avoid the danger of trying to cover extensively the field. It is often better to identify core or main topic and then make them stand out. It has been shown that topics taught are better remembered if the principal ideas are emphasized rather than covering too many grounds. The syllabus can then be made into a synopsis to be distributed to the students to enable them prepare ahead for lectures. Some well-run faculties distribute ahead of commencement of lecture the lesson plan for the course. If fortunate to have such a plan the teacher should study it to see how the plan fits with the principle of logical development of the course. This demands that the teacher arranges the syllabus or plan in such manner that make clear how the ideas from one topic relate to another so that at the conclusion of the course the students can appreciate the mosaic nature of what they learn. When information is presented in a logical manner, it is easier for students to learn, understand and remember. To determine whether the pedagogy is logical in development, the teacher should always keep in mind the question: what topic should my students first be exposed to to understand certain other topics? It in effect mean that the teacher should consider how the topics[4] may be sequenced to give students the best opportunity to understand the material intended for instruction. For example, in a civil procedure class it could be better to teach commencement of action before more complex topics like third party procedure and interlocutory injunction. Once they understand the various ways to commence action, it is likely that that would set the stage for them to appreciate parties to a civil claim and the pre-emptory powers of the court.

---

[4] Katz & O'Neil, above n. 2, 29.

Overarching Precepts

This is the point where the teacher should look at the classroom from the big-picture perspective. Katz & ONeil make a list of these precepts that ought to guide the new teacher. They include choosing what to teach, playing the role of teacher in a professional manner, finding personal voice in class, injecting something personal in teaching, being transparent with student, creating classroom atmosphere conducive to learning, inspiring students' participation, reading students responses to learning, and identification of the thread that runs through the course.

It is advised that the beginner negotiates a light load of related *courses to teach*.[5] The wisdom in this is obvious. It lightens preparation for the beginner and enhances self-confidence. In making an informed decision on this the beginner would need to consider selecting courses according to this order of priority: (i) substantive areas where she has extensive exposure in law school or practice; (ii) subject areas where she has extensive exposure in law school or practice; (iii) subject areas where she has some exposure; (iv) and areas in which she has a high degree of interest but little exposure or experience in.[6]

Baker states why: "teaching a familiar subject is that it substantially reduces your fear that a smoking gun may lie buried in the yet uncovered materials, a gun that will blast into oblivion most of the legal principles studied to date."[7]

Things may however not work out that way. Sometimes the choice is not there. The Dean simply tells the beginner as newest faculty member what the assigned course is. The course could be a strange one to the beginner, not within area of her competence or favourite subject. That is nothing to fear. The reason for the Dean's course assignment could well be that the beginner is the least person likely to resist a course other older faculty members do not like to teach. The subject may also be the Dean's favourite. The advice from the trenches is accept and work hard on the course remembering that the beginner has to explore a number of subjects before finding the right teaching niche. What is more, the beginner is not glued to the conscripted course forever.

Playing the *role of teacher* in a professional requires that no matter the age and experience of the teacher, she must assume the role of a law teacher in the faculty. The role infuses a sense of responsibility that prevents the teacher from being casual and informal. While the role does not imply high handedness on the part of the teacher, it implies that friendliness expressed should be in the context of explicit, necessary boundaries of teacher-student relationship. The advice from

---

[5] Douglas Whatley, Teaching Law: Advice for the New Professor (1982) 43 *Ohio St. L.J.* 125.

[6] Susan Baker, Advice for the New Professor: A View from the Trenches (1992) 42 *J. Leg. Educ.* 432.

[7] Susan Baker, above n.6 at 434.

Whaley is that the beginner should not inject too much of the real you into the classroom, in revealing sense of humor or cynicism because excessive personality leakage erodes the barrier separating the teacher from student. An appropriate amount of distance is necessary to maintain professionalism and right classroom atmosphere. [8]

Voicing continual academic self-doubt is to be avoided to preserve credibility. Since the primary purpose of legal education is to train students for the profession, a teacher behavior must reflect the model of professional behavior expected of the students when they enter the profession.

A beginner will be anxious in choosing course text material. In choosing course material, the beginner is advised to simply choose the most popular text in the subject from the number of course materials available.[9] A text that includes problems is extremely helpful in promoting class discussion. But one that poses too complex questions should be avoided by beginners. Once mastery comes with teaching experience, the beginner can hand such materials, but it is better to start and master the simple before proceeding to the complex. The beginner will find that even after recommending the appropriate text students may still turn to commercial study guides. That should not discourage her. It is not a bad idea to undertake your private review of these guides at least advise students which ones to avoid.[10]

No teacher is too new not to find her *own voice* in the classroom. All teachers are expected to bring their peculiar individuality to the classroom. By our nature some are tough and demanding, other not so tough. Whatever is the teacher's individuality should be kept temperate by the overriding consideration that a teacher is a fiduciary and is obligated to promote learning by creating classroom atmosphere conducive to learning, which inspires students' participation.

Every teacher is expected to *inject something personal in teaching*. No rule demands that teacher "A" must teach like teacher "B." Every teacher has the opportunity to shape and mold students to become responsible professional. It is recognized that our different, unique skills and experience can aid in building rounded, responsible future lawyers. For example, a teacher of equity and trust with banking or transactional experience who joins the faculty could take a more market approach to the subject in teaching. While a traditional teacher would concentrate on how the principles are stepped in family and friendship setting, a transactional modern could emphasize the commercial bent of the course,

---

[8] Douglas Whatley, Teaching Law: Advice for the New Professor (1982) 43 *Ohio St. L.J.* 125 at 131.
[9] Douglas Whatley, Teaching Law: Advice for the New Professor (1982) 43 *Ohio St. L.J.* 125 at 129.
[10] Susan Baker, Advice for the New Professor: A View from the Trenches (1992) 42 *J. Leg. Educ.* 432 at 436.

showing how the doctrines of equity grown beyond its original setting and now informs commercial dealing.

Being *transparent* with student requires that they are from the start of the course explicitly told the goals of the course, what the criteria for assessment would be, what knowledge, skills and values are expected of them, the style for teaching and the reason for choosing the style. The presence of an advance lesson plan or synopsis can help clarify matters.

For teaching to be effective the teacher must create a *conducive learning environment*. Achieving the feat is more an art than science. There is no magic formula for it, but certain parameter makes it easier to create. For example, fluent communication, proper animated delivery keeps the mind from wandering, creates strong feeling about the value of what is being learn. Qualities like proper visual contact, good personal appearance, choice of words, logical development of material, and the conversational manner of teaching ought to impact positively in creating the conducive environment. Bad qualities like intimidation, and belittling students must be avoided. They estrange participation.[11]

Effective learning is student-centred. This being so the primary strategic objective of the teacher is to inspire students' participation. This can be accomplished in a variety of ways. The learned commentators, Katz & O'Neil state that the following techniques can be helpful in this regard: (i) tactical use of seating chart,[12] (ii) calling upon students at random,[13] (ii) breaking the class into small groups for collaborative.[14]

Though the new teacher is likely to be concerned with how well she performs the basic duties in the classroom, she must alongside *pay attention to how the students are responding* or even reacting to learning. Reading the audience can help the teacher adjust teaching style to get the enhance learning. Certain qualities can create positive responses in the audience, such as ensuring that expressed words are easy to understand. It requires proper use of the teacher's speech organs and that the teacher structures her expressed words in a clear understandable manner. A level of gesture and eye contact can also help elicit the proper response

---

[11] Gerald F. Hess, Heads and hearts: The Teaching and Learning Environment in Law School (2002) 52 *J. Leg. Educ.* 75.

[12] Some overseas law schools provide the teacher a seating chart (a simple blank diagram of seats in the class) for the teachers use to fill in her students' names. Alternately, the teacher could ask her students to choose their seats and then enter their names to the chosen seat in the chart. This enables the teacher to quickly know the names of her student for purposes of creating conversational, student-centred dynamics. See Katz & O'Neil, above n. 2, 34

[13] One effective way of minimizing intimidation in random interrogation and calling of students to participate is to inform ahead of the lecture the particular students who would be interrogated. See Katz & O'Neil, above n. 2, 36.

[14] Katz & O'Neil, above n. 2, 33.

from the class.[15] A good way to get the pulse of your audience is to maintain proper eye contact and pay attention to distracting noises in the class. It can tell the teacher so much as to how well learning is effective. Some could accomplish it directly by asking for a show of hands. The methods for gauging pulse are many and every teacher will need to learn and individuate her technique in this respect.

Every teacher must be able to identify what is the supposed *thread* (theme) that runs through the course. This can be a daunting task requiring familiarity with legal philosophy, especially those that interrogate legal epistemology. Happily, the teacher's basic undergraduate learning of jurisprudence is likely to have supplied her the necessary roadmap. Some have suggested that the political inclination of the teacher can distort the process of mapping out the basic thread. Much as this can be true to a large extent, it must be admitted that whatever thread the teacher chooses can help the class temperate topical learning debates and provide background explication of the rules, doctrines and principles studied in the course. What is more, finding the theme does not prevent its validity questioning by the class or prevent finding a less political neutral theme by investigation. The good thing about finding and explicating the basic thread of a course is that it makes it easier for the class to understand the historical and contextual perspectives of the course, invariably sharpening appreciation for critical thinking.

For example, in an attempt to use a neutral explanation theme to the law of trust, a teacher could in her lecture simply ask the class for a dictionary meaning of the word "trust." Thereafter could ask the class to make a list of three persons they trust, giving reasons why they trust them. The exercise can be revelatory as each brings out their list and reasons for trusting. Most will likely list as persons they trust, their parents, spouse, sibling or a close friend. The reason for trusting them being confidants, seeking their best interest always, etc. This sets the stage for the big-picture-trust developing from principles of equity rooted in friendship and family setting. What is more, the fiduciary duties of loyalty, and all its additional paraphernalia can then be translated to how law institutionalizes the arrangement in the relationship between trustee and *custi que trust* (beneficiary).

For the purpose of choosing the recurrent theme, it is advised that those which reveal connection between different topics in the course offers useful insight into the thread running through the subject.

First Day Teaching Techniques

It is now time to start the first day teaching. An effective first thing to do as the teacher enters the class is to greet the students, introduce herself and state the

---

[15] For a list of good public speaking qualities, see Benefit Book.

reason why there, namely to teach the particular subject. Some teachers in the first lecture day have found it useful to ask that the students introduce themselves soon thereafter. While this can be a useful style, it could be less effective for a large class, may take too much valuable time, and guess what the teacher is not likely to really remember most names from the process. It may prove rather beneficial to use the seat chart styles for the purpose and incrementally learn students' names.

It is now time for serious business of teaching. Since effective learning is often interactive and student-centred, the teacher should be quick to create that conducive environment. This requires that the teacher let the students know that she *cares about helping them to learn*. The practice where some teachers frightening their students about that the course is difficult to understand or by some form of intimidation or superiority claim has no place in the classroom. Care is demonstrated in thoughts, words, and actions all underlined in sincerity.

Next the teacher should establish her *expectations*-what is expected of the students in terms of classroom advanced preparation and participation; method of interrogating participation; what constitutes good performance; pre-and post-course knowledge, skills and values expected, criteria for assessment and evaluation and the like.

Let us see one designed by Professor Gilda Daniels for Critical Legal Theory as our sample.[16]

The design follows this order:

Name of Teacher

Venue of Lecture

Telephone Number

E-mail Address

Website

Office Hours: (state availability days and time of consultation save by appointment)

Instruction: Please read the syllabus carefully before the first class, to understand the course requirements.

Course Description: (state the course content)

Course Objectives: (state course objectives and teaching techniques, such as that there will be group activities, use of MCQs, simulations, discussion questions, midterm and final term essay/MCQ testing, etc. to assist in learning. The teacher can state further what core competencies, the substantive knowledge and lawyering skills the course will assist the students to attain.

---

[16] See teaching of Critical Legal Theory at University of Baltimore School of Law, available at http//law.ubalt.edu, accessed September 23, 2015.

For example, on competencies of professionalism the syllabus could list the following: that it would assist them develop professional values, including judgment, reflectiveness and decision-making, cultural sensitivity and interpersonal skills and the like.

For substantive knowledge, it could state: knowledge of doctrinal law, including its economics, history, theory, policy and context.

While for lawyering skills, it could state: critical analysis, deep reasoning and reflection, problem-solving, persuasion, and rhetoric.

Reading List: This should include the book(s) considered most suitable for the course and state the primary source for the course shall be the course website (course website is recommended for every course taught).[17] All students offering the course would be required to register at the given site. This section should also state that the webpage shall be used for announcements, and so all should regularly visit the site.

Assessment-Exam and Grading: This section should explicitly spell out how final grades will be totaled. Some teachers find it useful to do the breakdown very comprehensive. For example, the teacher may state that discussion questions (DQ) shall attract 10 points; continuous MCQ, 20 points; seventy percent class attendance, 10 points; and all essay final course term 60 points, etc. depending on the teacher/faculty grading policy.

Attendance Policy: This would usually state when deemed excessive absence shall be awarded a fail grade, etc.

Classroom Policy: This would list requirements for preparation and participation, laptop use, etc.

Syllabus: This should contain the week of study, subject topic, reading assignment and discussion question, etc. (include the lesson note style of the NLS).

The interaction should then snowball to the hundred and one *housekeeping* matters-passing round the seating chart [if it is a style chosen to identify names), going through the syllabus (as stated in the synopsis or lesson plan), reviewing the administrative ground rules for the course. In today's world of computer and e-learning, it would for example be expedient to tell the students that all cellular phone be switched off or put in the silent profile to prevent distraction of other, etc.

The teacher can go further to introduce the substance or theme thread of the course by interaction discussion. Care must be exercise in choosing an effective introduction that rouses interest in the course. It is important that the opening introductory statements say something pertinent that will get the class attention to be interested in the course. There are several ways to do it. Relating the course to

---

[17] see discussion on technology and new teacher.

be studied to the daily concerns and challenges in the social world can be useful in this respect. The use of questions that stimulates thinking is another technique. Some teachers have found it helpful to relate real-life experience or relate a recent news item, a quotation or statement from a recognized authority to build interest in the course.

As example of using possible daily concerns and experience, a criminal law teacher can skilfully employ the *Speluncean Explorers* case to stimulate interest on how the legal system generates a theory of punishment, treats (in)voluntary acts and generally draws a distinction between acts and omissions.[18] It would be simply okay to state the facts as stated by Truepenny, CJ, only to create the necessary attention and expectation.

The trust example above is another skilful way to rouse interest using social world challenges and expectation.[19] An example of authoritative quotations or statement a teacher can use in land law (like my teacher employed)[20] is to relate how the first man was formed by God. Obviously, for the dust (land). He expected to also live on the produce of the land. Yes, the creation account tells that he was blessed, ask to multiple and fill the earth (land). When he fell into sin the prescribed punishment was to return to the dust (land). In effect, the essence of life is rooted on the land. It is the properties of formation, basis for sustenance and eventual destiny on death. Drawing on this necessary analogy the teacher could have succeeded in rousing the interest on her class in the study of land law- an essential if not the most important subject of learning in the faculty.

After the cursory introduction, it would be beneficial for our new teacher to do an *overview* of the course, which lays out the full range of topics to be covered in the course. Expectation is often heightened if the teacher can connect in concise manner how which topic fits the introduction. Keeping the big-picture in focus for them create keen interest in subsequent class. By modest count the first day in class is over and effective.

Routine Teaching Techniques (course review and exams)

While American law schools use the Socratic interrogators style of teaching, the Nigerian teaching technique is different.[21] The Nigerian style is lecture and

---

[18] The Case of the Speluncean Explorers (1949) 62 *Hard. L. Rev.* 1(a case constructed by Lon. L. Fuller).

[19] Above see p. 3.

[20] Prof. Jelili Omotola of the University of Lagos referring to the Biblical account of creation in Genesis.

[21] Socratic Teaching. It is a technique which only teaches how to think like a lawyer and is generally deficient in transferring skills and values. Karen Tokarz, et al, Legal Education at a Crossroad: Innovation, Integration, and Pluralism Required (2014) 43 *Washington Univ. J Law & Policy* 11, John B. Garvey & Anne F. Zinkin, Making Law Students Client-Ready: A New Model in Legal Education (2009) 1 *Duke Forum Law & Soc. Change* 101. P.A. Jones, Theory and Practice in Professional Education (2000) 7 *Int. J. Legal Profession* 239. James R. Maxeiner, Educating Lawyers Now and Then: Two Carnegie Critiques of

seminar oriented. Teacher often dictates notes accompanied with occasion explanation as teaching pedagogy. The lecture style is characterized by teacher delivering a prepared lesson, students' contribution not encouraged and where necessary, it takes the form of clarification questions. In contrast, the seminar or tutorial style, the majority of contributions come from the students, and they engage in a dialogue with each other, as well as with the teacher. This prevalent Nigerian technique does not require any performance whatsoever from the students. It is not only teacher-centred and passive, it is totally deficient in training students for the profession. It resembles more instruction stepped in teaching liberal arts or humanities, unfit for professional training.[22] Effective teaching demands collaborative, student-centred learning. So, rather than the style in use, faculties should design a system that allows for active learning like that now in use by the Nigerian Law School.[23] It is a pedagogy based on lesson

---

the Common Law and Case Method (2007) 35 *International J. Leg. Info.* 1. See also William M. Sullivan, et al. eds. *Carnegie Fund for the Advancement of Teaching, Educating Lawyers: Preparation for the Profession of Law,* 2007 (hereinafter called the *Carnegie Report*) Foundation for the Advancement of Teaching, Preparation for the Professions Program (PPP) 2007, Legal Education Report based on a survey of more than two hundred law faculties (schools) in the US and Canada in 1999. For example, Robert MacCrate in forward to *Best Practices* said: "The central message in both Best Practices and in the contemporaneous Carnegie Report is that law schools should broaden the range of lessons they teach, reducing doctrinal education that uses the Socratic dialogue and case method: integrate the teaching of knowledge, skills and values, and not treat them as separate subjects in separate courses: and give greater attention to instruction in professionalism." See also Roy Stuckey et. al., *Best Practices for Legal Education: A Vision and a Roadmap,* 2007 (hereinafter called *Best Practices*) and generally, Association of American Law School, Conference on the Future of Law School Curriculum: Brochure (Seattle, 2011). The Nigerian lecture type is also susceptible to the same pitfalls. That also explains why interdisciplinary courses been taught in faculties of law by NUC benchmark standards are truly not interdisciplinary in the sense of making them applicable to legal studies. For instance, professional courses like medicine does not graft interdisciplinary courses in the module form from the humanities, but rather embed them within the skills compartment in their applied form. Ethics for instance is not taught through pure philosophy to doctors. Rather its applied form is what is used as basis for instructing doctors. So, a pupil doctor would receive ethics instruction on say how to ethically manage treatment choices, organ donation issues and neonatal treatment decisions. See Festus Emiri, *Medical Law and Ethics in Nigeria,* Lagos: Malthouse Press, 2012. That is the same path the legal profession should walk. American law schools already are doing so. For example, the central message to all of them is to reduce doctrinal teaching by giving greater attention to instruction in professionalism. That explains why most top school curriculum does not contain subjects like literature, philosophy etc. Rather professional skill courses such as legal writing, negotiation, construction of facts etc. make up the content of their interdisciplinary approach to legal education. Unfortunately, the picture that emerges from our present NUC benchmark for law curriculum falls short of typical professional law faculties. Our faculties' programme of instruction in law more closely resembles typical programme of instruction for preparing liberally-educated students.

[22] Refer Ado lecture on train doctors etc. Mark Yates, The Carnegie Effect: Elevating Practical Knowledge Over Liberal Education in Curriculum Reform (2011) 17 J. Leg. Writing Institute 232, Debra M. Schneider, Refashioning Legal Pedagogy After Carnegie Report: Something Borrowed, Something New (2009) available at http://works.bepress.com/debra_schneider/1, Rosco B. Turner, Changing Objectives in Legal Education (1931) 40 Yale L.J. 575, James R. Maxeiner, Educating Lawyers Now and Then: Two Carnegie Critiques of the Common Law and Case Method (2007) 35 Int' J. Legal Info. 1; Peggy Maisel, Expanding and Sustaining Clinical Legal Education in Developing Countries: What We Can Learn from South Africa (2006) 30 Fordham *Int'L.J.* 374 at 419.

[23] refer to teaching method at NLS. Peter D. Swords & Frank K. Walwer, Cost Aspects of Clinical Education, in Clinical Legal Education: Report of the Association of American Law Schools-American Bar

plan generating active student-participation in form of role-play, simulation, live clinic, etc.[24]

Association Committee on Guidelines for Clinical Education, 1980, 153, Robert R. Kuehn, Pricing Clinical Legal Education at 23 (the article reveals clinical education has no cost and need not cost students more in tuition and is more of a school's will to provide it than of cost because data shows that nearly 80% of American law schools have present teaching capacity to provide clinical education without adding courses and faculty members. See also Daniel Thies, Rethinking Legal Education in Hard Times: The Recession, Practical Legal Education and the New Job Market (2010) 59 J. Legal Educ. 598.

[24] Elliott S. Milstein, Legal Education in the United States: In-House Clinics, Externship and Simulation (2001) 51 *J. Leg. Educ.* 375; For reading on techniques and strategies for legal education, teachers should familiarize themselves with readings from such as Gerald F. Hess & Steven Friedland, *Techniques for Teaching Law,* Durham, North Carolina: Caroline Academic Press, 1999, Howard E. Katz & Kevin F. O'Neill, *Strategies and Techniques of Law School Teaching: A Primer for New (and Not So New) Professors,* New York: Aspen Publishers, Wolters Kluwer, 2009. Additional useful reading can be gleaned from Paul G. Haskell, Teaching Moral Analysis in Law School (1999) 66 *Notre Dame L. Rev.* 1025 (explores the importance and feasibility of applying moral principles to legal problems in law school instruction), Bennett, Making Moral Lawyers: A Modest Proposal (1986) 36 *Cath. U.L. Rev.* 45, Lowell Bautista, The Socratic Method as a Pedagogical Method in Legal Education (2014) *Univ. Wollongong Research Online,* Kuan-Chun Chang, The Teaching of Law in the United States: Studies on the Case and Socratic Methods in Comparison with Traditional Taiwanese Pedagogy (2009) 4 *National Taiwan Univ. Rev.* 3, Jenny Morgan, The Socratic Method: Silencing Cooperation (1989) 1 *Leg. Educ. Rev.* 151, Orin S. Kerr, The Decline of the Socratic Method at Harvard (1999) 78 *Nebraska L. Rev.* 113 (argues that the method is on the decline as it is more of myth than reality), Karen Gross, Process Reengineering and Legal Education: An Essay on Daring to Think Differently (2005)49 *New York Law School L. Rev.* 435 (presents a reengineering approach to legal education by asking the blunt question how legal education would be designed if we were to start from the scratch, cognizant of the present, but not constrained by it), Frances McGlone, Student Peer Mentors: A Teaching and Learning Strategy Designed to Promote Cooperative Approaches to Learning and Development of Lifelong Learning Skills (1996) 12 *Queensland Univ. Tech. L.J.* 201 (illustrates how the peer mentoring programme was developed to teach undergraduate courses in contract and tort in Queensland University of Technology), Gregory S. Munro, Outcome Assessment for Law Schools, Spokane, Washington, Gonzaga Univ. School of Law, Inst. For Law School Teaching, 2000 (generally on origin, purpose and how to do assessment that are valid, reliable and fair for law subjects), James B. White, Law as Language: Reading Law and Reading Literature (1982) 60 *Texas L. Rev.* 415 (connects law with literature), James Boyd White, *Legal Imagination*, Boston: Little, Brown, 1973, Festus Emiri & Ayuba Giwa, above n. 35, but cf. Richard Posner, Law and Literature: A Relation Reargued (1986) 72 *Virginia L. Rev.* 1351 (where the writer argues that the use of literature in the interpretation of legal texts by method of literary criticism and its use to improve judicial opinions are overstated), Douglas J. Whaley, Teaching Law: Advice for the New Professor (1982) 43 *Ohio St. L.J.* 125, Susan J. Becker, Advice for the New Law Professor: A View from the Trenches (1992) 42 *J. Leg. Educ.* 432, Karen Tokarz, et. al., Legal Education at a Crossroad: Innovation, Integration, and Pluralism Required (2014) 43 *Washington Univ. J. Law & Policy* 11, John B. Garvey & Anne F. Zinkin, Making Law Students Client-Ready: A Model in Legal Education (2009) 1 *Duke Forum Law & Social Change* 101 (questions the 1870's Christopher C. Langdell's teaching method of studying cases combined with the Socratic questioning for failing to make students' client-ready., for while the method may meet the needs of eventual judges and legal scientists, it leaves the student ill-prepared to practice), Kent D. Syverud, Taking Students Seriously: A Guide for New Law Teachers (1993) 43 *J. Leg. Educ.* 247, Gerald F. Hess, Heads and Heats: The Teaching and Learning Environment in Law School (2002) 52 *J. Legal Educ.* 75, Paul Wangerin, Technology in the Service of Tradition: Electronic Lectures and Live-Class Teaching (2003) 53 *J. Leg. Educ.* 213, George M. Cohen, When Law and Economics Met Professional Responsibility (1998) 67 *Fordham L. Rev.* 273, Peggy Maisel, Expanding and Sustaining Clinical Legal Education in Developing Countries: What We Can Learn From South Africa (2006) 30 *Fordham Int' L.J.* 374 (reviews the development of clinical legal education in South Africa and the valuable lessons such an analysis provides for those seeking to promote it elsewhere), Robert R. Kuehn, Pricing Clinical Legal Education (empirical examination that defeats the claim that clinical education is too expensive), Peter A Joy, The Cost of Clinical Legal Education (2012) 32 *Boston College J. Law & Social Justice* 309 (argues that though clinical legal education should not be immune to cost constraint, so should any ither type of law school

Under the traditional pedagogy, the system intermittently allows room for *questions*. In answering questions the teacher should be kind, respectful and understanding no matter how ridiculous the question appears to be.

For now, other concerns related to everyday teaching such as the use of technology, grading and examination would be addressed in other section in this book.[25]

---

expenditure, all of which should be put through a cost-benefit analysis for cost-saving potential), Richard J. Wilson, Western Europe: Last Holdout in the Worldwide Acceptance of Clinical Legal Education (2009) 10 *German L.J.* 823.

[25] See chapters.

Chapter 4

Assessment and Evaluation

Introduction

Assessment and evaluation of learning is important in legal education for basic reasons: in promoting students learning and making law schools effective centres of law in society.[1] Curriculum teachers are familiar with the arsenals of assessment and evaluation in teaching. It is a required course for graduating as a student in the faculty of education.[2] Law teachers however, are yet to catch up in this area. Traditionally, legal education is conservative and not generally susceptible to innovation, so it is to be expected that law schools are impervious to developments in what has been termed the assessment movement.[3] Proper assessment demands that a law faculty should explicitly adopt and state categorically its mission statements and outcomes, explain how the curricula is designed and implemented to achieve the outcomes, and identify its methods for assessing students' performance and institutional outcomes promoting student learning. This no doubt is strange to legal education in Nigeria. I was a student over three decades ago in one of the top faculties in the country. I never saw published the mission and outcome statement of my faculty, talk more of an explanation how the curricula are designed to achieve them for purposes of evaluating students and faculty performance in meeting the targets. I have also taught law for nearly the same period. No faculty known to me does anything near the demands to assessment movement.

The value of outcome assessment to accreditation of academic programme and the faculty can be enormous in terms of advancing excellence and pursuit of effective academic programme. When a faculty has clear mission statement of what it sets out to do, possess a clear plan of how to achieve it, then it comes under a vintage to measure its successes or failures in prosecuting the mission, either or from both the perspective of students' and faculty sidedness. Outcome

---

[1] Gregory S. Munro, *Outcome Assessment for Law School*, WA: Spokane, Inst' Law Sch. Teaching, 2000.
[2] For general reading see Nigerian texts.
[3] See Munro, above n. 1, 4. Gregory S. Munro, *Outcome Assessment for Law School*, WA: Spokane, Inst' Law Sch. Teaching, 2000.

assessment mechanism focuses a faculty, helping it to coordinate its activities and programmes to fit purpose.

True, BMAS requires every faculty in the country seeking accreditation from the NUC or CLE to explicitly state their mission statement and how the curricula is designed to achieve them, but the truth is that faculties hardly review those accreditation documents for purposes of assessing students' and faculty performance after going through the rituals of accreditation.

This chapter design is to a call for law teachers to critical engage issues of curricula design, teaching pedagogy, and grading with the seriousness they attend to examination and the need to institutionalize sound, clear and coherent assessment of their students and faculties.

Please state how faculties and students' assessment affect rating and job prospects.

What is Assessment?

Assessment isn't a strange lexicon to many. Job employers assess their employees. Individuals often assess situations to take rational decisions. In education, assessment brings to mind a form of scaling for students to weigh performance. Socrates is reputed to be the originator of students' assessment. He accomplished it by interrogating his students.[4]

According to Munro, "assessment connotes a set of practices by which an educational institution adopts a mission, identifies desired student and institutional goals and objectives (outcomes), and measures its effectiveness in attaining those outcomes."[5] From this it is clear that assessment is not just about examination, testing to grade student. Assessment is also a learning tool for institutions to get feedback for purpose of strategizing. With call for professionalism in the teaching of law it is to be expected that assessment would take on greater significance to include assessment of lawyering skills and values. This would require new techniques for grading student outside the usual doctrinal assessment in the form of MCQ and essay examination. Multiple evaluation of students' performance is bound to include assessment that implicates thinking and performing lawyering tasks, such as those related to simulation and live clinics with necessary feedback. The end product of assessment in professionalism brings about more active teaching and learn for all the actors in legal education.

---

[4] Lowell Bautista, The Socratic Method as a Pedagogical Method in Legal Education (2014) U. Wollongong available http/ro.uow.edu.au/lhapapers/1481, accessed March 10, 2016 (posits that Socrates posed questions to his students reveals their hidden ignorance on the subject, thereby bringing the person questioned to a revelation of knowledge or truth that she innately possessed. It is a method of teaching characterized by question and answer to elicit knowledge) at 2-3.

[5] Munro, above n. 1, 11. Gregory S. Munro, *Outcome Assessment for Law School,* WA: Spokane, Inst' Law Sch. Teaching, 2000.

Since assessment isn't one-sided, but includes institutional assessment, it follows that it is also a sort of feedback technique for the faculty to evaluate itself using its parameters as set out in its mission. It is in this respect a "process that provides feedback to faculty, staff, and various publics about patterns of student and alumnae performance on a range of curriculum outcomes."[6] It is therefore, not just summative (measuring students' or institutional performance), but is formative (instrument of learning) as well.

Essentials of Assessment

If assessment carries all the benefits so stated, it is important to know what the characteristics of effective assessment. Certain principles stand out clear as signpost for effective assessment. They are as follows:

1. Its primary focus should be to enhance students learning

The priority of a faculty should be difficult to find. Most persons will tell you it is to properly and effectively enhance learning of students. But here is where the paradox lies. The priority of law teachers may differ fundamentally with that view. New comers into the teaching business are quickly greeted with the slogan, 'you in the place of publish or perish.'[7] So, the law teacher comes under pressure from day one to publish in order to make academic progress. That being the case, it can be said that the institutional goal is in direct conflict with the set goal of its operators. Both however need not be competing goals. They can complement each other. No question about it. Ranking of a faculty has much to do with its innovative research and scholarship, but it must not be forgotten that the piper who pays for research and scholarship (as music so to speak) is student fees. That being so it would not be out of place to make central student learning as the primary goal of an educational institution. While scholarship is an integral part of a faculty's mission, it is not the main purpose for establishing a faculty.

2. Integrated Professional Education

The shift from law as study in liberal/humanities to professional study constitutes best practice to make students' client-ready. That being so, assessment must enhance not just analytical reasoning and thinking but also emphasize abilities required for effective performance.

3. Active and Collaborative Learning

One good characteristics of adult education is that it should be active and collaborative in nature. Cognitive science reveals that what people hear is easily

---

[6] Munro, above n. 1, 12.

[7] John S. Elson, The Case Against Legal Scholarship or, If the Professor Must Publish, Must the Professor Perish? (1989) 39 *J. Leg. Educ.* 343. See also innovative scholarship paper.

forgotten. But is remember more if they perform what they hear. Customarily, law teachers in Nigeria teach by note-dictation and side explanation. American law school pedagogy is dominated by the Socratic teaching style. Both are not fundamentally different save that the Socratic method infuses doses of student participation in 'finding the ball, which may be absent in the dictation style.'[8] That notwithstanding both do not exhibit the status of law teacher as facilitators of learning and student as initiators of learning. Simulation and clinics supply these missing ingredients.[9] (state how).

Collaborative learning makes it possible for students to downplay the usual individualistic and competitive nature of learning law. Rather, students cooperate in clinic classes to develop lawyering skills and values which are vital ingredients for alternative resolution of disputes.

4. Assessment Is Integral to Learning

One purpose of assessment is help measure how student and institution perform in achieving outcomes, that being so, it is corrective therapy in the learning process. The learning scenario is such that the teacher as facilitator of learning helps the student to initiate learning by performance, with teacher and student serving as assessors and the teacher provides the necessary feedback to help improve the learning of student. Student evaluation is therefore a combination of formative and summative examination.

The traditional practice of utilizing only summative assessment to the exclusion of formative assessment for grading examination is accordingly not useful in engendering integrated learning process and so should be depreciated.[10] Any assessment which excludes the formative is unrepresentative of students learning and abilities. For example, judging students be mere summative assessment can hardly test skills and values of problem-solving, oral communication, advocacy, writing and drafting, which are the very essence of lawyering.

It is suggested that formative assessment is more consistent with the way people learn. For example, in a typical tort simulation using the *Osemebor v Niger Biscuit Ltd* played out in chapter ---- the students learn firsthand skills of problem-solving, ethical issues involved in the prosecution and defence of personal injury and negligence claim, how to research on relevant laws outside the negligence square that relate to consumer protection and the like, how to write letters, make presentation to company and government officials, draft pleadings and many others connected with lawyering. They are able to self-assess or peer

---

[8] Finding the Ball. Paper on ontology.
[9] Festus Emiri & Ayuba Giwa, Simulation and Lawyering Skills.
[10] Bar Exam Failure article.

assess their performance with facilitator's feedback. At the end of the exercise they would retain the true essence of negligence by performance.

5. Assessment is Measured in Multiple Modes and Contexts

One characteristics of assessment for it to conform with the requirement of "validity" is it should be measured in multiple modes and context. For it to be reflective of student ability it should not be a one-off measure, such as the end of session examination type, we used to call "Almighty June," our faculty used to administer to us when we were undergraduate student many years ago before the advent of course semester system. Measurement using a single mode (oral or written) and a single instrument (multiple-choice or essay exam) may be ineffective and invalid.[11]

Adherence to the principle of multiple modes of assessment may demand faculties to vary modes of assessment to include in curricula subjects like legal writing and research (LWR), legal clinic, etc. in addition to tradition subjects as stand-alone module or as integrated with traditional subjects.[12] Also, in term of multiple contexts, faculties may need to profoundly change their traditional single of instrument for judging students' performance.

Since assessment isn't only designed for students but also for institutions, then faculties performance evaluation similarly demands multiple measurement. For example, a faculty should feel comfortable to measure its standing on survey from multiple sources, such as those from its students, alumnae, law firms, courts, etc. Considering different perspective from say first year or third year students, judges, recent graduates etc, about the effectiveness of the faculty's law programme can be useful in outcome measurement.

6. Articulating Outcomes

It is believed that learning is enhanced when its goals are explicitly articulated at the outset. That way students, faculty and the constituencies can be guided by the outcomes. No one is in the dark. In this respect, it is suggested that all the actors should pay close attention to faculties mission statement in the BMAS accreditation or faculty brochure.

7. Implementation

Because assessment is designed to facilitate improvement in learning by the adoption of a mission, identifying desired student and institutional goals and objectives (outcomes), and then measuring its effectiveness in attaining those outcomes, it follows that academic planning must be a continuum. The continuum can be institutionally enhanced with the establishment of an academic

---

[11] Essay and MCQ serve different purposes. Refer to article.
[12] For examples of integrated clinic in traditional subjects see article. See also Ado-Ekiti Keynote Address.

planning or quality assurance department or both. The measuring process ought to involve reengineering of teaching pedagogy, curriculum, course materials, evaluation of extent of learning, assessment methods, successes and drawbacks and many others. This calls for frank dialogue and collaboration between students, faculty, university, its constituencies, and if need be the wider society.

8. Improve Students' Performance

Assessment assumes that the teacher is responsible for determining what students learn and whether to change teaching method to improve learning. This principle does not subscribe to the common belief that mass students' failure is a result of students' inability or disinterest in studying hard. That being so, mass failure at bar examination or faculty exams may not be representative of students' fault but rather of teachers' ineffective assessment.[13] This is because effective assessment goes beyond the motions of teaching and testing by exam. It includes very importantly, an evaluation of teaching pedagogy, curriculum, course materials, evaluation of extent of learning, assessment methods, how well students' can perform what they learn, and evaluation of information to determine what changes are needed in curriculum and the like to improve learning.

9. Standard for Performance

It is not enough for the teacher to analysis what is expected as learning outcome to students, the teacher must identify the set criteria for judging competent performance. Generally, law teachers don't make explicit what constitute competent performance. The criteria are often vague and arbitrary, known more to the teacher than those being judged by it.

For example, in a tort class using the *Osemobor* scenario[14] the teacher may ask the students to make oral application to say officials of the injurer, Niger Biscuits, requesting to know safety and precaution standard put in place in the factory to prevent defective product. The teacher judging the negotiation skill may watch out to see how the encounter between the victim's lawyer and company official is conducted. In assessing performance, it would be necessary to tell the student before the role-play what qualities of negotiation skills they would be assessed for and how best they can seek to meet the standard. For instance, if the teacher chooses to watch say, the skill of listening, how lawyers can benefit from paying attention to what the parties or their adversaries say, the teacher should clear the dominant quality for which performance is being assessed: skill of listening. But she must go further before the role-play to also tell the students ways that enhance paying attention. This she could do by stating that one way to

---

[13] Bar failure article.
[14] *Osemobor* v. *Niger Biscuit Ltd.* [1973] NCLR 382, (per Kassim J. High Court of Lagos State).

pay attention is to keep eyes on the speaker as a helping to concentrate or taking brief notes of main points, isolation of main points etc. this way the students are know what outcome is being judged and the criteria for it and so would improve in proficiency. According to Munro, this sort of learning is "student-centred and ability-based."[15]

10. Integrated Education

Assessment presupposes that learning is an integrated, coherent activity, not simply a collection of discrete activities. While it is not doubted that the law curricula is made up of modular subjects which for convenience can be divided into discrete groups of say public and private law or doctrinal and clinic etc. and two teachers teaching the same subject may instruct in different ways, all members of the faculty must key into a planned academic structure (mission statement, students and institutional outcomes, teaching techniques and strategies, and assessment programme) built around principles of assessment. In effect teachers as a group should invest in learning ability-based, student-centred learning and performance assessment.

Effective Assessment

For assessment to be effective it must exhibit the character of validity, reliability, and fairness.

1. Validity

Validity is a sort of fitness test. The process must accomplish its set objective. In this regards it resemble the regulatory manifesto of Breyer[16] or what commercial lawyers in sale of goods contract, that goods must be fit for purpose.[17] In the context of assessment, validity means that the mode of assessment must affect what it designed for, whether for students or the institution. Anyone who has attended a law graduation or call-to-bar ceremony would likely hear the head of the training institution proclaim: "these are fit and proper person competent in learning and character." What it brings to the mind is that the graduates are sound in learning and character. But it is plausible to ask, if the semester or end of year essay (sometimes mixed with MCQ) correlates to making the graduates fit for purpose: does performance in the exams translates to make new wigs client-ready? Hardly. In fact, it has been suggested that law school exams don't test the

---

[15] Munro, 76.

[16] Professor Stephen Breyer (now Justice of the United States Supreme Court) in his seminal work on regulation, generally referred to as the *regulatory manifesto* stated this simple axiom for creating and implementing regulatory programme: determine the objectives, examine the alternative methods of obtaining the objectives, and choose the best methods for doing so. See, Stephen Breyer, *Regulation and Its Reform*, 1982.

[17] See s. Sale of Goods Law. See also PS Atiyah,

skills required for effective lawyering.[18] Validity here requires that the test or other assessment of students' performance measures whether the course or subject goals and objectives are satisfied.

With respect to institutional assessment validity demands knowing whether the measure of success in its teaching translates to the quality of graduates occupying positions of responsibility and prestige?

For subject effectiveness, there should be connection between what is taught and what is assessed, requiring that the teacher makes clear course goals and what she teaches. For institutional measure, faculty evaluation should meet its institutional outcome. Where for example, a faculty sets out to contribute to society in champion a market approach to teaching law stepped in economics with a view of building a crop of graduates contributing to economic development, the instrument must assess the faculty's success in fulfilling the role.

2. Reliability

Reliability calls to question the extent to which an assessment instrument yields scientific predictability. Whether it yields consistent, reliable answers or results when repeated.

In terms of course content, reliability should reflect the extent to which the student meets the goals for the course. Thus, if exams samples too little of a course content, then it cannot reflect the extent to which the students meet the objective of the course. Excelling or failing is made to depend on learning an aspect only of the course. So, if restitution is agreed to be triggered by three causative events of say unjust enrichment, reversal of benefits from acquisitive wrongs, and the vindication of proprietary rights, testing the students on only one head of restitution would not reflect whether the student learned the causative events that generate restitution. Un this respect, MCQ questions could provide a better tool than essay and formative assessment in furthering course content reliability.[19]

Reliability also implicates scoring consistency. If three teachers were to mark same answer of an exam would they arrive at the same score? It is likely that if the answer is the essay type, grades awarded may show some marked difference. The inconsistency situation is exacerbated by the mandatory bell-shaped curves for exams[20] and the prevalence of norm-reference grading style by law teachers.[21] Even where assessment is done by a single teacher, experience tells that grading over a long time, grading fatigue or frame of mind and mood all combine to make

---

[18] refer to article on law school exam.

[19] Essay versus MCQ

[20] Joshua M. Silverstein, In Defence of Mandatory Curves (2012) 34 *U. Ark. Little Rock L. Rev.* 253.

[21] See discussion on norm-reference at p.

unreliable and inconsistent grading style. These challenges are made prevailing with MCQ examinations.[22]

3. Fairness

Fairness requires that assessment be equitable both in process and result. Students learning is often inhibited by perception of inequitable assessment. Some teachers are known for avoiding awarding "A" grade even for exceptional answers. In fact, some tell their students that the grade is reserved for the teacher. Such a stance not only inhibit learning, it could create a situation of what can be called "course-shopping-" students seek to offer courses being taught by teachers perceived as fairer not minding relevance to future usefulness to proposed specialty.

Fairness can also come to play where assessment exercise is based on cultural, ethnic, gender peculiarity could present challenges for those not familiar with the peculiarity. For example, a set of exam questions with facts not familiar to say minorities gives unfair advantage to those familiar with the facts while disadvantaging those unfamiliar with the scenario.

Unfairness can also result from unequal access by some students to the teacher and information, such as private discussion with teacher before student performance, use of prior examination questions, testing skills not taught in the course, etc.

Benefits of Assessment

The growing demands for quality, accountability and responsibility in education, especially university education provides the driver for assessment. This demand comes from the Nigerian Universities Commission, Council of Legal Education, and the Nigerian Bar Association-the primary accrediting agencies for faculties of law. This is especially so now that the NBA is expressing concern about the preparedness of law students for the practice of law.[23]

Absence of assessment in most, if not all faculties of law, mean that there is merely a near universal reliance on an exam system in faculties of law as the measure for improving students learning and enhancing institutional effective when we all know that the real purpose of examination is not to evaluate both but is merely device for sorting and ranking students by assigning grades.[24]

---

[22] Essay versus MCQ article.

[23] NBA needs assessment. Both the MacCrate Report and the Carnegie Report decry the weakness inherent in the homogenous methodology of American legal education. Having identified the fundamental skills and values that every lawyer should acquire, they go on to recommend the roles the practicing profession and academy should assume in preparing students to be client-ready. See, (cite both reports). See also, Robert MacCrate, Lecture on Legal Education, Wake Forest School of Law (1995) 30 *Wake Forest L. Rev.* 261 (discussion of a history of the task force set up on American law schools and its report).

[24] Roger C. Cramton, The Current State of the Law Curriculum (1982) 32 *J. Leg. Educ.* 321.

Generally, examination pattern in the faculties follow this order: students are evaluated at the end of semester or course, the questions are hypothetical essay focusing on application of judicial rules and doctrines, and in some rare cases a mix of multiple-choice questions, to be attempted under constraint of time, averaging two to four hours. Simple. After grading there is usual no feedback save that the faculty just publishes the grades. There are hardly any institutional objective grading criteria. Some faculties however pretend that they have one by use of some form of grading normalization or grade curve to control distribution of grades.[25] The pattern is summative for all intent and purposes. It is designed to test learning after teaching. There is no post-mortem diagnosis so to speak for students to learn from less than competent performance. This contracts with the formative evaluation processes, in which students perform, they are evaluated and provided feedback to learn how to perform competently.

Formative evaluation is often not a staple in legal education except for the few faculties that run clinics. Even at that, the trend reveals that clinical performance rarely gets a percentage in the grading summation of examinations. There is marked absence of multiple evaluation in legal education, unlike in other professional disciplines like medicine, architecture, performance arts etc. Because final exam is traditionally the only formal evaluation in legal education and sole determinant of grades, law exams can hardly serve as a learning tool. Since final exam (referred to as bluebook or essay exam) is the basic evaluative tool in law, legal education stands accused as a violator of accepted principles of assessment and therefore lacks a sound basis for proper learning and instruction in

---

[25] Joshua M. Silverstein, In Defence of Mandatory Curves (2012) 34 *U. Ark. Little Rock L. Rev.* 253; Robert C. Downs & Nancy Levit, If It Can't Be Woebegon . . . A National Survey of Law School Grading and Grade Normalization Practices (1997) 65 *UMKC L. Rev* 819; Barbara G. Fines, Competition and the Curve (1997) 65 *UMKC L. Rev* 879

professionalism.[26] Law faculty and school exam relies on a narrow band of evaluation and the legal academy pays insufficient attention to the issue.[27]

The flip side of students' assessment is institutional assessment. It would appear that the NUC-CLE self-study or accreditation process is the only institutional self-assessment in place for most faculties in Nigeria. Comprehensive as the process would seem, insiders acknowledge that it is close to window-dressing. Accreditors sadly, focus solely on present condition of the faculty, its programmes, library, finances, teaching and examination time-tables, hours of lectures, who teaches what, physical facilities on ground and the like. The process isn't an assessment of how the faculty is achieving outcomes (its mission statement, programme objectives and assessment of the programme objectives). Accreditation does not interrogate the very important questions of what students should learn, how best to teach them, and how to determine whether they have learned it.

Sadly, ranking criteria that attempt to measure the quality of faculties limitedly focus on factors like name recognition, finance, placement network, alumni and faculty prominence, university entrance cutoff scores, educational innovation and research, hardly on outcomes.[28]

It is therefore plausible to think that the root of cause of a continuing downward slide in competence and character of new wigs is traceable to the inattention faculties ad the law schools pays to principles of assessment. Conversely, the problems that have plagued legal education in Nigeria are problems for which assessment can offer solution.[29] Undoubtedly, many faculties

---

[26] Refer to Ughelli lecture and the moot against legal academy. The bluebook exam is criticized for these drawbacks and being too subjective. See, Ben D. Wood, The Measurement of Law School Works (pt. 1-3) (1924) 24 *Colum. L. Rev.* 226 cited in Munro, 37. See also Phillip C. Kissam, Law School Examination (1989) 42 *Vand. L. Rev.* 433 (discusses the political and social context of bluebook examinations, how grades affect chances of hiring law graduates, why it is injurious to effective and democratic legal education); Janet Motley, A Foolish Consistency: The Law School Exam (1985) 10 *Nova. L. Rev.* 732 ("law school exams, . . fail to serve an educational purpose and may be counter-productive to our educational goals, particularly the goal of teaching our students to learn from experience. Furthermore, the present system is guaranteed to create artificial categories and classes of students, which, in turn stigmatize and dramatically affect their lives.") at 723-724; Steven H. Nickles, Examining and Grading in American Law Schools (1977) 30 *Ark. L. Rev.* 411; John Mixon & Gordon Otto, Continuous Quality Improvement, Law and Legal Education (1994) 43 *Emory L.J.* 442; Steve Sheppard, An Informal History of How Law Schools Evaluate Students, with a Predictable Emphasis on Law School Final Exams (1997) 65 *UMKC* 657; Douglas A. Henderson, Uncivil Procedure: Ranking Law Students Among Their Peers (1994) 27 *U. Mich. J.L.* Reform 399 (bluebook essay exam is "psychometrically unsound.") at 407.

[27] Annual law teachers conference address peripheral matters of state, development and economy save the Ado-Ekiti one. State how.

[28] Gregory S. Munro, *Outcome Assessment for Law School,* WA: Spokane, Inst' Law Sch. Teaching, 2000, 43.

[29] Munro, above n. 28, 45; Carl A. Auerbach, Legal Education and Some of Its Discontents (1984) 34 *J. Leg. Educ.* J43 (states that current debates on why there is deficiency in learning and character of lawyers' echo so many past controversies, adds nothing new, while avoiding the real root cause). For example, in Nigeria, the debates have harped on poor reading culture, corruption of educational system, lack of

lack mission, are not guided by students and institutional outcomes, their curriculum is deficient in both structure and coherence, employ ineffective teaching methods, lack assessment measures, have no feedback learning system, and lack a comprehensive programme of assessment, all of which are the basic root cause of *rot* in present legal education.

Adopting and implementing outcome assessment carries several advantages:

1. Addresses Problem of Legal Education

Assessment is the answer to present challenging slide for competence and character deficiency in legal education. Statement of outcomes helps a faculty to identify competencies which in turn puts pointedly an evaluation of a faculty's obligation to its constituencies. By reviewing from time to time its set of outcomes, the faculty comes to appreciate areas needing improvement which invariably will impact on its teaching methods and more.

2. Promotes Continuity in Academic Programme

It is expected that the structure provided by competencies would promote academic programme continuity. The outcomes enable the faculty determine whether it meets its benchmark. By articulating competencies faculty members are driven to coordinate the teaching of outcomes I appropriate classes with the proper teaching techniques required. A faculty's competence helps determine the qualification of faculty graduates for hiring purpose.[30] What is more, competence can go a long way to shape how individual law subject are taught, thereby creating a level of coherence in method, style and underlining philosophy of learning. This can engender some great team spirit and collaboration of teachers in a faculty.

For example, if a faculty has one of its philosophy to design it academic programme to incorporate social and economic parameters within which law operates as a basic tool of legal analysis, it would be expected that that kind of analysis would inform it teaching style or every subject module would end with a round-up of an economic analysis of the course. So, for say an economics congenial subject like Law of Taxation, the round-up could be like this: 'an analysis of an economic theory of taxation and social welfare programmes-the tax and transfer system and how it can accomplish redistributive goals in modern societies more efficiently than can be done through modifying private legal rights.' While for even a non-congenial subject like Nigerian Legal System the round-up

---

funding, etc., while omitting the important question of interrogating principles of assessment-how law faculties and schools should serve their constituencies, teaching pedagogy, responsibilities of legal academy to the profession and society, and how the academy should determine if it is discharging the responsibility.

[30] Munro, above n. 28, 63. For example, the Chicago Law School is known for its competence in an economic analysis of law. It would then not be surprising if corporate firm would prefer to hire their graduates in commercial departments.

would be like this: 'an examination of whether the intricacies and expense of the legal process is unavoidable cost of justice or is the tribute extracted from the public by the powerful legal profession.'

Employers of labour can quickly identify such a faculty as one likely to breed good corporate lawyer who are better able to slice through social and political conflicts through the prism of economics as an evaluative tool. Faculty members recognizing the competence structure of economics are more susceptible to bind closer in research thereby enhancing faculty team spirit. The competence would also determine the qualification of new entrances into the faculty. We should expect that one of its entry requirement would be credit pass in economics and mathematics. Furthermore, guided by this competence, faculty members would better understand what her colleagues are doing.

3. Measure of Relevance

Competencies thereon moderates as a standard for determining what matters or subjects from the academic programme that lack relevance to it and so should be removed.[31]

Note for the Legal Academy

Traditional faculty members are comfortable with present legal education techniques and would naturally consider the call for the introduction of assessment principles too cumbersome and worrisome. Assessment as defined for purpose of improving students learning and institutional effectiveness is woefully absent in faculties of law in Nigeria. Faculties merely relies on the examination system as the driver for assessment. There is therefore a reluctance the challenge present mindset. This reluctance notwithstanding, the legal academy cannot remain impervious to emerging changes in learning theories, techniques, and strategies for improving learning and performance. Since assessment is an effective and innovative learning tool, the legal academy has to come to terms with it and understand how to do it effectively. There is no question about it, if a faculty is to effective it must be guided by student outcomes-a statement of the knowledge, abilities and values its students should derive from legal education. Also, it should be guided institutional outcomes. This section is concerned with how the legal academy can effectively introduce and manage the principles of assessment in the faculty.

1. Steps to Initiating the Assessment Process

Recognizing the enormous benefits of assessment and the fact that most faculties are yet to key into the process it plausible to ask who should feel able to initiate

---

[31] Munro, above n. 28, 64.

the process. The likely initiators ought to be the deans of a faculty, as the academic leader or a concerned faculty members interested in academic excellence. The existence of a quality assurance or academic planning department in the university should aid driving the process. The collective body of law teachers through the Nigerian Association of Law Teachers (NALT) could also be a possible initiator for the assessment movement.[32]

The beginning of the process is an articulation of the *mission* statement of the faculty. A cursory look at most mission statements of faculties reveal that many simply copy from others without giving deep thought to how it should impact on their peculiarity as an evaluation criteria, whereas it ought to take cognizance of dialogue with the faculty's constituencies in formation. The statement should centre on the function a faculty is to serve and the values of the particular institution. For example, after articulating the general, primary mission to educate students to enter the legal profession, it should go further to define specific areas of its competencies. Such peculiarities could be like: "support scholarship and provide professional services to the oil, maritime and host communities in the Niger-Delta belt;" "emphasize those areas of law significant to North-East region, including natural resources, environmental, and Islamic law;" "inculcate in our students the ideas of economic efficiency as tool for explication of legal problem solving;" "promote among students, faculty, and the profession a sense of community enriched by a diverse group of people devoted to freedom of inquiry and freedom of expression," etc. Particularizing in this manner sets a faculty apart from others, directing competencies and collaboration towards them.

The next step would be to determine *student and faculty outcomes.* Here the faculty is required to adopt outcomes regarding student achievement and the faculty's role in the community and society. In involves interrogating the questions, what do we expect the students to know, think. Or do upon graduation; what knowledge, skills, values, attitude, motivation, and self-perception do we expect of them upon graduation, and the like.[33]

---

[32] Sadly, NALT has rarely concerned itself with matters connected with improving teaching and learning in faculties of law nor is it interrogating properly how learning theories impact on their students. In its over fifty years existence its annual conferences have focused on national issues such as (state)

[33] For a guide on this, see H. Russel Cort & Jack L. Sammons, The Search for Good Lawyering: A Concept and Model of Lawyering Competencies (1980) 29 *Clev. St. L. Rev.* 397; MacCrate and Carnegie Report. Analytical skills, problem-solving, writing, negotiation, communication etc. The MacCrate Report states that the following seven principles will help a faculty determine its outcomes: (i) outcome should be formulated in collaboration with the bench, bar, and perhaps other constituencies, (ii) outcomes should be consistent with and serve the institutions mission, (iii) outcomes should be adopted upon consensus after dialogue and deliberation, (iv) outcomes should be measurable, (v) outcomes should be explicit, and simple, (vi) outcomes are not to be limited by numbers, because number is a function of mission, resources, and time, but it should contain those the faculty can reasonably address, (vii) students outcomes should be reasonable, fixed in the light of their abilities and that of the faculty. See American

Thereafter, the assessment process reaches the *curriculum design* stage. The curriculum would then be designed to achieve the student outcomes. Faculty would at this stage be required to interrogate what curriculum best facilitate student development of the knowledge, skills and values reflected in the outcome. For example, if one of its primary outcomes is inculcate the ideas of economic efficiency as an evaluation, explicative and explanative tool of law, it should be expected that all it modular subject would have incorporated in them an economic analysis of the particular subject being taught. In formulating the curriculum faculty members should keep in mind the necessary characteristics of an effective curriculum, namely, that it be: coherent; mission and outcome focused; provide for incremental and developmental formation of student ability; faculty coordinated; provide for valid assessment and continual feedback to faculty and student; and be stepped in core courses tilted to create the required competencies.[34]

2. Measuring Outcomes

Outcomes have to be measured to provide opportunity for incremental improvement. Measurement can be from alumni or general interviews, through questionnaires and surveys, use of statistical indicators, examination, performance appraisals, student and faculty teaching portfolios, alumni follow-up reports, employee's reports, and student self-assessment of competencies.[35]

Bar Association (ABA) Section of Legal Education and Admission to the Bar, Legal Education and Professional Development-An Educational Continuum Report on the Task Force on Law Schools and the Profession: Narrowing the Gap, 1992 (often referred to as the MacCrate Report).

[34] Munro, 96.
[35] Munro, 117.

Chapter 5

Examinations

Introduction

Blue Book Essay Examination

Examination is a feature of assessment known to all law faculties. Assessment are of two kinds, formative and summative evaluation. Formative evaluation takes place during the course and it provides feedback for teacher and student. Summative testing is given at the end of course to determine how well students have achieved the course goals.[1]

Its usual form is the blue book essay exam requiring issue-spotting. Law examination is a dread for teacher and student. Teachers dread the heap of blue books waiting for grading, and while grading often complain about the performance of their students. Students on the other hand, are no better from the process. They complain and worry about poor performance despite all the time they devote to study. All of this is strong evidence that law school is poorly designed as an effective teaching and learning tool.[2]

Exam performs many functions all related to teaching and learning, namely: (i) to measure the learning competencies of the examinee; (ii) provides valuable feedback and to serve as a motivator for further study; (iii) it provides information to teacher regarding student's comprehension and ability of what is learned; (iv) it provides the teacher feedback regarding teaching effectiveness and preparation of students to enter the profession; (v) teaches student lawyering and learning skills.[3]

---

[1] See generally Phillip Kissam, Law School Examination (1989) 42 *Vand. L. Rev.* 433; Greg Sergienko, New Modes of Assessment (2001) 38 *San Diego L. Rev.* 463.

[2] Nickles, Examining and Grading in American Law Schools (1976) 30 *Ark. L. Rev.* 412 (discussion about the testing methodology of American law schools showing that their exam styles are outdated and discredited in research); Jay M. Feinman, Law School Grading (1996-1997) 65 *UMKC L. Rev.* 647 (discussion that law school courses traditionally have done very badly at formative evaluation). But cf. Kenny F. Hegland, On Essay Exams (2006) 56 *J. Leg. Educ.* 106(discussion that essay plays an important role in helping students become better writers. The writer suggest call to abandon essay exams isn't borne out of the educational deficiency of essay exams, but because the academy emphasizes scholarship as a more important thing than grading).

[3] Janet Motley, Foolish Consistency: The Law School Exam (1985-86) 10 *Nova. L. J.* 723 at 725; Kenney F Hegland, On Essay Exams (2006) 56 *J. Leg. Educ.* 140 (discussion on the use of all-essay exams).

Sadly, law school exam rarely meets these requirements. In the traditional way exams are being administered and used in the legal academy, exams fail to serve educational purposes and are susceptible to being counter-productive to educational goals, especially the goal of teaching students to learn from experience. The unfortunate effect of this is that law exams creates an artificial class of students, those pass well, those pass fairly and the others who fail, which goes on to stigmatize and affect work placement and fortune in life.[4]

The deficiencies of essay exams are as follows:

(i) Test Small Subset of Knowledge

Essay exams are time-consuming and can only test a subset of the course. It is therefore prone to sampling error in items tested which reduces it reliability. Unfortunately, it is difficult to eliminate sampling error because multiply administration of essay exam is difficult considering the considerable time it takes to grade them. Sampling error thus benefit students how concentrate on the areas the exam covers.

(ii) Fails to Test Skills Taught

One primary goal of education is teaching is for students to learn what they are taught. Law teaching is often devoted to teaching of doctrines, skills of interpretation, reasoning, and application to factual situations. The issue-spotting essay exam calls for the application of recalled law to facts situation.

(iii) Limitation of Frequency and Test Variety

Grading essay exam is time-consuming so the teacher tends to do a single course testing. Even if the teacher can give several essay examinations during the semester, the time it takes to grade often prevents quick feedback.

(iv) Inconsistent Grading

According to Munro, a teacher grading essay question assumes that "I know a 'D' when I see one," when studies clearly show that when the same examiner grades an exam answer twice there is only a seventy-five percent chance of grades being consistent in deciding whether an answer passed or failed.[5] The challenge is exacerbated by faculties not having internal coordination among faculty members in scoring exams even when teachers are teaching sections of the same course. Some faculties however try to conceal the unreliability deficiency of essay grading

---

[4] Janet Motley, Foolish Consistency: The Law School Exam (1985-86) 10 *Nova. L. J.* 723 (discussion that law school performs a poor job of assessment requiring its re-evaluation and reform).

[5] Gregory S. Munro, *Outcome Assessment for Law School,* WA: Spokane, Inst' Law Sch. Teaching, 2000, 108.

by the use of grade normalization policy regardless of who teaches what.[6] Much as the policy can polish the rough edges of inconsistency in grading, it cannot determine whether teaching and learning are effective. Thus, even with the policy, it is difficult to know whether the students have learned well or whether teaching is weak or not.

The subjectivity and unreliability of essay question opens it to denunciation as an invalid process for measuring ability and learning.[7] There is convincing evidence that law school exam provides no feedback which can be used to develop skills, because assessment only tells whether a student performs well or not. While the no feedback pass or fail grade may prompt a fail student to work harder, it sadly does not provide an explicit learning goal for the hard work. The student may just well be induced to spend more time memorizing rules, as the grading does not ordinarily teach her about analysis or reasoning. This is unfortunate because if law school exam must serve and advance educational goals then it must necessarily state what makes the performance less than appropriate. The exam thus creates the impression that unless students are threatened or rewarded through the grading process they will not be serious about study. Since motivation is directly related to feedback and explicit skill instruction, to the extent that the all-essay exam is generally summative it is devoid of validity and reliability.

This is to say in the least sad because law exams ought to hold great potentials as a teaching and learning devise designed to train student for the profession. If nothing law exams should test reasoning, and skills required for lawyering. Despite admission by some in the legal academy that law school exam is deficient on several fronts, many still stick to the traditional mode because the assessment function of exam dominates the consciousness of formal legal education making it difficult to conceive of an expanded role for examination.

Teachers are often reluctant to re-examine mode of examination thinking that what we have is just good enough. After all, it was the same mode they were examined with when they were students and they did well. Recognizing that there are many lawyers who succeed in spite of the degree brand placed on them as students ought to indicate that students who do not do well in law exams are not necessarily destined to professional incompetence. Therefore, if students do not perform well, teacher should rethink better mode for transmitting lawyering skills.

It is not all knocks for essay exams. One skill it teaches students is how to work under severe time pressure. Useful as this may seem it appropriateness in

---

[6] Grade normalization policy refers to. Robert C. Downs & Nancy Levit, if It Can't Be Lake Woebegon... A Nationwide Survey of Law School Grading and Grade Nominalization Practices (1997) 65 *UMKC L. Rev.* 819 at 831.

[7] For example, it is difficult to know precisely what is being tested for and graded in a typical law essay exams, because it could range from a conglomerate such as knowledge of rules, writing style, grammar, reasoning, handwriting, spelling etc.

real practice of law is not as prevailing. Much of legal problem-solving in the real world demands more of reasoning than speed. Students who have no speed in writing would be disadvantaged in essay exam even if they can think and analysis well.

It is also suggested that the essay exam teaches skills of memorizing. The value of the skill is dubious, because memorizing isn't a core skill. Competent lawyers do not memorize rules. They consult materials before advising clients. Essay exam disadvantage students with poor memories, regardless of possessing other fundamental lawyering skills.

Good grades in essay exams often depend on issue-spotting, which does not necessarily translate include the ability to analyse and reason. Sadly, grades derived from essay exams are used to categorize and stigmatize students with significant consequences. In our competitive society where employment placement is made to depend on grades, law exams create a culture of competition and an avoidance of collaboration, the development of "every person to herself attitude, which promotes combative dispute resolution mentality in the profession. Grades and competition at the cost of friendship and collaboration is said to have as its basis the rewards of power and money.[8] The result is adverse for the sustenance of empowering public consciousness. This is to be expected. As law students near the finish line of study, they find little interest in public interest lawyering, especially lawyering for the powerless and poor. Their initial dreams of righting much of social injustice exhibited in early law learning simply evaporates. They become concerned with how to make money and join the high-network world.

What all of this simply reveal is that law traditional essay exam is counterproductive to teaching and the learning process from experience. Sticking to it as the academy does demonstrates that teachers are like their students failing to learn from experience, in what works and what doesn't work in training our students. We have become fossilized to certainty, and are unable to adjust even in the face of invalidity and unreliability of our exams.

Suggestions to Improve Essay Exams
(i) Use of MCQ
A mix of essay and MCQ can reduce law exam susceptibility to these deficiencies.[9] MCQ enjoys a lot of advantages over essay exam. Assessment on it covers a

---

[8] Janet Motley, Foolish Consistency: The Law School Exam (1985-86) 10 *Nova. L. J.* 723 at 741.

[9] See however, Richard Lempert, Law School Grading: An Experiment with Pass Fail (1971-1972) 24 *J. Leg. Educ.* 251 (discussion on the suggestion that giving individual students the choice about how grading should be done is a realistic option so long as the student only has the option of determining whether she is to receive a letter or pass-fail grade in all or some of her courses. If individuals were to have the option of deciding whether they should be graded on the basis of their advocacy skills, brief-writing abilities, in-

broader area of course, grading is less burdensome, so enables quick, better feedback. Also, because it is easier to calibrate and reuse it is a good gauge for evaluating different teaching methods.

(ii) Use of Non-Teacher/Outsider Evaluation

While the norm in law is teacher-based assessment, that itself should not rule out alternative some universities use, such as non-teacher-based assessment. Non-teacher based assessment is a practice where postgraduate students grade examinations. The exam (formal and informal) would be based on problem sets, papers, midterm, final term exams, oral assessment, etc.[10] Much as this mode would allow for more frequent assessment, it is plausible to think that students and teacher would resist for different reasons. Students could fear outsider assessment. Teachers may interpret it as control and power erosion. But it must be recognized that alternative like this could broaden students' perspective from believing that their teachers answer is the only right answer to believing that there are many ways to approach a problem. Outsider assessment can be expanded to include assessment by judges, practicing lawyers and members of the community. This again provides and enhances learning by providing wider perspective to students, counteracting the belief that there is a single right answer, the teacher's answer to legal controversies. Outsider assessment can be a useful means of providing increased support for a faculty in the community and greater credibility for the faculty's programme.[11]

(iii) Student/Peer-Based Assessment

This form of assessment is not uncommon in law. It is just that its use is largely limited to informal and spontaneous use by teachers in class. Student self or peer assessment is recommended because the ability to self-assess one's work is critical to lifelong learning because it teaches them how to monitor and learn from their responses to novel situations.[12] To the extent that it is a mode of assessment that promotes self-reflection, it is a recommended way to building student self-reflection which is a critical component of successful professional life.[13] Journaling, especially in clinic and simulation classes, is a good way to encourage self and peer assessment. There is however no good reason why it cannot be made to apply to other components of teaching and learning. Admittedly, self and peer

---

class finals, or take-home examinations or the option of deciding whether a faculty member should write evaluation rather than a notational grade, such innovations, though expensive is likely to have educational value than the switch from letter to pass-fail grading).

[10] Greg Sergienko, New Modes of Assessment (2001) 38 *San Diego L. Rev.* 463 at 475.

[11] Munro, above n. 5, 125.

[12] Ibid.

[13] Donald A. Schon, Educating Reflective Practitioner: Towards a New Design for Teaching and Learning in the Professions, 1987, 317, cited in Sergienko, above n. 10, 478.

assessment is challenging on several grounds. One such is its susceptibility to unreliability. For example, an incompetent student can overstate her performance and award high score to her work or that of a peer. The element of bias is another challenge. It is human to think highly of oneself. So, scores may not reflect true performance. Peer assessment can reduce the challenge of bias. Bias can also be minimized by the teacher creating incentive for honest self-assessment. The incentive can take the form of explaining to students the role of self-assessment in the future career life of student and the lifelong benefits of doing honest self-assessment. A teacher's periodic, random review of scores awarded can also provide incentive for honest self-assessment.

(iv) Objective Examination

Objective exam is a system of grading essay exam as though they were not essay exams, but grading them as though they were objective exams. The teacher dissects the answers to the essay question into smaller sub-issues to which points are assigned. The primary purpose is to avoid the fear of subjectivity often experienced in grading traditional essay examinations. So, the teacher grades the essay as though the questions had actually been asked in MCQ or true/false format.[14] Objectifying essay exam provides some quantifiable basis upon which to evaluate performance. In this respect (grading) it resembles more the MCQ than essay exam. When objectifying the answer to the essay exam, the teacher predetermines the total number of points that the student will earn in several areas of issues identification, sub-issues identification, statement of rules of law and policy, analysis of facts, and conclusion. These points are used to create an answer key against which performance is measured.[15] Commendably, the Nigerian Law School has a practice akin to objective examination in grading bar examinations using the template of marking scheme.[16]

Another way to get around the reliability challenges of essay exam is the format of essay questions set with many sub-issues requiring point answer as though they were MCQ requiring fill in the gap type. Students are required to give direct answer to issues, identify sub-issues, statement of rules, policy and conclusion. In this respect also, the Nigerian Law School is to be commended. Some essay questions for bar examination demand direct, pointed answer, with very little essay and analysis. All of these reduce fear of subjectivity in grading.

Some however have argued that despite its perceived deficiencies essay exams should remain the traditional mode for law exams. They point to its conceivable

---

[14] Linda R. Crane, Grading Law School Examination: Making a Case for Objective Examination to Cure What Ails 'Objectified' Exam (2000) 34 *New Eng. L. Rev.* 785 at 788

[15] Linda R. Crane, Grading Law School Examination: Making a Case for Objective Examination to Cure What Ails 'Objectified' Exam (2000) 34 *New Eng. L. Rev.* 785 at 790.

[16] See note to marker of bar examinations.

benefits. For instance, Hegland, sticking to the tradition argues that essay exams signal to students that the academy and profession takes good writing seriously, and that other than this important symbolic point, essay exams make students better writers.[17] As support for the assertion, the writer points out that we all come out of the faculty better writers because that is the traditional exam pattern. This is especially true of old teachers who graduated at a time when legal writing was not part of law curriculum, as the bulk of legal writing was then the three or four-hour long essay exam. Claim that the absence of feedback makes it bad enough to teach writing is considered a virtue rather than vice, because it agrees with how best to write and become an expert in writing. Expert writers encourage free writing as effective way to become effective. Thus, to the extent that essay exams demands concentration on *what* student writes in the exam under time constrain in aligns with training to become effective writer.[18] Essay exam intensive performance is thought to fit the description of how to become effective writer because student is 'doing law when it matters most, when grades on are the line: analyzing tough problems, organizing fleeting thoughts, and facing the daunting task of capturing them on paper, perhaps best of all, there is no time for a hundred indecisions, no time for a hundred revisions.'[19]

Another good case for essay exam is that it may well be an effective way to learn the law, because one can learn from writing about a thing. Recognizing the importance of writing to learning, kings were obligated under the Mosaic law to copy the Law of Moses in his own handwriting. The purpose was to deepen appreciation and understanding of the law.[20] A good way to learn about something is to write about it. Since memory involves retention and retrieval writing enhances both, so does the essay exam.

While it is generally stated that essay exams are unreliable because grading is often subjective, Hegland for example, posits that essay exam only seem more subjective than MCQ, because its subjectivity is more public, and that even at that, subjectivity isn't really an educational problem as such., unless confused with arbitrariness. The writer gives a good example of why the distinction between subjectivity and arbitrariness must be conceptually and practically kept distinct. He states: I was once on a committee to interview candidates to be our local police chief. The committee was composed of twelve people, with different backgrounds

---

[17] Kenny F. Hegland, On Essay Exams (2006) 56 *J. Leg. Educ.* 106
[18] Peter Elbow, *Writing Without Teachers*, 2nd ed. Oxford, 1998, ("The idea is simply to write.... Go quickly without rushing. Never stop to look back, to cross something out, to wonder how to spell something, to wonder what word or thought to use, or to think about what you are doing.... The only requirement is that you *never* stop.") at 3.
[19] Kenny F. Hegland, On Essay Exams (2006) 56 *J. Leg. Educ.* 106 at 144.
[20] Holy Scriptures/Bible

and law enforcement interest. After a few days of interviewing we were asked to pick the top three candidates. We were given no criteria. We all wrote our three choices of the twenty candidates, only four received top three votes."[21] The lesson is that although individual selection was subjective, it was remarkably consistent. So, subjectivity didn't make the votes arbitrary. Analogically too, essay grading may be subjective, but that in itself does not make it unreliable and arbitrary, because it can by all means be consistent.

Further support for essay question is that while MCQ rewards students who *know* legal rules, essay exam rewards those who can *manipulate* the rules. Since the shelf life of rules are more transient, the choice should trump in favor of manipulation. Essay exams is more of doing than knowing. No one becomes a great footballer by knowing all the rules of football. So is law. Legal education does set out to train those who know legal rules only, but importantly, to train professionals who will practice law. What is more, drawing analogy from food that we may not be what we eat, but may be how we test, just like it can be said that rules don't decide legal issues (a realist take on law), that does not detract from the true fact that rules nonetheless help decide legal issues, it cannot be doubted even by moderns who deride essay exams, that essay exams enhances analytical ability, a highly priced commodity in law, than the mere right or wrong answer of MCQ. A tilt from essay exam to MCQ may well bring legal education back into where it rescued itself-primitive formalism. The very thinking that exam is MCQ resurrects a thinking of relative fixation in law.

Assessment is generally designed to observe seven principles of good undergraduate education, namely: to encourage contact between students and faculty; develop reciprocity and cooperation among students; uses active learning techniques; gives prompt feedback; emphasizes time on task; communicate high expectations; and respect diverse talents and ways of learning.[22] These goals are rarely advanced by the traditional essay mode of examination. Long essay exam fails to assess learning and quick feedback for students and teachers to improve. There is therefore a need to re-evaluate to supplement it with new testing techniques at are valid, reliable and fair. No doubt these new techniques would increase teachers' workload, but it is worth the effort for effective teaching and learning.[23]

---

[21] Kenny F. Hegland, On Essay Exams (2006) 56 *J. Leg. Educ.* 106 at 146.

[22] P Ramsden, *Learning to Teach in Higher Education,* London: Routledge Falmer, 2003), 176 (discussion on Chickering and Gamson's seven principles of good undergraduate education).

[23] LuCSee Lucy C. Jacobs & Cunton I. Chase, Developing and Using Tests Effectively: A Guide for Faculty, 1992.

Multiple Choice Question Examination

Blue book essay exam is the traditional examination pattern in the faculties of law. It is characterized by issue-spotting by students.[24] Over time this testing method have been criticized for its many deficiencies. The call and use of multiple choice questions (MCQ) is therefore an attempt to improve the essay type exam and possibly supplement it with a component that more closely address the deficiencies of essay exam.[25] MCQ refers to questions which offer students the choice of selecting the correct or best answer from a number of choices. It could be the short form of "true" or "false" option, or one requiring the test-taker to select from four or five multiple answers. In some cases, the choice requires student to fill in a brief response to a specifically devised question that has a pre-established correct response.[26] That being so objective questions can be classified as multiple-choice questions alone include "choose the best answer," "choose the worst answer," "choose the applicable rule," and "choose the proper analysis" types.

Despite the flaws of essay exams on grounds of test-taking and evaluation, critics of MCQ continue to justify essay exam as generally preferable on ground that it is good bases for testing analytical ability and writing skills. The flaws of essay exam demand supplementing it with MCQ.

Advantages of MCQ

MCQ as a mode of examination enjoys the following advantages: (i) primarily it is an efficient evaluation process. Grading the exam takes less time. Because the answers are predetermined, it can be graded by a machine or teaching assistant, thereby freeing the law teacher's time for other things; (ii) the efficiency of it makes it an appropriate vehicle for short tests to gauge student's grasp of topic; (iii) though it is frontloaded test, so may take more thought and care to create than essay exam, the investment is worth it. It saves overall time compared to the lengthy essay grading process; (iv) it enables easier cooperation of faculty staff

---

[24] Norman Redlich & Steve Friedland, Challenging Tradition: Using Objective Questions in Law School Examination (1991) 41 *DePaul L. Rev.* 141.

[25] For reading on deficiencies of essay examination as a valid, reliable and fair tool for testing see, Philip C. Kissam, Law School Examinations (1989) 42 *Vand. L. Rev.* 433.

[26] Norman Redlich & Steve Friedland, Challenging Tradition: Using Objective Questions in Law School Examination (1991) 41 *DePaul L. Rev.* 141. For a discussion on the advantages and disadvantages of MCQ, see Michael S. Josephson, *Learning & Evaluation in Law School,* Washington DC, 1984, 318; Michael S. Jacobs, Law School Examinations and Churchillian Democracy: A Reply to Professors Redlich and Friedland (1991) 41 *DePaul L. Rev.* 159 (1991); Norman Redlich & Steve Friedland, A Reply to Professor Jacobs: Right Answer, Wrong Question (1991) 41 *DePaul L. Rev.* 183. See also, Howard J. Gensler, Valid Objective Test Construction (1986) 60 *St. John's L. Rev.* 288; Linda R. Crane, Grading Law School Examinations: Making a Case for Objective Exams to Cure What Ails "Objectified" Exams (2000) 34 *New. Eng. L. Rev.* 785; Marcella David, A Funny Thing Happened on the Way to the Multiple-Choice Exam: Or, The Schoolroom Lessons from Bush v. Gore (2001) 51 *J. Legal Educ.* 1.

who teach various components of a course to generate questions covered by them to make the whole of MCQ questions for testing purposes; (v) because MCQ can easily be answered in a relative shorter time than essay exam, it provides opportunity for the teacher to test a wide variety of topics; (vi) because it can cover a wider variety of taught topics it enhances fairness of exams and materially conforms to the reliability ingredient of effective assessment; (vii)susceptibleness to wider coverage is consistent with legal education goal of course coverage; (viii) it is compactable with concerns of issue-spotting underlying essay exams because MCQ questions are formulated on the basis that there is a predetermined correct or better answer to a question. It can be used to measure knowledge, skills and values, especially if the teacher utilizes a fact-pattern and focuses on interpretation of rule of law that requires analysis or application of rule; (ix) it is also compactable with testing analytical skills if they are well constructed not simply to test memorizing rules and principles; (x) it can be a useful way to familiarize students in the faculty for bar examination, with component of MCQ; (xi) the widespread use MCQ to as primary mode of mental measurement not only for professional examinations, but also for employment-related exams all support its validity and efficacy; (xii) because it is a time-saver mode of exams, it provides opportunity for quicker feedback.

MCQ suffers inherent deficiency that it permits guessing and have a greater potential fo ambiguity. Educators have suggested that the guessing challenge arising from accessibility to correct answer can be minimized by offering test-takers incorrect alternative answers called distractors.[27] Alternately, guessing can be minimized by a system of deducting points for incorrect answers.[28]

Improving Proficiency in Setting MCQ
No doubt setting effective MCQ questions that test knowledge, skills and values of the test-tacker can be challenging. First teacher can minimize unfairness in an MCQ exam by actually answering her set questions under exam conditions. It would in no small way offer insight to the teacher if the questions are fair. Question could also be formulated for students to choose the "best" answer, not necessarily the "correct" answer. This way substance over form is encouraged. Because MCQ exam lend itself more readily to statistical analysis, it can be useful at the end of test to review the questions. In the process, teacher can detect defective questions, observe whether a particular incorrect answer is chosen by a large number of test-takers, which can provide useful insight into whether the question is flawed or that teaching (and learning) of the particular topic is

---

[27]Norman Redlich & Steve Friedland, Challenging Tradition: Using Objective Questions in Law School Examination (1991) 41 *DePaul L. Rev.* 141.
[28] Howard J. Gensler, Valid Objective Test Construction () 60 *St. John's L. Rev.* 288 at 291.

ineffective.

Some Concerns About MCQ

We have chosen to address some educational concerns about MCQ because of reluctance by some still greet it with suspicion. One important psychometric property of an exam is that it must be valid, i.e. it must measure what it is designed to test. Unquestionably, law exams are designed to measure students learning and achievement of course content, skills and values. While an all-essay exam can measure performance at a deep level, time constraint of the exam tends to measure a small subset of concepts and skills. Performance thus depends on whether the few tested concepts and skills are the ones a particular student happen to learn well, which weaken validity. On the other hand, MCQ has a wider course breath range to measure mastery of concepts, skills and values. So, when course grades are based on a combination of both essay and MCQ it enhances psychometric validity.[29]

Another important test is reliability. Students' scores must not vary considerably for the wrong reasons.[30] The flexibility of broad variety coverage of course and its amenability to be used in testing performance more than once during course period enhances the reliability of grading.

Effective assessment often is both formative and summative.[31] Because MCQ format can be graded quickly with computer or by an assistant teacher, it offers prompt opportunity for feedback as a formative testing.

Law school grading have both norm-referenced and criteria-reference components. MCQ computerized scoring readily provides useful data information for norm-reference evaluation by showing whether individual exam items are successfully separating out levels of performance on one hand or appear to have significant technical difficulties on the other; and for criteria-reference it

---

[29] Lynn M. Daggett, All of the Above: Computerized Exam Scoring of Multiple Choice Items Helps To: (A) Show How Exam Items Worked Technically, (B) Maximize Exam Fairness, (C) Justly Assign Letter Grades, and (D) Provide Feedback on Student Learning (2007) 57 *J. Leg. Educ.* 391 at 395.

[30] Reliability can be measured from the perspective of comparing the same students' scores on different forms of the same exam (alternate form reliability); or by comparing student scores on odd- versus even-numbered exam items on the same exam (split-half reliability), or some other psychometric tests. See Lynn M. Daggett, All of the Above: Computerized Exam Scoring of Multiple Choice Items Helps To: (A) Show How Exam Items Worked Technically, (B) Maximize Exam Fairness, (C) Justly Assign Letter Grades, and (D) Provide Feedback on Student Learning (2007) 57 *J. Leg. Educ.* 391 ("Exam reliability is necessary, but not sufficient, for exam validity. In other words, an exam cannot be valid if it is not reliable. Measurement can be reliable without being valid. If, for example, I measured each of my torts student's height at several points during a semester and assigned letter grades based on average measured height [for example, students 6 feet 2 and taller receive an "A"], that measurement would be highly reliable, since adult student height is quite consistent. However, this evaluation technique would have no validity, since height has no relationship to mastery of torts concepts and skills.") at 396.

[31] Formative assessment offers feedback on performance. It is essentially diagnostic, designed to help the student improve on performance. Summative assessment on the other hand, looks backward and judges' student on what it learnt. See

reveals overall class performance.[32]

With all the virtues of MCQ it is surprising why faculties have greeted MCQ with cold welcome. It has been suggested that present reluctant to introduce or supplement MCQ as an exam mode is rooted in an "unmitigated dependence upon traditional three-hour written examination given at the end of the course."[33] It is to be expected. That was how present crop of teachers were examined at their undergraduate study. So, in insisting on essay exams, they are only charting familiar terrain and keeping to what is imagined, the dominant tradition of legal education. Traditionalist are quick to think that MCQ is incompatible with legal education and its accompanying sophistry intended to test abilities and qualities of reasoning, issue-spotting and imaginative rule application. It is also reasoned, that MCQ isn't congruent with what lawyers do in practice. In practice, lawyers write legal opinion, do brief of argument and the like, not answer objective questions as though they were some machines of law. Furthermore, the simplicity of constructing essay questions can be a cynical reason for teacher's preference for it. Unlike MCQ, essays questions can easily be drawn based on three or more fact-pattern covering a few issues taught. All of these obstacles to MCQ are surmountable if teachers' pay particular attention to how it can be utilized for issue-spotting and imaginative reasoning. It is time for the legal academia to supplement at least essay exam with MCQ which provides efficiency, greater coverage and other benefits not inherent in essay examination.

Formative Assessment

Formative assessment is designed to provide students with continuous feedback throughout the semester to enhance learning and performance.[34] Formative assessment is not a staple diet for evaluation in law where preference is given to a single cumulative final exam. This is understandable. Multiple grading format could be tasking for busy law teachers, who justify the single exam as a structure fitted to give the big picture of legal doctrine, rather than piecemeal grading. The limited use of formative assessment is partly attributable to the fact that law teachers are largely unaware of the benefit of formative assessment because study reports are published in educational journals generally not read by law teachers. Academic freedom makes imposing it unlikely. The result is that formative assessment is left largely to teacher's preference.

---

[32] M. Daggett, All of the Above: Computerized Exam Scoring of Multiple Choice Items Helps To: (A) Show How Exam Items Worked Technically, (B) Maximize Exam Fairness, (C) Justly Assign Letter Grades, and (D) Provide Feedback on Student Learning (2007) 57 *J. Leg. Educ.* 391 at 401.

[33] Norman Redlich & Steve Friedland, Challenging Tradition: Using Objective Questions in Law School Examination (1991) 41 *DePaul L. Rev.* 141 at 156.

[34] Carol S. Sargent & Andrea A. Curcio, Empirical Evidence that Formative Assessments Improve Final Exam () *J. Leg. Educ.* 379.

This is however an area that the academy ought to pay attention to because study provides evidence that formative assessments help law student performance on a cumulative final exam, and addresses some of the concerns expressed about integrating formative assessments into large-section doctrinal courses. [35]

For formative assessment to increase learning and serve as motivation for better performance, its feedback must explain the gap between current and competent performance desired. The effectiveness of the feedback depends on what the teacher gives the student and the way students receive the feedback and interpret it. Explanation of feedback can take various forms, but it is useful not to grade because students tend to focus on grades not suggestion for improvement. Feedback should allow the learner to calibrate her progress toward desired outcomes. Feedback for simple task and assignments yield better results than for the complex. It is therefore advisable to keep student task within cognitive capacity of students. Feedback is more effective when it provides details of how to improve rather than just an explanation of what is competent performance. Peer comparison should be avoided because it may inhibit motivation to improve. It should be given mindfully.

Empirical study reveals that formative assessment helps improve the overall CGPA of law students and so should be encouraged.[36]

Open Book Exam

In recent times the debate rages as to whether open-book examination (OBE)[37] is preferred to close-book examination (CBE), and how the choices affect effective teaching and learning. It is suggested that the issue of choice is not simply a question of choice of assessment methods because it carries wider implications related to evaluating approaches to teaching, learning and curriculum design. In the final analysis whether choice is made should take into account an alignment between the course design, teaching, learning and assessment methods on one hand and the desired learning outcomes to teaching and learning activities.[38]

---

[35] Gregory S. Munro, *Outcomes Assessment for Law Schools* 143 (Inst. for L. Sch. Teaching 2000); Michael Hunter Schwartz, Sophie Sparrow & Gerald Hess, *Teaching Law by Design:* Engaging *Students from the Syllabus to the Final Exam* 154–58 (Carolina Acad. Press 2009); Wiliam M. Sullivan, Anne Colby, Judith Welch Wegner, Lloyd Bond & Lee S. Schulman, *Educating Lawyers: Preparation for the Profession of Law* 164–67 (Jossey-Bass 2007); Carol S. Sargent & Andrea A. Curcio, Empirical Evidence that Formative Assessments Improve Final Exam () *J. Leg. Educ.* 379 at 380. See also Andrea A. Curcio, Gregory Todd Jones & Tanya M. Washington, Does Practice Make Perfect? An Empirical Examination of the Impact of Practice Essays on Essay Exam Performance (2008) 35 *Fla. St. U. L. Rev.* 271.

[36] Carol S. Sargent & Andrea A. Curcio, Empirical Evidence that Formative Assessments Improve Final Exam () *J. Leg. Educ.* 379 at 383.

[37] Open book exam is an exam system that permits student to use textbooks, statute, notes, journals and other reference materials while writing examination.

[38] Amanda Cahill-Ripley, Innovative Methods of Assessment in Law: The Value of Open-Book Exams as a Catalyst for Improving Teaching and Learning in the Law School ([2016] *Law Teacher* 205; G. Philips,

While CBE is the established procedure for exams in the faculties of law, some legal educators are suggesting its replacement with OBE as alternative and more effective method of assessment. Still others suggest a mix between both for effective assessment.[39] Let us consider the advantages of one against the other. They are as follows.

The CBE is useful if the purpose of testing is to test student ability to use knowledge to recall what is learned. It is a procedure used to grade student ability to memorize facts and what is learned. CBE encourages cramming, particularly of facts, cases and legislation before exam. It therefore encourages swallow learning.

On the other hand, OBE is associated with an evaluation of high level cognitive skills of reasoning, problem-solving and conceptualizing. In effect, OBE is useful in promoting higher-order thinking by having students draw upon information from materials available to them in answering exam questions.[40] OBE improves understanding and is a gauge for the teacher to assess students' analytical skills of identifying and retrieving information to ground legal reasoning.

OBE discourages memorizing and rote learning, leading to deeper appreciation of what is learned, thereby improving learning outcomes. What is more, OBE creates a feeling of confidence in students about exam performance thus reducing the usual anxiety associated with CBE. It has been suggested that preparation for open-book examinations requires the student to practice study skills such as note taking and identifying and retrieving relevant information from materials including going beyond set textbooks, encourages students to look for the links across the curriculum and to apply higher-order thinking: critical analysis, evaluation, synthesis.[41]

Much as the OBE allows students to adopt a more thoughtful approach to exam questions and a calmer approach to exam, it could create a feeling of over confidence, triggering less preparation for exams. Students offered the option of OBE provides less time to formulate and write answers because much of the time is spent looking up materials and reading.

Using Open Book Tests to Encourage *Textbook* Reading in College (1995) 38(6) *Journal of Reading* 484; L. Tussing, A Consideration of the Open Book Examination (1951) 11 *Educational and Psychological Measurement* 597; P. Maharg, "The Culture of Mnemosyne: Open-Book Assessment and the Theory and Practice of Legal Education" (1999) 6(2) *International Journal of the Legal Profession* 219–239.

[39] C. Theophilides & M. Koutselini, "Study Behaviour in the Closed-Book and the Open-Book Examination: A Comparative Analysis" (2000) 6(4) *Educ. Research and Evaluation: An Int'l. J. Theory & Practice* 379; L. Donnelly, "A Modest Proposal: The Case for the Open-Book Law Exams" (2005) 2(2) *European J. Leg. Educ.* 105. For a definition of surface learning see Edward Phillips, Sandra Clarke, Sarah Crofts and Angela Laycock, "Exceeding the Boundaries of Formulaic Assessment: Innovation and Creativity in the Law School" (2010) 44(3) *Law Teacher* 334.

[41] Amanda Cahill-Ripley, Innovative Methods of Assessment in Law: The Value of Open-Book Exams as a Catalyst for Improving Teaching and Learning in the Law School ([2016] *Law Teacher* 205.

OBE turns exam workload from student to teacher. The teacher will have the onerous task of setting exam questions that can draw out high order thinking and analysis, otherwise the OBE would be easy workover for the students who can copy straight answers from their open-book materials. Exam questions sets must be such that require the students to draw on vertical and horizontal knowledge of what is learned to form interconnections which would be applied to answering questions. The teacher has to consider the type of questions necessary for effective OBE, especially its complexity and comprehension so that the questions are made to stimulate creative thinking of the students. OBE can therefore be problematic for a teacher who is not an expert in her course and cannot raise to set problem-based questions which encourage application of knowledge, skills and values. OBE can also be used for essay question that test inter-connective reasoning. Questions that require data-dumping must be avoided. So too are questions designed for OBE. For example, a trust question like, "list the elements of a valid express trust," is a data-dumping question. It does not set to test deep order thinking or analysis. In an OBE, all the student would need to do is copy from any useful material the answer. The question may be useful for CBE is the teacher is interested in testing student ability to use knowledge to recall what is learned. An example of an appropriate OBE essay question could read like this: "From settlement of the greatest wars down to the simplest of inheritance on death, from the audacious Wall Street scheme down to the protection of grandchildren, the trust can be seen marching before it the motley procession of the whole of human endeavor . . . The trust is the guardian angel of the Anglo-Saxon, (in fact of all person under the common law legal system) accompanying her everywhere, impassively, from cradle to the grave. Is Equity necessary to perform all these functions?" An essay question like this requires the students to identify and retrieve information and apply it to the question and critically analyse the function of trust law.

OBE is also significant to learning outcomes. It can be a useful learning process in generating study and thinking skills. It is therefore suggested that teachers could deepen this by making clear to the students that marks will not be lost if they treat exam as a learning exercise rather than an exercise of regurgitating facts. The assessment must therefore centre on objects not used to measure CBE. For while CBE may test ability to regurgitate, OBE ought to facilitate the acquisition of lawyering skills: grounding in skills of reasoning, critical analysis, and application of knowledge to problem-solving. That being so, it would be appropriate for the teacher design teaching and learning outcomes with high cognitive skills in mind. Going by the learning progression theory, it would appear that OBE would be most suitable after the designer stage of learning, when the students would have outgrown the use of the (P)IRAC structure because it is not needed in their legal analysis although it is implicit in their discussion, and they can organize analysis around concepts instead of parties. Students under the present five years law programme are only likely to reach this stage of intellectual development in the third year. It would thus not be advisable to employ OBE before the stage.

It would be helpful to tell the students from the outset if a teacher chooses the OBE and what materials would be allowed in for the exam. If notes are permitted, the information can be helpful for students note taking. The debate rages as to which a faculty should adopt. We would only suggest a choice based on a consideration of some factors: (i) there may not necessarily be significant difference in learning outcomes between the two;[42] (ii) faculties must explore the compatibility nature between teaching, learning and learning outcomes and the exam, whatever the choice is as key factor impacting on students' achievement; (iii) much as OBE can be a useful driver for encouraging deeper learning, it would be fraught with pitfalls if the curriculum is not designed to include tasks to develop higher-order skills; (iv) faculty or institutional tradition of exam types and limitations specified.[43]

It is expected that most faculties would be reluctant to progress from the traditional CBE assessment style because historically it is the style prevalent in legal education. What is more, prior to the frontloading of court process, much of lawyering is conceived as grounded in wittiness, oral advocacy and ability to draw on memory. All of these must be less prevailing with the presence of e-learning materials and court simplification processes. To the extent that modern lawyering increasingly demands more of problem-solving, analysis, and synthesizing of information under time constraint, coupled with the fact that practicing lawyers commonly consult legal materials when undertaking cases, all heightens the usefulness of OBE as probably more authentic than CBE.[44]

No doubt, skills of application of learning are more important than memorization is further reason to prefer the OBE to the CBE. Because OBE aligns more with the professional purpose of legal education to deepen higher-order cognitive skills it is worth trying, even as a mix with CBE. Recognition that

---

[42] The research experiment conducted at the University of Cyprus found that there was no significant difference in achievement between students who sat CBE and those who sat OBE when both types of exam were designed to test higher-order skills and critical thinking. Cahill-Ripley relates that the 72 students used for the research were divided into two groups to undertake CBE and OBE exam (sections with multiple-choice, problem- solving, and essay type questions measuring ability of argumentation) on the same topics. The result showed that those who sat the OBE were found to perform less well overall due to the time spent consulting materials which had a negative impact upon their achievement. See Cahill-Ripley, above n. 2.

[43] Generally, there are no teaching and examination methodology and strategies prescribed by the regulatory bodies of NUC, CLE or the NBA. Not to be overlooked however is a difference in assessment by faculty's choice of either CBE or OBE can significantly result in marked difference between faculties and can weaken the patent validity process as a whole of faculties.

[44] See Cahill-Ripley, above n. 2; R. Aizen, "Four Ways to Better 1L Assessments" (2004) 54 *Duke L.J.* 765

effective assessment requires validity, reliability and fairness, should be good enough reason why faculties ought to increase the variety and quality of their assessment methods, if need be, to include OBE.[45] What is more, OBE would likely reduce incidences of the usual exam malpractice associated with students bring into the exam venue extraneous material. To this end, it reduces pre-exam invigilation stress.

Whether decision is arrived at, whether to continue the use of traditional CBE or introduce OBE or do a mixture of both should be an informed a faculty's teaching and learning curriculum combined with its choice of learning outcomes preference. If its preference is for developing higher cognitive skills rather than rote and memorization, then the skills should dictate more of the use of OBE. The converse should be the case. To some extent the choice of exam method has wider implications for the purpose of legal education. If faculty takes the position that learning outcomes should reflect preparing students to join the legal profession as practicing lawyers, the use of OBE should be most appropriate. If on the other hand, it adopts as its preference law as an academic/liberal study, the traditional CBE would fit its objective. A mix of both CBE and OBE, where appropriate would be recommended if the skills cut across both preferences and the course is structured as it presently is, for five years, with a mixture of foundational law courses and not-so foundational law courses, and a good mix of compulsory interdisciplinary humanities courses like history, economics, languages, philosophy, general studies, computer, etc. We however, suggest that it is time to progress beyond the inward-looking English liberal version of law curriculum as opposed to global best practice professional law curriculum which tilts more in transmitting lawyering skills to students.[46] Unquestionably, OBE if considered as an element of wider curriculum design can contribute to effective teaching and learning.

Degree Classification

Some in the legal academy question why law degrees should be classified, especially the qualifying certificate for call to bar issued by the Council of Legal Education. Proponents of declassification ague that degree classification make little sense within a diverse and expanded higher education system, more so that the classification does not genuinely compare between institutions or even across different university courses.[47] What is more, they have suggested that

---

[45] See generally, R. Burridge, K. Hinett, A. Paliwala & T. Varnava, *Effective Learning and Teaching in Law* (ILT Effective Teaching & Learning) (Oxford, Routledge, 2002); J. Smits, European Legal Education, or: How to Prepare Students for Global Citizenship? (2011) 45 (2) *Law Teacher* 163.

[46] J. Smits, European Legal Education, or: How to Prepare Students for Global Citizenship? (2011) 45 (2) *Law Teacher* 163.

[47] Bruce Macfarlane, Degree Classification: Time to Bite the Bullet (1998) 3 *Teaching Higher Educ.* 401.

classification bears little connection with workplace skills which law exam rarely measure. These have therefore suggested that in line with professional awards of proficiency in learnings like medicine, pharmacy etc. the current classification system should be replaced with "awards" and "awards with distinction."

Oral Examination

Traditional law school exam rarely has a place for oral exam. Interestingly, law students in Russia are tested entirely on their performance on oral exams.[48]

Bar Final Examination

Talking about bar final examination at the law school is very touchy matter. One general complain about it has been the failure rate. Abysmal performance is recorded year after year. The blame for this is diverse. The students are not serious enough for professional exams. Students come to the law school with less than the prerequisite knowledge to equip them for learning the professional courses at the law school. Some turn the nozzle the other way. Bar exams do not exam the skills needed for practice and so fails otherwise students who would be good lawyers. No, the challenge has to do with the stiff nature and unfriendly learning environment of the law school. Trafficking this blame game is unhelpful. Commendably, the CLE has unquestionable rigged it curriculum to make it student-centred. It has embarked on a few enhancing academic services to strengthen teaching and learning to combat falling passage rates.[49] The failure rate is not peculiar to Nigeria. Even in America, concerns about falling rate is widespread. [50] In the U.S. pass rate fell from 70% in 1996 to as low as 64% in 2004.[51]

Pass rate at the bar final is a national concern. When results are published the public debate it. Universities, dean of law show concern as to how their

---

[48] John M. Burman, Oral Examinations as a Method of Evaluating Law Students (2001) 51 *J. Leg. Educ.* 130. (the procedure in Russia takes this form: 'Five students enter the classroom while the others wait in the hall. Each chooses one question from about fifty; the questions are typed on separate slips of paper and placed face down on the desk. Each student is then allowed time to think about the answer (without books or notes). As soon as one of the five is ready, she meets with the teacher. After she answers the written question, along with any follow-up questions, the teacher assigns her a grade, which is then entered into the student's grade book and on the official grade sheet that is later given to the administration. The student then leaves the room. As one student leaves, another enters and selects a question, and the process repeats itself, for hours, until each student has met with the teacher. Those students who do not pass muster the first time around may return at the end of the session and try again. Since each student has a different question, at least theoretically, no one worries about the four students who are in the room listening while one student meets with the teacher)' at 134.

[49] Academic retreat, bar revision for stragglers, quality assurance, lesson notes, etc.

[50] Lorenzo A. Trujillo, The Relationship Between Law School and the Bar Exam: A Look at Assessment and Student Success (2007) 78 *Univ. Colo L. Rev.* 69. (discussion on national concern about bar failure rate and suggesting strategies for bar passage)

[51] National Conference of Bar Examiners, Bar Passage Statistics, http://www.ncbex.org/ stats.htm (last visited September 23 2016).

students perform. Even the law school saddled with the responsibility of training students for the bar qualifying exam is concerned with falling bar passage rates to the extent that those rates reflect the quality and effectiveness of legal education or lack thereof.

Deficiencies of Bar Exam

There is need for introspection by CLE to address the real challenge without trading the blame-game. Critics of bar exam assert that the bar exam does not verify minimum competence necessary for the practice of law because it does not evaluate proper lawyering skills and professionalism, it relies to a large extent on memorization, it does not test the law itself, and does not implicate current challenges of incompetence.[52] This is certainly a weighty criticism considering the ten core lawyering skills outline in the MacCrate Report.[53] The skills include problem-solving, counselling, organization, negotiation, fact investigation, legal analysis and reasoning, research, written and oral communication, litigation and ADR procedures, recognizing and resolving ethical dilemmas. Bar exam only test some of the skills while ignoring entirely the others. For example, a cursory look at bar final exams for the past thirty years show that it entirely ignores testing skills of organization, negotiation, fact investigation, research, written and oral communication. That by simple count is half of the ten core skills outlined in the MacCrate Report. So, as it stands, pass at the qualifying exam is no insurance that the students possess the minimum lawyering skills. If anything, may they are half qualified.[54]

Some go a step further. They argue that beyond the ten-core competence of MacCrate, bar exam does nothing to encourage or test the development of other qualities beneficial to the profession, such as quality of listening, empathy for client, desire for pro bono or public interest services, poor peoples' lawyering. Others assert that it overemphasizes memorization of legal rules thus discount true understanding of rules, while much of lawyering involves research.[55]

Some critics of bar exam state that the exam is inherently flawed given that

---

[52] See, Society of American Law Teachers Statement on the Bar Exam (2002) 52 J. Leg. Educ. 446, 446; Lorenzo A. Trujillo, The Relationship Between Law School and the Bar Exam: A Look at Assessment and Student Success (2007) 78 *Univ. Colo L. Rev.* 69

[53] See American Bar Association Section of Legal Education & Admission to the Bar, Legal Education Development- An Educational Continuum, Report of the Task Force on Law School and the Profession-Narrowing the Gap, 1992.

[54] Some academics have recently suggested that bar entrants can be better assured if the present cut-off pass mark is moved from 40% to 50%. Such a move will only be counter-productive, because the real is that if bar exam does not measure enough of the skills for testing competence raising the cut-off score would make little practical sense. See, Andrea A. Curcio, A Better Bar: Why and How the Existing Bar Exam Should Change (2002) 81 *Neb. L. Rev.* 363.

[55] All of this make prevailing the open book examination, a thing not encourage for bar qualifying exam. See discussion at

most students take extra-school commercial tutorial to prepare for the exam. They point that this is designed to teach the tricks of bar exam and immerse students in blackletter rules. That students narrow their effort to rules demonstrates that bar exam ignores the nuanced understanding of the law and synthesizing of rules, which are skills for effective lawyering.

Still others critique the mode of examination for adopting artificial testing techniques having little bearing to the practice of law. For instance, the MCQ component which carries 100 marks overall of the total obtainable 400 marks is limited to a time constrain of 50 to 60 minutes exam. What that translates to is that a student must attempt an answer to every question in an average of 30 seconds to be able to complete the 100 tested questions. Students usually complain about this time constrain. This portion of the exam is often offered as evidence establishing the artificial testing technique of bar exam. A practice lawyer never has to answer a novel multiple-choice question in such a time frame. When presented with a unique question a competent lawyer resort to legal research, ask questions to clarify legal and factual details and issues before reaching conclusion. What is more, lawyers are never given defined groups of answers and forced to choose the most correct in the real world of practice.[56]

Proponents for Bar Exam

For those who side with present mode of bar exam, they justify it on grounds that though the exam fails to test the ten-core skills, it nonetheless tests the most basic and essential analytical skills required for the practice of law.[57] They argue that skills of organization, writing ability, ability to follow direction, reading comprehension, recognizing of legal issues are all (implicitly) tested as embedded in the essay and MCQ exam modes.

Suggested Reformation

One of the justification for licensure is the belief that professional would be able to regulate their profession so that those who deal with them can be rest assure that all who render professional services would be at least competent and ethical.[58] Essentially bar qualifying certificate is therefore is designed to certify competent, ethical students as fit for the profession. That being so, bar falling rates necessarily implicates an interrogation of how best the law school can

---

[56] Lorenzo A. Trujillo, The Relationship Between Law School and the Bar Exam: A Look at Assessment and Student Success (2007) 78 *Univ. Colo L. Rev.* 69. But cf. the argument that MCQ testing prepare them for universal common style placement exam. Refer to portion on MCQ.

[57] Suzanne Darrow-Kleinhaus, A Response to the Society of American Teachers Statement on the Bar Exam (2004) 54 *J. Leg. Educ.* 442 (discussion that bar exam identified the skills that can be accurately tested with a standardized test, and examine only those skills).

[58] Ira Horowitz, The Economic Foundation of Self-Regulation in the Professions in Roger D. Blair & Stephen Rubin, (eds.), *Regulating the Professions: A Public-Policy Symposium,* 1980.

improve and strengthen its academic services to combat falling passage rates, or whether some alternative means can be devised independent of CLE to improve competence and character components of would-be-lawyers or what can be termed alternatives to bar exam (if the CLE is the only licensed body to train for qualifying certification). This does not discount the value of what faculties can do to enhance perquisite knowledge of their students who enter the law school sequel to the bar qualifying exam. For example, faculties can introduce bar preparatory tutorials aimed at assisting incoming students to law school as part of their ancillary academic services. Such tutorial can be handled by voluntary or paid practitioners and other constituents. Alternately, a faculty could consider offering bar revision schooling to its final year students.

Increasingly, people are doubting the capacity of the Law School to train lawyers. Its present carrying capacity is about 6,000 students. Going by the number of student seeking admission now put over 10,000 it follows that there will ever be a backlog in admitting students for the qualifying exam.[59] Not only is its carrying capacity challenge, the situation is exacerbated by the teaching strength of the school, less than 100 academic staff. What that translates to is 1-60 teacher-student ratio, far and above the 1-25 ratio for effective teaching and learning.[60] The state of the law school learning (including boarding) facilities compromise conduciveness despite funding from government. Worse is the requirement of compulsory in-class attendance as prerequisite to write the bar exam. All of these contribute to its immediate constituents (lawyer) call to rethink the place of the CLE/NLS in legal education. Some have advocated for its outright abolishment of the NLS component of CLE. Other more sympathetic call for its privatization or commercialization and other for a liberalization of the qualifying exam preparatory school to allow private competition with the NLS, while preserving the CLE as a pure exam body only.[61] The arguments and against the NLS are many and diverse.[62]

Teaching and learning techniques to sure up pass.

Suggested recommendations. Liberalize law school to competition, scrap it, let CLE become an exam body like ICAN

A Final Word on Reforming Law School Assessment

There is no question about it, all forms of assessment ranging from bluebook essay, MCQ, OBE, CBE, formative and summative assessments all have their up

---

[59] Epiphany Azinge

[60] despite shortfall in ratio, the faculty members must be commended for keeping an auto-driving calendar and implementation of student-centred techniques of learning that many universities have either failed or neglected to implement despite their ratio advantage over the law school.

[61] Alegeh, Bayo Ojo, Hayirat Balogun

[62]

and down sides. They in one way or the other fail the test of content validity in interrogating knowledge, skills and values taught for the professional study of law.[63] They test very narrow range of the three components of professional education, and where that is not the cases, they assess them within a narrow range of test methodologies. This being so, legal educators should continually strive for assessment methods that help to properly captures the essence of legal education- the training of students to enter the legal profession by developing valid, reliable and cost-effective assessments that better test a wider range of knowledge, skills and values competent lawyers need in an integrated rather than segregated form.[64]

To improve the range and method of assessing to integrate knowledge, practical, and professional identity dimensions, it is suggested that teachers should do the following in testing:

(i)   Test Factual Development

Fact gathering and analysis is a key core competence skill of lawyering. As skill, it can be incorporated in doctrinal teaching and testing with minor adjustment to existing teaching and assessment methodologies. The teacher can do this by asking students to tie fact gathering with rule application. For example, in a tort test students' can be asked to identify the questions they would ask an injured client to determine whether an injury comes with the square of negligence, a task that can be repeated for all doctrinal courses. Devising questions in which facts are necessary to analyze doctrines teaches facts gathering and analysis.[65] Answers to these testing even in a pure doctrinal class devoid of simulation or law clinic or skills courses could involve students' facts gathering online, from courts and other empirical sources which enriches appreciation for learning.[66]

---

[63] Joan Howarth, Teaching in the Shadow of the Bar Exam (1997) 31 *U.S.F. L. Rev.* 927; Kristine S. Knaplund & Richard H. Sander, The Art and Science of Academic Support (1995) 45 *J. Legal Educ.* 157; Marjorie M. Schultz & Sheldon Zedeck, Final Report: Identification Development and Validation of Predictors for Successful Lawyering, 2008, 13, available at http://www.law.berkeley.edu/files/LSACREPORTfinal-12.pdf accessed September 23, 2015.

[64] For general reading, see, Andrea A. Curcio, Assessing Differently and Using Empirical Studies to See if it Makes a Difference: Can Law Schools Do It Better? (2009) 27 *Quinnipiac L. Rev.* 899 (the paper discusses how to develop empirical studies to measure the validity and reliability of the various testing tools to create more effective and cost-efficient testing. It suggests an assessment methodology able to desegregate legal analysis, skills and professional identity, while making the strong point that if teachers give their teaching and assessment work the same scholarly scrutiny given to other research interest, they would help students become more effective lawyers).

[65] Andrea A. Curcio, Assessing Differently and Using Empirical Studies to See if it Makes a Difference: Can Law Schools Do It Better? (2009) 27 *Quinnipiac L. Rev.* 899 at 905.

[66] Ideally, skills will be taught across the curriculum rather than in a specific course. For a discussion of how an Australian law school integrated skills teaching throughout its curriculum, see Bobette Wolksi, Why, How and What to Practice: Integrating Skills Teaching and Learning in the Undergraduate Law Curriculum (2002) 52 *J. Legal Educ.* 287.

(ii) Assessment through Listening or Watching Performance

One other way the three dimensions of professional learning can be interrogated is through students' watching performance and being tested to analyze what is watched on performance, e.g. through the course webpage or video.[67] For example, the doctrinal teacher can play a simulation interview between lawyer and client in a sexual harassment scenario to her class by video and ask the students to analyze from it gaps in listening, taking notes, and the like, what the client's objectives are, what ethical issues the facts interrogate, what questions should be asked, what sort of evidence the case requires, how the lawyer can solicit the necessary facts involved, analyse skills of empathy involved, and suggest potential legal courses available to the client using appropriate remedial regimes applicable to the facts.

(iii) Drafting Exercises

Drafting exercises provides a fine opportunity to test students learning in the three dimensions of professional learning. Teachers recognize that a doctrinal class an understanding of legal rules and facts application can be enhanced by drafting exercises. That being so, drafting exercises which require students to allege the predicate facts for a claim as well as the applicable elements can well assess students understanding of doctrines and their application. For example, in a regular contract class where the teacher has taught offer as one of the essential ingredients for a valid contract, she could ask students to students to present three applications on counter-offer, invitation to treat, draw up an offer to all the world; and even present short quizzes on likely issues of ethics all of these raises. Further class discussions and feedback on the place of promise or the morality of promise in the law of contract can in no small measure integrate students learning on what facts to investigate in a contract claim. Even a before-class activity say requiring students to prepare a list of counter-offers, and the likely issues of skills and professional responsibility that could arise after assigning them reading of materials (like *Carlil* v. *Carbolic Smoke Ball Co*,[68] *Akinyemi* v. *Odu'a Investment*; [69]PS Atiyah, *An Introduction to the Law of Contract* 44 (3d ed. 1981)[70] could enhance students facts finding and application capacities.

(iv) Assessing Oral Communication Skills

Oral communication skills are core competence requirement for lawyering. Sadly, most doctrinal courses have no testing component for oral communication skills.

---

[67] Andrea A. Curcio, Assessing Differently and Using Empirical Studies to See if it Makes a Difference: Can Law Schools Do It Better? (2009) 27 *Quinnipiac L. Rev.* 899 at 906.

[68]

[69]

[70]

This assessment deficiency can be made less prevailing by teachers utilizing simulated client interviews and counselling exercises to assess students' ability to analyse and orally communicate. Teachers could also employ motion arguments on doctrinal issues that arise in the course.[71]

(v)   Assessing Issues of Values

Bluebook essay exam and most of the other modes of examination in the law school rarely assess students' ability to identify and address issues of value or professional responsibility. But in a doctrinal course it is possible to address them by raising problems that interrogates values. For example, an equity teacher can use the reasoning in *The Siskina* as case-scenario to test how students recognize the ethical dilemma and professional responsibility issues the case throws up for commercial players and the public. In a land law class, *Savannah Bank Ltd* v. *Ajilo* can provide exercise to assess how much of values our students appreciate. In virtually all doctrinal courses students can be assessed on their ability to recognize and resolve professional responsibility issues.

(vi)   Assessing Empathy

The ability of a lawyer in listening to a client to empathize makes for competent performance. The skill can be taught via video showing of a client interviewing or counselling session. Thereafter, students may be asked questions such as, 'did the body language of the client send a wrong signal? Did it encourage a non-legal solution approach, how does your worldview and upbringing influence your view of the client, etc.?

(vii) Assessing Teamwork Skills

Ability to work as a team is indisputably a skill lawyers should possess, especially in an era seeing the profession metamorphosing for a vocation more to a business. Solo practice is not the in-thing today. So, lawyers have to learn and work as team players. The law school is a good place to inculcate the skill and for enhance learning by students of professional identity and professional responsibility.[72] The skill can be assessed in doctrinal setting after group assignment by the teacher both by team members and through self-reflection by asking questions relevant to

---

[71] Andrea A. Curcio, Assessing Differently and Using Empirical Studies to See if it Makes a Difference: Can Law Schools Do It Better? (2009) 27 *Quinnipiac L. Rev.* 899 at 908.

[72] Cristina D. Lockwood, Improving Learning in the Law School Classroom by Encouraging Students to Form Communities of Practice (2013) 20 *Clin. L. Rev.* 95 at 98 ("Since the beginning of history, human beings have formed communities that share cultural practices reflecting their collective learning: from a tribe around a cave fire, to a medieval guild, to a group of nurses in a ward, to a street gang, to a community of engineers interested in brake design. Participating in these 'communities of practice' is essential to our learning. It is at the very core of what makes us human beings capable of meaningful knowing)."

the students' participation in the team effort.[73]

The six suggestions by Andrea Curcio are just illustrative examples of how teachers can thinker with assessment to make it reflect the three dimensions of professional studies in law. They basically allow a wider range of testing knowledge, skills and values.[74] Teachers need to rethink and reformulate testing methodologies because present law school assessments have proven inadequate to measure the skills necessary for effective lawyering, yet it is an assessment technique with significant consequences for students- affecting prospect of job placement, defining students' self-worth, and even admission into the profession. The assessment status quo should change to more align with principles of validity, reliability and fairness. Given the high stakes that rest on examination the legal academy should be especially interested in exam reform as a scholarly pursuit motivated by a desire to explore wider issues that may make a difference in the lives of students, and ultimately, the legal profession.[75]

Law School Accreditation and the Bar

Accreditation is a ritual known to the legal academy. It is intended to quality assure teaching and learning of law schools. By legislation, the NUC and CLE are the accreditation bodies for licensing and quality assuring the adequacy of law schools.[76] Over the years, these agencies have designed basic minimum standards for effective teaching and learning. Unfortunately, these standards have proven

---

[73] Timothy J. Ellis & William Hafner, Peer Evaluations of Collaborative Learning Experiences Conveyed Through an Asynchronous Learning Network, in Proceedings of the 38th Annual Hawaii Int'l Conference on System Sciences, 2005 available at csdl.computer.org/comp/proceedings/hicss/2005/2268/01/22680005b.pdf, accessed March 10, 2017 (an excellent guide on how to designing a valid and reliable teamwork assessment model), cited in Andrea A. Curcio, Assessing Differently and Using Empirical Studies to See if it Makes a Difference: Can Law Schools Do It Better? (2009) 27 *Quinnipiac L. Rev.* 899 at 911.

[74] Andrea A. Curcio, Assessing Differently and Using Empirical Studies to See if it Makes a Difference: Can Law Schools Do It Better? (2009) 27 *Quinnipiac L. Rev.* 899 at 911

[75] Andrea A. Curcio, Assessing Differently and Using Empirical Studies to See if it Makes a Difference: Can Law Schools Do It Better? (2009) 27 *Quinnipiac L. Rev.* 899 at 911. The legal academy has largely shown reluctance to assessment issues because good and effective teaching and learning rarely counts for professorial promotion. See Douglas A. Berman, Scholarship in Action: The Power, Possibilities and Pitfalls For Law Professor Blogs (2006) 84 *Wash. U. L. Rev.* 1043, 1057 (discussing how deans and colleagues value legal scholarship, especially scholarship about big abstract issues that appeal to other academics, more highly than classroom teaching); Roger Scordato, The Dualist Model of Legal Teaching and Scholarship (1990) 40 *Am. U. L. Rev.* 367, 375 (states that the emphasis on scholarship creates incentives to minimize time spent on classroom teaching). But it is suggested by Curcio that if studying assessments can result in publishable scholarship, although it may not be credited in the same way by colleagues as more esoteric law review articles. If there are such studies, however, and they indicate that alternative assessment methods improve student learning, produce more effective lawyers, or eliminate the discriminatory impact of existing assessment methods, the studies may help persuade law schools that they owe students a fiduciary responsibility to value teaching and assessing, and its resulting scholarship, to the same extent as more abstract legal scholarship, and the data may even create market demand for changing current practices- Andrea A. Curcio, Assessing Differently and Using Empirical Studies to See if it Makes a Difference: Can Law Schools Do It Better? (2009) 27 *Quinnipiac L. Rev.* 899.

[76] Refer to statute

nebulous and accreditation outcomes have been reddened with palpable unfairness.[77]

Accreditation is often a ritual requirement for every new law school, and reaccreditation of older law schools. Central to the process are minimum standard for approval to be granted. The standards for accreditation generally cover many aspects of the operation of a law school, such as curriculum design, faculty, administration and finance, admissions, library resources, and physical facilities. It includes rules specifying length of the undergraduate study, limitation on student-faculty ratio, etc. The standards are said to be objective, but it is mistaken to think that objectivity by itself renders a standard appropriate.[78] The criteria involved implicates physical infrastructure, curriculum design, finance, teaching infrastructure like staff mix, class and tutorial time-table, library holding, teaching methodologies, town and gown relationship, and many likes. This book already makes tangential reference to some of these accreditation signposts, and why some of the criteria require re-examination in moving legal education away from liberal studies towards professionalism.[79]

Commentators sadly are suggestive that accreditation standards implicitly effectuate elitism in enrolment selection, relative low student-faculty ratio, requirement of full-time faculty, rather than part-time adjunct, emphasis on scholarly research and writing in addition to teaching, an academic rather than utilitarian approach to legal education, libraries with extensive collections, and good physical facilities.[80]

We are however narrowing the discourse here to the role the bar should play in accreditation. Unlike in Nigeria where accreditation is the business of government agencies, in the United States the bar administers law school accreditation through its section of Legal Education and Admission to the Bar (Section of Legal Education).[81]

---

[77] For example, old-boy connection plays a significant role in the process of choosing accreditation team, its reports and recommendations. Some law schools have even gone as far as attempting and implementing unlawful designs of window-dressing in infrastructure, staff hiring, etc.

[78] Objectivity paper.

[79] See Carnegie and other reports. Refer also to curriculum design on economics, literature etc. in law when what should be taught is how skills in those learning interconnect with law. See Ado lecture.

[80] Marina Lao, Discrediting Accreditation? Antitrust and Legal Education (2002) 79 *Wash. U.L.Q.* 1035 at 1042.

[81] Marina Lao, above n. 80. Accreditation in Nigeria however does not interrogate issues of antitrust unlike in the U.S. For antitrust implications in accreditation see Peter James Kolovos, Note, Antitrust Law and Nonprofit Organizations: The Law School Accreditation Case (1996) 71 *N.Y.U. L. Rev.* 689.

Should law school also be accredited by the bar just as the universities. Is it not fairer than present government funded accreditation. Movement towards business than vocation makes prevailing liberalisation of legal education.

Chapter 6

Learning Environment

Introduction

When law students arrive for the first time in the faculty, they are usually full of excitement. They walk around the building admiring their new study place. First, they are happy to get admission into the faculty after so much competition. They are also happy to be privileged to join a supposed elite club of learners. For the first lecture, it is a hundred percent attendance, most entering the class with broad smiles, new notebooks, laptops and bags. What excitement this can be for the observing teacher. In this respect, they resemble first-day children at the kindergarten school.[1]

Sadly, over the years our students' excitement wanes. Many factors are said to cause it. Learning takes a curve that demands their 24/7 attention. They have to learn how to write, think and act like lawyers in so short a space of time. New rules, concepts, doctrine and policy has to be learned and mastered for exams that require more of memorizing than they contemplated. All of these is made worse be a learning environment not generally conducive for the task of effective learning.

Law school adversely affects students. Studies show that the intense, competitive learning environment contributes to the psychological health of students and that the environment plays a critical role on the quality of teaching and learning.[2] This unfortunately turns away a few the not too strong to extra-curriculum, non-curriculum activities and drug dependence.

---

[1] Gerald Hess, Heads and Hearts: The Teaching and Learning Environment in Law School (2002) 52 J. Leg. Educ. 75. See also Emily Grant, The Pink Tower Meets the Ivory Tower: Adapting Montessori Teaching Methods for Law School (2014) available at: http://ssrn.com/abstract=2483130, assessed on September 23 2015 (discussion can incorporate Montessori's ideas to foster a more robust educational environment for law students as they join a profession of life-long self-directed learners).

[2] For a discussion on the psychological health situation of law students resulting from intense competitive environment exacerbated by rising costs of legal education, see, Susan Daicoff, Lawyer Know Thyself: A Review of Empirical Research on Attorney Attributes Bearing on Professionalism (1997) 46 *Am. U. L. Rev.* 1337 (an empirical study on anxiety and distress amongst law and medical students in the U.S.); Stephen B. Stanfield & G. Andrew Benjamin, Psychological Distress Among Medical and Law Students (1985) 35 *J. Legal Educ.* 65; Barbara Glesner Fines, Competition and the Curve (1997) 65 *UMKC L. Rev.* 879; Stephen C. Halpern, On the Politics and Pathology of Legal Education (1982) 32 *J. Legal Educ.* 383. But it must be stated that generally, moderate levels of stress improve student performance while low or high levels of stress decrease performance. See, B. A. Glesner, Fear and Loathing in the Law Schools

As a result, several suggestions have been proposed to reduce students' stress and alienation. Alternative grading system that reduces stress and motivates learning is one such. For example, some educators advocate faculty less reliance on closed bluebook exam, and a shift to more of formative assessment. Law schools are encouraged to educated students on time, stress, and substance abuse and where possible, facilitate peer and family support systems, and access to institutional counselling services.[3] The law school should quickly address stress related challenges of students because if left unaddressed for too long it could affect cognitive learning, emotions and attitude of students to teaching and learning.

Theories of Effective Environment

Hess has suggested four models for an effective teaching and learning environment, namely: (i) the Lowman's two-dimensional model;[4] (ii) Palmer's notion of teaching as creating space;[5] (iii) Gamson and Chickering's seven principles of good adult education;[6] and (iv) the U.S. National Research Council learning environment model.[7]

Lowman's Two-Dimensional Model

The model is based on two articulations: intellectual excitement and interpersonal rapport. The former requires mastery of the course by the teacher to occupy students mind and animation to capture the heart of students, while the latter recognizing that the classrooms are highly charged interpersonal spaces, states that emotional reactions to the education environment affects both teacher and

---

(1991) 23 *Conn. L. Rev.* 627, 631 ("a certain amount of tension and anxiety can be useful in motivating individuals to do their best)." at 644, cited in Gerald Hess, Heads and Hearts: The Teaching and Learning Environment in Law School (2002) 52 *J. Leg. Educ.* 75 at 80.

[3] The NLS does in its first week of students' orientation, a practice that should be emulated by faculties. See lesson plan.

[4] Joseph Lowman, *Mastering the Techniques of Teaching* 2nd ed. San Francisco, 1995.

[5] Parker Palmer, The Courage to Teach: Exploring the Inner Landscape of a Teacher's Life, San Francisco, 1998.

[6] Arthur W. Chickering & Zelda F. Gamson, *Seven Principles for Good Practice in Undergraduate Education*, AAHE Bull., Mar. 1987 at 3. After Arthur Chickering and Zelda Gamson published "Seven Principles" in the March 1987 issue of the *AAHE Bulletin,* more than 150,000 reprints were requested by college administrators and teachers over the next 18 months. Subsequently, books, faculty development conferences, and numerous articles reviewed the research behind the seven principles and their practical application in higher education. For a description of the development of the seven principles and their impact on undergraduate education, see Gerald F. Hess, Seven Principles for Good Practice in Legal Education: History and Overview (1999) 49 *J. Legal Educ.* 367. In 1998 the Institute for Law School Teaching sponsored a conference that brought the seven principles to the attention of law teachers. The seven principles were featured in programmes of the sections on teaching methods and clinical legal education of the Association of American Law Schools.

[7] Committee on Developments in the Science of Learning & Committee on Learning Research and Educational Practice, Commission on Behavioral and Social Sciences and Education, National Research Council, eds. John D. Bransford *et al.*, Washington, 1999, 131.

student. Thus, effective teachers evoke positive emotion by communicating their respect for students and their expectations that students will perform competently. This in turn motivate student learning.[8]

Palmer's Space Creation

For Palmer space is "the physical arrangement and feeling of the room, the conceptual framework that I build around the topic my students and I are exploring, the emotional ethos I hope to facilitate, and the ground rules that will guide our inquiry. He then formulated six paradoxes that can motive or hinder effective teaching and learning. They are: (i) the space should have open boundaries-while the course should have boundaries determined by syllabus, the space should nonetheless, permit alternative ways to deeper learning; (ii) the space must be hospitable and charged-yes hospitable to encourage active student participation, but charge to give it the seriousness deserving of learning; (iii) individual and group voices should be preserved-individuals should be able to express their ideas, emotions, confusions, and perspectives, and the group should be allowed to affirm, question, and challenge the individual. Individual and group voices should not be muted by teacher; (iv) voices of individuals and the big stories of the course should be accorded ventilation-individual experiences should be meld to the course big stories to create learning and consciousness; (v) respect for solitude-solitude allows for reflection, so a learning norm that the community all speak in one voice should be discouraged; (vi) silence and speech should be welcomed-as both are modes of teaching and learning.

Chickering and Gamson Seven Principles for Good Practice

The principles are: (i) encourage frequent faculty-student contact-such in and out of class contacts motivate students' learning and commitment to competent performance; (ii) encourage cooperation among students-team learning deepens understanding and builds comrade spirit useful for the real world; (iii) encourage active-learning-a student-centred curriculum is a good way to implement it; (iv) quick feedback-help improve performance; (v) emphasize time on task-efficient time management improve overall efficiency in teaching and learning; (vi) communicate high expectations-expecting students to perform well becomes a self-fulfilling prophecy when teachers and institutions hold high expectations of themselves and make extra efforts; (vii) diverse talents and ways of learning should be respected-there are many roads to learning, none necessarily inferior to the other.

---

[8] Gerald Hess, Heads and Hearts: The Teaching and Learning Environment in Law School (2002) 52 *J. Leg. Educ.* 75 at 82.

National Research Council (U.S.) Learning Environment

The Council postulates that effective teaching and learning consists of four interconnected components, namely: (i) learner-centred environment-learning should harness student background to ground and link new learning; (ii) knowledge-centred environment-students' should learn concepts and skills of the course and how to apply it to new situations; (iii) assessment-centred environment-effective assessment provides feedback provides opportunity for revision to achieve competent performance; (v) community-centred environment-in the community students and teachers share a set of norms, students learn from one another and interact with others students and teacher.

Synthesized Theory of Effective Environment

From the models above, it is possible to synthesize eight ingredients for an effective educational environment applicable to legal education.[9] They are:

(i) Mutual Respect

Mutual respect among teachers and students is a core ingredient for effective teaching and learning. Respect is not something that is legislated by the teacher. It grows from classroom dialogue, gestures, students' doing the hundred and one things consistently well, the exploration of ideas, and problem-solving, etc.[10] Respect in this context is not be confused with condoning indolence. Respect does not mean that participants eschew conflict, hard work and criticism. These are sometimes necessary for challenges, motivation to do more and reflection.

Creating a respectful environment is a complex interpersonal process, which ought to begin with the teacher. That is what is the kick-starter for the conducive environment. It triggers reciprocity from the students. Effective teachers recognize that one of the best ways to accomplish it is for the teacher to learn the names of her students. The exercise is made less tasking by using a seating chart.[11] Calling students by name tells the class that everyone is valued in the enterprise of learning, and it creates a felt connection to competently perform.

---

[9] Gerald Hess, Heads and Hearts: The Teaching and Learning Environment in Law School (2002) 52 *J. Leg. Educ.* 75 at 87. See also also Emily Grant, The Pink Tower Meets the Ivory Tower: Adapting Montessori Teaching Methods for Law School (2014) available at: http://ssrn.com/abstract=2483130, assessed on September 23 2015 ("According to Montessori, there are six basic components necessary to the classroom environment, and the teacher plays an active role in developing each. The development of these six elements—freedom, structure and order, reality and nature, beauty and atmosphere, the Montessori materials, and the development of community life—depends heavily on the teacher's ability to adapt to the growth of the individual child);" Erik Gerding, A Montessori Law School? The Conglomerate, May 8 2010, available at http://www.theconglomerate.org/2010/05/a-montessori-law-school.html, accessed September 23 2016.

[10] Kent D. Syverud, Taking Students Seriously: A Guide for New Law Teachers (1993) 42 *J. Legal Educ.* 247.

[11] See discussion at page on what is a seating chart.

Learning about students' experience and background which can be meld to the big stories of the course in a way not too pointed and does not embarrass creates class energy. For example, when teaching negligence, the teacher can draw on the experience of a student who has served as a factory manager or is a medical doctor to explain the element of 'duty' which interrogates the neighbour test. One fine way to know of students' experience and background without necessarily probing is to read their faculty or course records. It should provide background information about our students.[12]

It is also important for our students to get to know us. The teacher should introduce herself at the course beginning. Introduction should include stating your name, professional and personal interest. The course webpage can be used to communicate teachers' work experience and students' course expectations. In-class and out of class interaction in formal and less formal settings enhances a conducive learning environment. But the teacher must know where to draw the lines. We use and encourage teachers to see the fiduciary nature of the relationship, especially as underlined in the old English case of *Keech* v. *Sandford*.[13]

Time is a precious commodity. It should be spent, not wasted. Even at that, it should be spent wisely. The time of students' is not less precious. Teacher should be prompt to time and end lectures as predetermined by time-table or other rules prevailing, recognized rules. The saying that 'it is in the habit of students to wait for lecturer, not the other way around' has no place for effective teaching and learning. For instance, teacher-student consulting hours must be respected by the teacher. The importance of this can be impressed on students by telling them that you will not schedule any other work during the time and that 'nothing is as important than meeting them.' It not only reassures care, but communicate seriousness in the enterprise of learning.

The environment is kept conducive by teacher stating the ground-rules for course, and an articulation of how respect is enhanced. For example, they need to know the rules on class attendance, use of computer, cell phone, etc. during lecture. They also should be explicitly told that respect is at least a three-way traffic. Teacher's respect for them, their respect for the teacher, and mutual respect for one another.

(ii) Expectations
The teacher should set high, but modest, attainable academic expectation for her students. The articulation on expectation should be continuous even after the

---

[12] Some faculties and course teachers require students to write short statements about themselves, their motivation to study law and how they intend to put to use legal knowledge and skills on graduation.
[13] (1666) state facts and the reasoning of the court.

first day in class. One fine way to do it is by modelling high expectation. For instance, showing the class a model of outstanding performance can be magical.[14] Students give high ratings to courses in which they had to work hard.

(iii) Supportive Teaching and Learning

Supportive learning involves teachers' attitudes, student-faculty contact, role modelling and mentorship. A teacher's interpersonal, supportive attitude of say, concern, encouragement and help, will motivate students to excel. So, does frequent student-faculty contacts.[15] It can help clear ambiguities. In playing the role of mentors, teachers encourage, guide and advise students.[16]

(iv) Collaboration

Collaboration is two-sided: collaboration between students, and collaboration with course teacher. The former involves students working together in pairs or groups in in class and out of class projects, while the latter involves students and teacher collaboration in course design, delivery and evaluation.[17]

(v) Inclusion

When students' background and experiences are included in course design and instruction, they get motivated, either extrinsically (motivation for reward, such as grades or money prize) or intrinsically (motivation based on interest, such as curiosity and desire to learn). Variety of perspectives of interest to the class can be

---

[14] Paula Lustbader, You Are Not in Kansas Anymore: Orientation Programs Can Help Students Fly Over the Rainbow (2008) 47 *Washburn L.J.* 327.

[15] Susan B. Apel, Principle 1: Good Practice Encourages Student-Faculty Contact (1991) 49 *J. Legal Educ.* 371.

[16] For a model of how NLS does it see Felicia Eimunjeze, NL&PJ. See externship handbook. Refer also to Gadzama scheme. Lynn C. Herndon, Comment, Help You, Help Me: Why Law Students Need Peer Teaching (2010) 78 *UMKC L. Rev.* 809; Ted Becker & Rachel Croskery-Roberts, Avoiding Common Problems in Using Teaching Assistants: Hard Lessons Learned from Peer Teaching Theory and Experience (2007) 13 *Legal Writing: J. Legal Writing Inst.* 269.

[17] D. Jacques, Learning in Groups, Kogan, Paye, London, 1992; David Dominguez, Principle 2: Good Practice Encourages Cooperation Among Students (1991) 49 *J. Legal Educ.* 386; Frances McGlone, Student Peer Mentor: A Teaching and Learning Strategy Designed to Promote Cooperative Approaches to Learning and the Development of Lifelong Learning (1996) 12 *Queensland Univ. Tech. L.J.* 201; P MacFarlane & G. Joughin, An Integrated Approach to Teaching and Learning Law: The Use of Student Peer Mentor Groups to Improve Student Learning in Contract ( ) 3 *Legal Educ. Rev.* 2 at 153-172; Paula Lustbader, Structuring Collaborative Exercises, in *Techniques for Teaching Law,* eds. Gerald F. Hess &Steve Friedland, 139 (Durham, 1999). Gerald F. Hess, Student Involvement in Improving Law Teaching and Learning (1998) 67 *UMKC L. Rev.* 343; Gerald F. Hess, Principle 3: Good Practice Encourages Active Learning (1999) 49 *J. Legal Educ.* 401. In learner-centered environments, teachers share power with students by involving them in decisions about their own education." Gerald F. Hess, Collaborative Course Design: Not My Course, Not Their Course, but Our Course (2008) 47 *Washburn L.J.* 367; Sarah Morath et al., Motions In Motion: Teaching Advanced Legal Writing Through Collaboration (2013) 21 No. 2 *Persp. Teaching Legal Res. & Writing* 119.

gender issues, matters of minority, etc.[18] The teacher should likewise pay attention to the different learning styles of students and adapt instruction to fit the varieties. The varieties could include lectures, seminars, group activities, externship, internship, dialogue, role-play, clinic, simulation, writing exercises, visual aids, etc.

(vi) Engagement

Effective teaching and learning engages both teacher and students. Teacher demonstrates it through active presence with students in and out of the classroom. Students show it by being active participants in their education. The teaching concept of immediacy has proved helpful in bringing closeness with students using verbal and nonverbal communication. Verbal communication can take the form of soliciting alternative viewpoint, praising student for competent performance, calling student by name, etc. Nonverbal communication can take the form of appropriate eye contact, listening, smile, etc. The use of a variety in teaching method enhances students' engagement as the teacher connects to the different learning styles of the class.[19]

(vii) Delight

The enthusiasm of the teacher is contagious to motivating students to learn. The teacher can do so in many ways. For example, she can tell her class why the course intrigues her, why teaching brings her much delight, etc.

(viii) Feedback

Feedback on performance is an essential factor in assessment. In this respect, formative assessment is encouraged over (not as substitute, but as complement) the traditional summative assessment of law schools. Feedback must however be prompt for it to be effective in enhancing competent performance.[20] While the teacher is the primary source of feedback, she can be through other sources, like students' themselves, their peers, external reviewers, computer programme,[21] etc.

---

[18] Paula Lustbader, Teach in Context: Responding to Diverse Student Voices Helps All Students Learn (1998) 48 *J. Legal Educ.* 402; Paula Lustbader, Principle 7: Good Practice Respects Diverse Talents and Ways of Learning (1999) 49 *J. Legal Educ.* 448.

[19] Vernellia R. Randall, The Myers-Briggs Type Indicator, First Year Law Students, and Performance (1995) 26 *Cumb. L. Rev.* 63 (discussion using the learning styles based on the Myers-Briggs Type Indicator).

[20] Terri LeClercq, Principle 4: Good Practice Gives Prompt Feedback (1999) 49 *J. Legal Educ.* 418. Sandra L. Simpson, Riding the Carousel: Making Assessment a Learning Loop Through the Continuous Use of Grading Rubrics, 6 Can. Legal Educ. Ann. Rev., 2011, 35, 51; Andrea A. Curcio, Moving in the Direction of Best Practices and the Carnegie Report: Reflections on Using Multiple Assessments in a Large-Section Doctrinal Course (2009) 19 *Widener L.J.* 159 (finding that use of rubrics and grading sheets resulted in easier self-assessment and contributed to students' lifelong learning process).

[21] For example, computer lessons allow students to learn at their own pace and provide continuous feedback as students respond to questions. See also Richard Warner et al., Teaching Law with Computers (1998) 24 *Rutgers Computer & Tech. L.J.* 107.

Teachers who apply these principles will not only create an effective teaching and learning environment, but will also help maximize students' achievements and build on the dreams they bring to legal education, a worthy promotion of our primary professional responsibility.

To all of the above can be added the 'hidden curriculum,' a term said to be rooted in sociology, reputed to be first utilized by Philip Jackson.[22] He posits that there is power in the implicit messages in schooling and school design. That explains why Montessori classroom are beautifully painted to enhance early learning. Stressing the aesthetics of beautiful physical environment to learning, Eric Margolis stated:

"Given that people constantly pick up messages from their environment, it is clear that the way a school is designed, the materials used...has an influential role in education. A building that looks and feels like a prison has one kind of impact, whilst a light and airy, inviting building has another. The school building sends out a message to pupils and staff about how much they are valued and also about how much their education is valued."[23]

---

[22] Philip W. Jackson, Life in Classroom,1968 (the commentator argues that what is taught in schools is more than the sum total of the curriculum and believed formal schooling should be understood as a socialization process where students pick up messages through the experience of being in school and interacting with faculty and peers, not just from things they are formally taught) cited by David M. Moss, The Hidden Curriculum of Legal Education: Towards a Holistic Model for Reform 2013 J. Disp. Resol. 1 (2013) available at: http://scholarship.law.missouri.edu/jdr/vol2013/iss1/3 accessed September 23 .2015.

[23] Eric Margolis, The Hidden Curriculum in Higher Education (2001); Ane R. Martin, What Should We Do with a Hidden Curriculum When We Find One? (1976) 6 (2) Curriculum Inquiry 143.

Chapter 7

Simulation

Introduction

The Carnegie Report and other assessment needs of legal education stress the value of simulation as a tool for teaching practical skills and professionalism.[1] Practical skills components such as clinical, field placement, and simulation provides students opportunity to learn the integration of doctrine, skills and professionalism.[2] At its embryonic stage of development, simulation was limited into trial practice, pre-trial practice, negotiation, mediation, counselling, legal writing and drafting classes. Its use is now wider across all curriculum. As envisioned in *Best Practices*, simulations involve "students assuming the roles of lawyers and performing law related tasks . . . under supervision and with opportunities for feedback and reflection. Shared reflection of the experiences of a class, debriefing, is a vital part of any simulation.[3]

The emergence of realist scholarship, legal writing curriculum, legal clinics and calls to tilt legal education towards professionalism have all combined to heightening the place of simulation in legal education and lawyering. Most legal writers and clinicians in fact suggest that simulation is a veritable tool for transmitting learning to students. This chapter sets out to discuss how law teachers can use simulation to deepen students' learning in the three dimensions of professional education, namely thinking, performing, and behaving. It is concerned with how simulation as a teaching pedagogy helps to illuminate and synthesize knowledge of abstract legal doctrines taught by traditional pedagogy, and it demonstrates how teachers have used stories in simulation classes to stimulate learning in the three dimensions of legal education, especially in expanding the meaning of "what happened." The chapter offer an example of how

---

[1] Refer to them.

[2] Paula Schaefer, Injecting Law Student Drama into the Classroom: Transforming an E-Discovery Class (Or Any Law School Class) With a Complex, Student-Generated Simulation (2011) 12 *Nev. L.J.* 130; Paul S. Ferber, Adult Learning Theory and Simulations – Designing Simulations to Educate Lawyers (2002) 9 *Clin. L. Rev.* 417 (discussing how simulations facilitate teaching substantive law, skills, and professionalism).

[3] Best Practice.

teachers have used simulation in large classes to teach using the hypothetical example styles *Yoyo* as case-study.

Place of Simulation in Legal Education

Why should teachers be interested in simulation as a medium to transmit lawyering skills? Both the *Carnegie Report* and *Best Practices in Legal Education* emphasizes that legal education should go beyond instruction in legal doctrine and analytical skills by teaching law students' practical skills and understanding of professional identity and obligations.[4] Simulation is an important tool for integrating doctrine and skills training in context-based courses and for teaching professionalism pervasively across the curriculum. While clinical education is often thought as the primary means of training professionals in practical skills, simulation can also fill the role.[5]

Simulation is an important tool for addressing the shortcoming identified by the profession in failing to train students that are client-ready. Much as clinical education can be the primary means to do so for professionals 9such as law and medical students) simulation can equally fill the role. For example, medical schools use simulation with great success in training doctors: actors play the part of patients and interact with medical students, who practice interviewing and diagnosing.[6] Law school can equally do same with hypotheticals.

Simulation is an activity that resembles something but is not the thing itself. It is a vehicle that illuminates and synthesizes abstract legal doctrines to better understanding. It is also a low-cost means for teaching skills and values in a manner that triggers students' motivation to learning by practice, thereby deepening learning in professionalism.[7] It is a pedagogy which demands that

---

[4] See above n. 2.

[5] Paula Schaefer, Injecting Law Student Drama into the Classroom: Transforming an E-Discovery Class (or Any Law Class) With a Complex, Student-Generated Simulation (2011) 12 *Nevada L.J.* 130. On the advantages of simulation over clinic in professional training see, Elliott S. Milstein, Legal Education in the United States: In-House Clinics, Externship and Simulation (2001) 51 *J. Leg. Educ.* 375; Paul S. Ferber, Learning Theory and Simulation-Designing Simulations to Educate Lawyers (2002) 9 *Clinical L. Rev.* 417 (e.g. gives room for the teacher to control the pace of simulation exercises, allows students to learn in a short period of time than live-clinic and without real consequences). But cf. Deborah Maranville, Infusing Passion and Context into the Traditional Law Curriculum Through Experiential Learning (2001) 51 *J. Legal Educ.* 51 (even though simulation can transfer skills, real client experience is better than simulation in increasing students' engagement and experiential learning)

[6] Christine N. Coughlin et al., See One, Do One, Teach One: Dissecting the Use of Medical Education's Signature Pedagogy in the Law School Curriculum (2010) 26 *Ga. St. U. L. Rev.* 361, 363 (explaining that medical schools format for acquiring medical skills as a three-step process of "[s]ee one, do one, teach one" with "do one" representing the step that students must perform the subject skill such as putting on a splint).

[7] Stacy Caplow, Autopsy of a Murder: Using Simulation to Teach First Year Criminal Law (1989) 19 *N.M. L. Rev.* 137; Phillip G. Schrag, The Serpent Strikes: Simulation in a Large First-Year Course (1989) 39 *J. Legal Educ.* 555; Jay M. Feinman, Simulation: An Introduction (1995) 45 *J. Legal Educ.* 469; Paula Schaefer, Injecting Law Student Drama into the Classroom: Transforming an E-Discovery Class (or Any

students act like lawyers in carrying out activities of lawyers in dealing with situations that confront practice lawyers. As a teaching technique, it is a style in-between two familiar spectrum of teaching, the traditional doctrinal hypothetical and the clinical programme, but unlike the former, it is more complex than it, while lacking the intense reality of the later.

According to Hess and Freidland:

"Simulation and role-playing are techniques somewhere between doctrine-oriented hypotheticals and life-client clinical programs. Simulation in legal education includes writing a contract, interviewing a client, or arguing in moot court. A simulation is an indirect, vicarious experience, like doctrinal hypotheticals in a casebook, but is often modelled to resemble direct, live-client situations. Simulation often involves fact-oriented, ethics-oriented, and client-oriented problem solving. In this manner, simulations are more directly concerned with the attorney's role in practical contexts."[8]

Simulation occupies the square between doctrinal learning and live-client clinical. In a typical doctrinal class hypothetical, students are presented with a basic legal problem that requires them to resolve using the *(P)IRAC* or other flexible styles of writing.[9] For example, first year students of contract law are introduced to the interesting concept of the possibility of an offer being made to the whole world. *Carlill* v. *Carbolic Smoke Ball Co,* is often used to drive home the concept that if a person makes to another a statement capable of being construed as a promise and the promise fulfils all the objective requirements of an enforceable contract, then the fact that there was no intention to perform a juridical act is irrelevant.[10] Following the case ratio, a hypo can be constructed by the teacher: "D makes an offer to the whole world that . . .etc. C, who on the basis of the advert buys the medication, uses it and yet suffers from. . .etc. Would D be liable to C on the legal count that he accepted the offer?" Such a hypothetical question requires the students to simply fit the facts to law and arrive at a

---

Law Class) With a Complex, Student-Generated Simulation (2011) 12 *Nevada L.J.* 130 (use of simulation to give students first-hand experience in e-discovery practice);. For reading on how simulation can be useful as pedagogy, see, Myron Moskovitz, Beyond the Case Method: It's Time to Teach with Problems (1992) *J. Legal Educ.* 241; Curtis J. Berger, Teaching "S&V" Beyond the Live Client Clinic: We Can Do Far More Without Spending Far More, in Joan S. Howland & William H. Lindberg, eds., *The MacCrate Report: Building the Educational Continuum,* St. Paul, 1994, 69 (comparative cost benefit of simulation against live law clinic).

[8] Gerald F. Hess & Steven Friedland, *Techniques for Teaching Law,* NC, Durham: Carolina Acad. Press, 1999, 193. *Best Practices* describes simulation-based courses as learning which "relies on students assuming the roles of lawyers and performing law-related tasks in hypothetical situations under supervision and with opportunity for feedback and reflection.") Id at 132. For a discussion on how simulation integrates doctrine, skills and ethics, see

[9] For the various legal writing styles, see Paul S. Ferber, Adult Learning Theory and Simulations – Designing Simulations to Educate Lawyers (2002) 9 *Clin. L. Rev.* 417.

[10] [1893] 1 QB 256. See also *Blackpool & Fylde Aero Club Ltd* v.. *Blackpool BC* [1990] 1 WLR 1195.

conclusion. The hypo only succeeds in making the students to "think like a lawyer." No more. Hypo learning is nothing than "learning by watching".

But simulation is unlike it because it often involves complex multidimensional reasoning. While a hypo generally raises one or two linear issues for analysis, simulation goes beyond. It is rather used to help students raise and reason on several issues, much of which they must organized before any of the issues can be separately analysed.[11] It is more complex than doctrinal hypos because it includes elements of performance, such as client interview, facts gathering, negotiation, drafting of documents and such activities built around lawyering activities designed to improve cognitive. While hypos merely show students how other solve problems, simulation on the other hand, helps them to solve problems themselves by mimicking lawyers' performance as they find, frame and analyse issues. Hypos are not problems as we know them in the real world. Clients who come to lawyers do not present to them hypos. Rather they present to lawyers' problems seeking solutions. So, a lawyer trained to analyse hypos is not really trained to be a problem-solver. No one really learns to play table tennis or football by simply watching it on video and taking some lectures on it, without elements of practice. Simulation bridges the gap between both. It is the mimic performance.

In contrast to hypo, live-client clinic demands more than doctrinal solution. In a live-clinic, students in addition to finding legal solution to disputes, must deal with the other concerns of the client as problem-solvers, be they psychological or economic. For example, (in our hypo above) while C may be happy to know that the *Carlill* ratio provides her a possible legal remedy, she may be concerned about future repeat business relationship with D (assuming that they are trading partners in a continuing business that may become frosty using litigation to redress the injury). This is itself a legitimate concern of the client outside the brackets of law. Simulation is unlike it because it lacks the intensity and reality of live-client experience.

Simulation continuum exercises often use one set of facts to grow many exercises at different points throughout the course instruction.[12] For example, the

---

[11] Moskovitz, above n 33 at 246. On the weakness of hypos in transmitting lawyering skills, see Edwin W. Patterson, The Case Method in American Legal Education: Its Origin and Objectives (1951) 4 *J. Legal Educ.* 1. But cf. Gerald F. Hess & Steven Friedland, *Techniques for Teaching Law*, NC, Durham: Carolina Acad. Press, 1999, 193 at 196, (where the learned writers admitted that simulation because it does not get down to live-client clinic may miss out elements of "irrationality and unpredictability of clients, de-emphasizing the important need for judgment as a legal skill.")

[12] For a range of courses and examples of how simulation can be deployed across curriculum, see, Paula Schaefer, Injecting Law Student Drama into the Classroom: Transforming an E-Discovery Class (or Any Law Class) With a Complex, Student-Generated Simulation (2011) 12 *Nevada L.J.* 130 (e-discovery in pre-trial litigation); *Best Practice*, above n. 2 at 179 (trial practice classes); *Carnegie Report*, above n.2 at 107 (drafting legal documents using case file in legal method); Id at 112 (alternative dispute resolution);

Carlill scenario can be used by the teacher to hone skills in drafting of offer and complaint, interrogatories and discoveries, moot court trials procedure, etc. Because simulation is built around lawyering activities, it can enrich didactic learning.

Simulation, at its embryonic stage of development was confined to moot court exercises and trial practice offerings. Its scope now covers the gamut of law curriculum as a legitimate method of instruction across legal subjects.[13] Simulation enhances learning in that it enables students to perceive more deeply how legal doctrines affect people in real life; and because it contains elements of entertainment (e.g. role-play), it provides a departure from too serious and stereotype learning and so it can be a refreshing diet in engaging students in lawyering roles. But its special attraction is its potential for stimulating retention of knowledge, because knowledge acquired in solving problem is better remembered.[14]

Simulation problem-solving technique in legal education is closely connected with Bloom's taxonomy of learning, analysis and ranking of types of learning (in ascending order of importance): (i) knowledge; (ii) comprehension; (iii) application; (iv) analysis; (v.) synthesis, and (vi) evaluation.

Karen Barton et al., Authentic Fictions: Simulation, Professionalism and Legal Learning (2007) 14 *Clinical L. Rev.* 143 (transactional lawyering skills); Andrew L. Strauss, Creating and Conducting In-Class Simulations in Public International Law: A Producer's Guide (1998); Carol R. Goforth, Use of Simulation and Client-Based Exercises in the Basic Course (2000) 34 *Ga. L. Rev.* 851 (business association class); Sally Frank, A City Council Examines Pornography: A Role-Play for a Law School Class (2000) 21 *Women's Rts. L. Rep.* 169 (city council debate on pornography); Caro McCrehan Parker, Writing is Everybody's Business: Theoretical and Practical Justifications for Teaching Writing Across the Law School Curriculum (2006) 12 *J. Legal Writing Inst.* 175 (writing assignments); Harriet N. Katz, Evaluating the Skills Curriculum: Challenges and Opportunities for Law Schools (2008) 59 *Mercer L. Rev.* 909 (client-counselling); John B. Garvey & Anne F. Zinkin, Making Law Students Client-Ready: A New Model in Legal Education [2009] *Duke Forum Law & Soc. Change* 101 (negotiation); John Lande & Jean R Sternlight, The Potential Contribution of *ADR* to an Integrated Curriculum: Preparing Law Students for Real World Lawyering (2010) 25 *Ohio St. J. Disp. Resol.* 247 (ADR); Charlotte S. Alexander, Learning to be Lawyers: Professional Identity and the Law School Curriculum (2011) 70 *Md. L. Rev.* 465 (law practice management); 4 *ILSA J. Int'l & Comp. L.* 669 (public international law course); William R. Slomanson, Pouring Skills Content Into Doctrinal Bottles (2011) 61 *J. Legal Educ.* (civil procedure class).

[13] Phillip G. Schrag, The Serpent Strikes: Simulation in a Large First-Year Course (1989) 39 *J. Legal Educ.* 555Schrag (allays fears expressed in some quarters that simulation is costly in terms of time and resources it demands from teachers, students and school administration) Id at 556. See also Hess & Freidland, above n. 10 at 196 ("simulation require primarily human resources, which cost little or no money if students and staff perform their roles.") See for example, Kenny F. Hegland, Fun and Games in the First Year: Contracts by Role-play (1981) 31 *J. Legal Educ.* 534; F. Bloch, The Andragogical Basis for Clinical Legal Education (1982) 35 *Vand. L. Rev.* 321; Robert P. Davidow, Teaching Constitutional Law and Related Courses Through Problem-Solving and Role-play (1984) 34 *J. Legal Educ.* 527; Barry J. Stern, Teaching Legislative Drafting: A Simulation Approach (1988) 38 *J. Legal Educ.* 391; Edward D. Cavanagh, Pretrial Discovery in the Law School Curriculum: An Analysis and a Suggested Approach (1988) 38 *J. Legal Educ.* 401.

[14] Geoffrey R. Norman, Problem Solving Skills Versus Problem Based Learning (1989) 79 *Cornell Veterinarians* 307.

The traditional law school lecture-type pedagogy can be helpful in learning of stages (i) and (ii). Teaching in the form of lecture or seminar can transmit knowledge and comprehension of legal doctrines, rules and concepts. But is the far it can go. It can rarely teach the application of legal doctrines because it lacks elements of performance and evaluation of performance. Simulation is what is helpful to master stages (iii) and (iv) and possibly further.[15] Since most scholars of adult education posits that a characteristic feature of adult education is that of mutual inquiries by both teacher and students on experiential, active learning, simulation is a form of learning that is consistent with it.[16]

Simulation Example

Some teachers effectively teach simulation exercises by developing a hypo around the tort of negligence, that can be characterised as an infraction of legislation on safe foods and drug using facts patterned after *Osemobor* v. *Niger Biscuit Co. Ltd.*[17] In the case, negligence was raised against the defendant for manufacture of biscuits found to have a decayed tooth consumed by the plaintiff. A hypo could be constructed using similar scenario like this: Yoyo who buys biscuits manufactured by Delta Foods is injured consuming the biscuits with decayed tooth. What are the remedies available to her? You are required to interview Yoyo, your potential client. Make a record of the client-interview. Following the interview, you are to do case planning, considering the options of alternative dispute resolution, ethical issues raised in the scenario, etc. The *Yoyo* simulation is used by us to teach a range of lessons in problem-solving. Along with the Yoyo hypo, the students are given *Osemobor* to read. But in addition to understanding the facts of the case, its ratio, they are required to think and analyse the hypo in the matrix of problem-solving. It requires them to identify multiple issues, find rules that apply to the broad and narrow questions for determination, the policies underlying the rules and rule explanation, and how it possibly sits within the *Donoghue*[18] square and the mandate of government regulation on defect products.[19] The teacher can make the facts of the hypo fairly complex by injecting a series of memorandum on jurisdiction, regulatory statutes, substantive tort concepts of negligence and strict liability, scientific analysis of supposed injury to the client, interview sessions with

---

[15] Benjamin Bloom, (his famous taxonomy posits that possession of knowledge is a basic level of learning which ought to progress to application).

[16] Gerald F. Hess & Steven Friedland, above n. 10 at 194; June Cicero, Piercing the Socratic Veil: Adding Active Learning Alternative in Legal Education (1989) 15 *Wm. Mitchell L. Rev.* 1011; Gerald F. Hess, Principle 3: Good Practice Encourage Active Learning (1999) 49 *J. Legal Educ.* 401; Robin A. Boyle, Employing Active-Learning Techniques and Metacognition in Law School: Shifting Energy from Professor to Students (2003) 81 *U. Det. Mercy L. Rev.* 1.

[17] [1973] NCLR 382, (per Kassim J. High Court of Lagos State).

[18] Donoghue v.. Stevenson [1932] AC.

[19] NAFDAC, CPC, SON, etc.

defendant's company and government regulatory officials, needing them to organize interviews, draft complain letters and court processes, and the like. This is an exercise we have tried. Most of our students tell us that they find the simulation exercises insightful because at the end of the exercises they gain deeper insight to the civil procedure system, tort law, regulatory law and matters connected with real lawyering than could be conveyed through reading cases and abstract statute. The simulation exercises bring them to mimic human clients, drawing up strategies, draft papers, propound oral and written questions, negotiate with adversaries, and perform many of the task of lawyers.

Because our classes are fairly large, averaging 150, we divide our students into groups of ten on each assignment on the Yoyo hypo. The various groups are assigned roles and cues, much like the presentation of a play or movies, each given a written description of their roles. This tells them whether a lawyer will assist them in the process, whether their assignment requires research, and how it will be reviewed and critiqued. We use it for grading between 10-30%, (depending on the faculty policy) of their total exam score for the course. After grading, there is usually a quick feedback session.[20] That is how we engage our students in a simulation-tort class.

Using Stories in Simulation to Recreate Consciousness

Stories are an effective vehicle for simulation. One specific idea that skills teachers share is that students need to be taught that lawyering is often more about facts than it is about law. It is facts that often govern the formulation of what constitute the *ratio* of the case. That being so, simulation ought to make central the teaching of facts. But facts are not just out there for capture. They are often laden with patent subtleties that can confuse even the skilled lawyer.[21] Unfortunately, indeterminacy of law as opposed to indeterminacy of facts characterizes the focus

---

[20] This follows the recommended pattern by informed legal educators. Cite papers on assessment and evaluation. See Gregory S. Munro, Outcome *Assessment for Law School*, WA, Spokane: Inst. Law Sch. Teaching, 2000; Hess & Friedland, above n. 10, especially chapter 10 & 11 (classroom assessment responds directly to the questions 'how well are students learning' and 'how effectively are teachers teaching.') Id at 261; Thomas A. Angelo & K Patricia Cross, *Classroom Assessment Techniques*, 2nd ed. 1993; Jay M. Feinman, Simulation: An Introduction (1995) 45 *J. Legal Educ.* 469 at 478 ("Evaluation is part of the learning process. Student performance in a simulation needs to be evaluated, and the evaluation should count toward the student's grade in the course."). cite Nigerian and foreign articles.

[21] Critique of traditional legal education argue for storytelling to be taught as a skill in law schools. See Brain J. Foley, Applied Legal Storytelling, Politics, and Factual Realism (2008) 14 *J. Legal Writing Inst.* 17 at 18 ("Proponents of legal storytelling may find themselves in the position of criticizing legal education as sometimes falling to get at the human element of the conflicts that become lawsuits.") Id at 20. See also, Richard Neumann, *Legal Reasoning and Legal Writing: Structure, Strategy and Style,* 5th ed. Aspen Pub. 2005, 207 ("facts have subtleties that can entangle you if you are not careful. Beginners tend to have difficulties with four fact skills: (i)separating facts from other things; (ii) separating determinate facts from other kinds of facts; (iii) building inferences from facts; and (iv) purging analysis of hidden and unsupportable factual assumptions.")

of much traditional law teaching.[22] So lawyers are hardly taught how to construct facts and interpret them. The thinking is that legal construction of facts will be learned on the job of lawyering. Traditional law school pedagogy hardly has a place for teaching indeterminacy of facts because it is reasoned by the academy that when the students begin practice of law they will learn indeterminacy of facts on their own. It is this gap that simulation storytelling curriculum addresses. It is recognized that improving law through storytelling often encompasses the idea of injecting stories of "outsiders," bringing to limelight the stories and realities of people ordinarily shut out in law-making and adjudication. This explain the special attraction of stories to outsider jurists like feminism, critical legal studies and the like.[23] This likely explains why in simulation classes, stories have assumed a "pride of place as a tool to help students hear and incorporate the voices of outsiders as they engage in and practice various lawyering skills, and to challenge them to think creatively and compassionately."[24] Since stories bear an intricate connection with legal reasoning and argumentation, teaching students how to tell stories improves legal education.

Stories are told to create imagination, bring to bear clients experience and realities negotiated through law and its institutions. That being so, good lawyering ought to account for the client's theory of the case.[25] Unfortunately, despite the centrality of case theory in lawyering, most account of lawyering pay peripheral reference to it. Many advocacy or trial texts make no mention of it, despite its importance in the trial process.[26] Good lawyering demands recognizing the complexity of a client's story and desired outcomes. Client's problems may be messy, with difficult-to-determine facts, legal and non-legal aspects requiring telling the client's story in a conscious way that creates new understanding, rather simply funnelling them into legal rules. It is the theory of the client's the case that makes all the difference.

---

[22] Lorie M. Graham & Stephen M. McJohn, Cognition, Law and Stories (2009) 10 *Minn. J.L. Sci. & Tech.* 255 ("narrative plays a fundamental role in legal reasoning, in such areas as memory, moral decision-making, reasoning by analogy, explanation, and even organizing of vast amount of information that lawyers contend with. ... A narrative approach provides a more dynamic view of how people think about cases.") Id at 258; Robin A. Boyle, Employing Active-Learning Techniques and Metacognition in Law School: Shifting Energy from Professor to Students (2003) 81 *U. Det. Mercy L. Rev.* 1 at 19 ("facts are determinate in an ontological sense, but the facts of a lawsuit as argued by lawyers ... are indeterminate in an epistemological sense.")

[23] See generally, conference paper delivered at ALS London, UK, July 19, 2007. See also, Mary L. Coombs, Outsider Scholarship: The Law Review Stories (1992) 63 *U. Colo. L. Rev.* 683; White, above n. 7.

[24] Carolyn Grose, in Storytelling Across the Curriculum (2010) 7 *J. Asso. Legal Writing Directors* 37 at 39.

[25] See Symposium: Legal Storytelling (1989) 87 *Mich. L. Rev.* 2073; Symposium, Speeches from the Emperor's Old Prose: Reexamining the Language of Law (1992) 77 *Cornell L. Rev.* 1233; Symposium, Lawyers as Storytellers and Storytellers as Lawyers: An Interdisciplinary Symposium Exploring the Use of Storytelling in the Practice of Law (1994) 18 *VT L. Rev.* 565. See also, Emiri & Giwa, above n. 6.

[26] Cite Oputa and Niki Tobi to show its absence. Even books on professional ethics by Law School lecturers make no mention of it.

Stories are not told for the fun of it. They are told to recreate consciousness, incorporate the voices of clients, especially the voices of outsiders negotiating legal reality. Essentially, simulation storytelling inheres to curriculum in three important ways: helps students see that facts are not objective;[27] that they are not just hearers and tellers of stories, but importantly are constructors of stories;[28] and that in constructing stories, they must make conscious, intentional client-storytellers for persuasion.[29] To tell winning stories, our students need to master the law, the facts, and the client's goal. Weighing the client's goal makes central case theory. The client's theory of the case lies in the heart of effective trial advocacy and client representation, particularly that which incorporates the client's understanding of her case. Client's case theory is subtle appeal to the profession that client voices long muted by lawyers who tell their stories should be made central in lawyering. After all, the case is that of the client, so if anything, lawyers ought to allow clients play greater role in their case.[30] Case theory is therefore the explanatory statement linking the case to the client's experience of the world.

Skill teachers see case theory from perspectives. Some focus on the elemental role of case theory. Elemental case theory describes the concept in a manner that seek to force coherence on the disparate facts of a case in a way that resonates with the basic intuitions of the fact-finder.[31] So, for Peter Murray it is the totality of facts presented with reference to logic, consistency and human experience that ground them to the fact-finder as truthful.[32] From this wide perspective, case theory is seen as the totality of a case presented before the fact-finder. It includes four basic elements: the facts presented, the legal framework, the client's perspective, and their coherence with lived experience. However, for those who subscribe to its explanatory thesis, they posit that it is the explanatory statement linking the case to the client's experience of the world, which puts in the centre-

---

[27] There are no neutral facts in the world. See David Luban, Paternalism and the Legal Profession (1981) *Wis. L. Rev.* 454; Scheppele, above n. 6 (discussion of point of viewlessness); Festus Emiri, above n. 6.

[28] Anthony G. Amsterdam & Jerome S. Bruner, *Minding The Law,* Harv. U. Press, 2000 (established framework for narratives follow five literary paths: a steady state; the trouble begins; effort to redress the trouble; outcome and; an ending with a coda or moral.) Id at 114.

[29] See how outsiders have used constructed stories to recreate consciousness and open law to multivoicedness. See White, above n. 8; Miller, above n. 8.

[30] Critical lawyering is a term used to describe the emerging offshoots of critical legal theory from the standpoint of accessing legal knowledge through the storytelling approach to law from the standpoint of theory. See for example, Miller, above n. 21 at 486. See also Cunningham, above n 21; Anthony V. Alfieri, The Antinomies of Poverty Law and a Theory of Dialogic Empowerment (1987-88) 16 *N.Y.U. Rev. L & Soc. Change* 659; Anthony V. Alfieri, Speak Out of Turn: The Story of Josephine V (1991) 4 *Geo. J. Legal Ethics* 619.

[31] Kimberly A. Thomas, Sentencing: Where Case Theory and the Client Meet (2008) 15 (1) *Clinical L. Rev.* 187 at 189.

[32] Edward D. Ohlbaum, Basic Instinct: Case Theory and Courtroom Performance (1993) 66 *Temp. L. Rev.* 1.

burner the human experience of the client.[33] Binny Miller for example, states that case theory "serves as a lens for shaping reality, in the light of the law, to explain the facts, relationships, and circumstances of the client and other parties in the way that can best achieve the client's goals. The relevant reality combines the perspectives of the lawyer and the client with an eye towards the ultimate audience- the trier of fact."[34] Much of outsider jurisprudence sits within this square.[35] This is the real sense that creates an entailment between simulation storytelling and client-centred lawyering.

That being so, both parties in contentious matters will strive to tell their stories in a manner that ties up the facts to law and experience of the trier to get victory. For the defendant, case theory is a comprehensive and logical explanation of why the defendant is in court and why he is entitled to a favourable verdict. The claimant or prosecution will likewise have its own theory, expectedly, different from that of the defendant.[36] Case theory therefore encapsulates the multiple stories told in a variety of ways by the parties, making facts fluid, non-objective and contextual.

Effective teaching therefore demands that simulation classes should use the theory to stimulate reasoning and client centred lawyering. Let us see how some teachers have done so using the Elmer Davis story, especially in the context of helping our students see that facts are indeterminate, that legal education trains them not be hearers but also tellers, and constructors of stories; and that in constructing stories, they must make conscious, intentional choices as to how to tell stories. In fact, the case also reveals that where a story start or end can be deliberately chosen for purposes of persuasion.

---

[33] Miller, above n. 8.

[34] Ibid at 487 (using critical lawyering theory the commentator posits that client's voices have been silenced by the narratives that lawyers tell on their behalf). See also Binny Miller, Teaching Case Theory (2002) 9 *Clinical L. Rev.* 293

[35] In using stories to recreate reality, critical theorist distinguishes 'what' happened from the 'meaning' of what happened, believing that by opening the client's world, the meaning of what happened can be better understood.   See for example Miller, above n. 8, (where the narrative was expanded beyond 'what happened' scope of whether the $592 received by the defendant as damages benefit from an accident, spent by her in buying Sunday shoes for her children, should count as money deductible from her social benefit. Her lawyer chose a narrative that concentrated on the meaning of what happened to vindicate and justify the receipt). See also, White, above n. 8; Miller, above n.8 (Recognizing the importance of the client's life experience, critical lawyering involves clients in the choice of which story to tell and it expands the content of the narratives from 'what happened' to include the fabric of the client's life) Id. at 514; Peter Gabel & Paul Harris, Building Power and Breaking Images: Critical Theory and the Practice of Law (1982-83) 11 *N.Y.U. Rev. L &Soc. Change* 369; Lucie White, Mobilization on the Margins of the Lawsuit: Making Space for Clients to Speak (1987) 16 *N.Y.U. Rev. L &Soc. Change* 535; Jessica A. Rose, Rebellious or Regnant : Police Brutality Lawyering in New York City (2000) 28 *Fordham Urban L.J.* 619 (addresses current legal limitations in combating police brutality for subordinate groups and why and how the legal community must develop a more creative and rebellious methodology if it is to accomplish the goal of social transformation).

[36] Edward D. Ohlbaum, Basic Instinct: Case Theory and Court Performance (1993) 66 *Temp. L. Rev.* 1.

The Elmer Davis story is one storyline constructed by Kim Lane Schepple.[37] It is a narration of an African-American, Elmer Davis, who confessed to rape of a white woman in North Carolina. We shall only examine the case from the perspective of the voluntariness or otherwise of his confessional statement. The simulation class can be made to see that the facts of voluntariness are not objective facts out there for capture. Both the prosecution and the defendant would sure have their different case theories all stepped in facts that are true. It is expected that the prosecution will be happy to sustain the charge by showing the voluntariness of the defendant's confessional statement. That being so, its evidence will be as follows:

Prosecutor (P): Who is in charge of overseeing the interrogation of Mr. Davis?

Witness (W): I was.

P: Is there a Department protocol for interrogating prisoners?

W: Yes.

P: Describe that protocol to the judge.

W: We limit interrogation to twice daily, once in the morning and once later in the day.

P: What procedure did you follow for the interrogation of Mr. Davis?

W: We followed the Departmental protocol. I typically interrogated Mr. Davis in the morning, and another officer questioned him later in the day.

P: Did the procedure vary?

W: No, we followed that procedure the entire time Mr. Davis was in custody, up until the time he confessed.

With evidence like this, the simulation teacher could ask the students to identify the state's theory of the case and how it is constructed to tilt in favour of voluntariness of Mr. Davis confession. They can see it revealed in evidence that the Departmental protocol was followed, a policy in place against around-the-clock interrogation. The prosecution kept faith with (what seemed) good police practice, which should ordinarily satisfy the judge.

But this is only side of the coin. Simulation calls for deep reflection. Let us see how the defence can also construct the theory of the client's case to raise involuntariness.

Defence Attorney (DA): Mr. Davis, how long were you in jail before you gave the statement to the police?

Defendant (D): Sixteen days.

---

[37] Kim L. Scheppele, above n. 6. For purposes of this paper we would adopt the scenario played out of the story by Carolyn Grose, in Grose, above n. 24.

DA: Please describe the cell where you were being held?

D: It was a small cell in the back of the jail, with a bed and a chair. There was a little window out into the jail yard.

DA: Was there a clock in the cell?

D: No.

DA: Did you have a wristwatch?

D: No, they took my watch away from me when they put me in jail.

DA: During the sixteen days, how often did the police question you?

D: Pretty much all the time.

DA: When you say "pretty much all the time," what do you mean?

D: After I woke up in the morning, one of them would come and start asking me questions. That would go on all morning and then he'd leave. Then after a little while another one would come in and start up all over again.

DA: Was it light out while you were being questioned?

D: Sometimes it was.

DA: And was it ever dark out while you were being questioned?

D: Sure, it was.

DA: How long did the questioning go on?

D: Every single day until they got me to sign this statement.

The students can identify the client's theory of the case. It is radically different from the state's theory. It is all about the involuntariness of the confessional statement. Yes, the defendant was of the considered view that the interrogation was persistent, constant harassment, especially from the perspective that he didn't know what time it was and the questioning took place during dark hours.

The simulation role-play reveals to the students that two stories are true constructed of the facts, but from different viewpoints. It is true that the prosecution adhered to its protocol on questioning prisoners. It equally true that from the defendant's sense of time based on the changing light from the little window, the interrogation was sporadic. While the prosecution can argue that the circumstances were not sufficient to constitute coerced confession, the defence could argue that the repeated nature of the interrogation created a kind of duress which should vitiate the confession. What the story has done is to encourage the students to learn first-hand how they are themselves constructors of stories and eventual legal reality, and that reality is not fixed, as though cast in steel. What happened is nothing near objective. What position gets vindicated as fact may just turn out to be the story adopted by the decision-maker. They begin to appreciate experimenting with choices about how to use facts, frame examination of witnesses, how to structure facts, choose where a story should start and end, what evidence to highlight and the like.

The simulation-experiential learning technique can be furthered by moving the hypo somewhat into trial.[38] Assuming the judge disbelieves the defence and admits the confessional statement of Davis, how can you continue to centralize the client in defence? How will the centralizing motivation determine when and where to begin direct examination of your client? It is of course expected that the prosecution will frame a story with the simplistic thread like this: description of the murder committed by Davis, his subsequent arrest and his confession to the crime. Readily, the judge sees a bad black-man who enjoys killing. He should be convicted without more. But simulation requires that our students attempt to loosen the tight frame drawn by challenging the apparently objective and machine-like character of law and facts drawn by the prosecution. Some thinking and skills must come to play. The "when" and "where" to begin direct examination could provide the missile.

Grose tells us how he and his colleague do this by engaging in another direct examination of Davis. We unashamedly copy it in our simulation class. It goes like this:

Defence Counsel (DC): Mr. Davis, where did you grow up?

Defendant (D): Here in Alabama in Jefferson, just five miles from here.

DC: Do you remember the first time a policeman ever talked to you?

D: Yes.

DC: Tell the jury (judge) about that, please.

Prosecutor: Objection, relevance?

Ending the role-play here the students are asked why the line of argument by defence counsel will lead to relevant information. They only gain insight to this by visualising how the added construct goes to support the client's case-theory of involuntariness of the confessional statement. Even if the judge rules that the statement is voluntary and eventually convict Davis for murder, at least the defence would have built a structure of (seeming) coercion as ground for appealing the decision of the trial court on the voluntariness of Davis statement.

---

[38] In this respect, we simply follow the plan drawn by Grose by in our simulation class. See Grose, above n. 24 at 52.

At this point, we can assign to our student an article by Cunningham as a must read.[39] With the hindsight of the paper, they could be asked, why is the defendant's first contact with the police relevant? They know why from reading about legal literature on ethnographic lawyering which creates multiple consciousness. They quick see the picture-story. A poor black kid brought up in Southern America at the dawn of the civil rights movement, afraid of the police known (whether rightly so or otherwise) for intimidating people of colour. This background provides context to the confessional statement of Davis and supports his theory. It supplies the bridge for the judge to link the statement with coercion. The exercise makes pointed that it matters to lawyers their choices about how to use facts, frame examination of witnesses (that examination is not just about not asking leading questions in examination in chief or not asking offensive questions in cross examination and the like stipulated in the sections of Evidence Act), that case theory is a conscious, intentional choice lawyers must make in constructing persuasive and compelling stories. Case theory analysis in the context of storytelling teaches the lawyering skills. When stories are made with choices they are persuasive, compelling, and the choices can result in stories that achieve client's goals in ways they feel comfortable with.

Case theory is however, not only applicable to litigation. It readily also applies to negotiation, pre-trial proceedings and transactional lawyering. It is mistaken to think that stories enjoy a lesser place of prominence in transactional lawyering.[40] The reason isn't farfetched. Every transaction is a story. It is the

---

[39] Lucie E. White, *Goldberg* v.. *Kelly* on the Paradox of Lawyering for the Poor (1990) 56 *Brook. L. Rev.* 861; Anthony V. Alfieri, Reconciling Poverty Law Practice: Learning Lessons of Clients Narrative (1991) 100 *Yale L.J.* 2107; Cunningham, above n. 4. See also, related literature, John M. Conley & William M. O'Barr, *Rules versus Relationship: The Ethnography of Legal Discourse,* 1990 ("the law has come to define the problems of ordinary people in ways that may have little meaning for them, and to offer remedies that are unresponsive to their needs as they see them.") Id at 177. Generally, ethnographic lawyering brings lawyers into the construal world of those who experience disempowerment and marginalization to attain multiple-consciousness that enables them to imagine other kinds of marginalized viewpoints. Richard Delgado, Storytelling for Oppositionists and Others (1989) 87 *Mich. L. Rev.* 2411, Mari J. Matsuda, When the First Quail Calls: Multiple Consciousness as Jurisprudential Method (1989) 11 *Women's Rts. L. Rep.* 7; Miller, above n. 21 (a case of a black man charged with disorderly conduct, resisting arrest, assault after he was stopped and wrongly accused of shoplifting by three white security guards, thereby raising provocative questions about the defendant's life experience about the various case theories that lawyers construct); White, above n. 8. For reasons, why legal education should go beyond formalism and be expansive to context, see Phillip C. Kissam, The Decline of Law School Professionalism (1986) 134 *U. Pa. L. Rev.* 251 ("the study and practice of law would be improved by a more contextual approach that places a greater emphasis on both the application of law to concrete situations and the understanding of how law serves or fails to serve conflicting social values. This approach would improve professional education by initiating future practitioners into the uncertainties, complexities and value conflict of the 'practice situation.'") Id at 254; Edward D. Re, The Causes of Popular Dissatisfaction with the Legal Profession (2012) 68 *St. John's L. Rev.* 85 (discussion why the legal profession should re-access itself in the face of growing public dissatisfaction).

[40] Susan M. Chesler & Karen J. Sneddon, Once Upon a Transaction: Narrative Techniques and Drafting (2016) 68 *Okla. L. Rev.* 263

stories that give life to transactions. It is it that metamorphoses to become the basis of agreements, and the ultimate clauses of documents executed by the parties. For example, a conveyance is itself a story of negotiation, title investigation, and the purchase agreement. Therefore, the ability of lawyers to visualise and conceptualise transactions as stories benefits the negotiation, drafting, implementation, interpretation, and the ultimate enforceability of the transaction document.[41] It is all about client-centred lawyering.

Integrated Legal Education

Integrated education however demands that simulation should go beyond skills to also teach values. So, how can the simulation hypos of say the Yoyo negligence scenario and that of Davis be used to teach students professional responsibility in balancing client's case theory with interest of justice? More importantly, how can lawyers make client representation client-centred and empowering while observing the primary professional responsibility of ethical lawyering?

Traditionalist are bound to worry about striking the balance between client-centred case theory and professional responsibility. The reason is that they generally express too much objectivity about facts and so they can only conceive a limited universe for case theory. From their perspective, critical lawyering is discounted as unethical and a deviation from professional responsibility. Law to them defines the boundaries of stories. Classic, proper practice sees client stories through the law saturated lens. In the Davis scenario for example, the frame consists of only 'relevant' stories: 'what happened.' What happened is merely a story of how trouble started; where the defendant met the deceased, murdered her, his arrest, detention and subsequent trial. No more! Interestingly, that is the tight frame constructed by most criminal legislation and procedure statutes. Section 316 of the Criminal Code Act defines murder as the wilful killing of another. The Criminal Procedure Act makes provision for arrest, detention and trial process. The Evidence Act sets the ambits of what constitute confession etc. So, for traditionalist, (like the prosecution did in Davis case) once an account of *what happened* is given, all stories must be those that only fit within the frame constrained by law. No one is allowed to wrestle with the law to fit into their client's lived realities. Client's lived realities must be funnelled into what they understand the law requires. The paradigm gives facts a secondary role to law. Stories are subsumed in law, which is the starting and ending point of case theory. Facts are simply to be fitted to legal theory.

---

[41] Ibid.

Teachers however recognizing the learning progression theory know that all this tight stuff are characteristics of the technician and drafter stages of learning.[42] The real goal of legal education not yet attained, namely: to get their students to the designer and hopefully the creator stage of legal development. That is why a teacher would go further than the traditional boundaries of teaching. This requires injecting into the simulation class elements of critical lawyering to help recreate experience with law and consciousness.

The tight frame is all that critical lawyering disagrees with. *What* happened ought to constructed to include the *meaning* of what happened. That is what the simulation defence did by asking Davis "do you remember the first time a policeman ever talked to you?" It is a simulation story attempt to provide context and meaning to support the case theory of the non-voluntary nature of Davis statement. Meaning of what happened becoming intricate connected with the story of the client as to what happened. In contrast with traditional legal counselling model, which assigns a passive role to clients, case theory located in client-centred lawyering is rooted in the philosophy that lawyers should interact with clients in a way that allows clients to be decision-makers.[43] This demands that together the lawyer and client should consider various alternatives available in a case and the likely consequences in reaching the decision, a perfectly ethical position, which aligns with the concept of client autonomy.[44] Once taught in this way, the simulation helps students to see themselves in a brave new world of constructors of stories and closes the gap of learning difficulties, moving them to the level of creators of legal reality not afraid to stretch legal reasoning.

The simulation teacher would however need to give quick feedback on professional responsibility that client-centred theory recognizes that there are certain decisions which must be reserved for the lawyer. The client determines the goals of representation while the lawyer implements the goals. The end-means dichotomy can sometimes be difficult to draw, as most decisions in cases is a mixed question of ends and means.[45] That can constitute further analysis on

---

[42] Paula Lustbader, Construction Sites, Building Types, and Building Gaps: A Cognitive Theory of the Learning Progression of Law Students (1997) 33 *Willamette L. Rev.* 317.

[43] Critical lawyering aligns with rule 14 of the RPC which enjoins lawyers to be dedicated and devoted to the cause of their clients.

[44] Rule 14 (2) (a)-(e) of RPC demands lawyers to consult with their clients, keep them informed of important developments and possible strategies. On observation of client's autonomy as a key concept in representation, see, Miller above n. 21 at 503. See also, Mark Spiegel, Lawyering and Client Decision-making: Informed Consent and the Legal Profession (1979) 128 *U. PA. L. Rev.* 41; Marcy Strauss, Towards a Revised Model of Attorney-Client Relationship: The Argument for Autonomy (1987) 65 *N.C. L. Rev.* 315; Robert D. Dinerstein, Client-Centred Counselling: Reappraisal and Refinement (1990) 32 *Ariz. L. Rev.* 501; David A. Binder, et al. *Lawyers as Counsellors: A Client-Centred Approach*, 1991.

[45] Rule 14 (3) of RPC implicitly recognizes it when it states that: "when representing a client, lawyer may where permissible, exercise his independent professional judgment to waive or fail to assert a right or position of his client." See *Opia* v... *Ibru* (1992) 3 NWLR (pt. 231) 658. See also Robert F. Cochran, Jr.,

values and deepen students understanding of the scope of professional responsibility played out in client representation. Simulation has helped the teacher teach so much that the traditional law school pedagogy cannot achieve.

The teacher at this stage may assign the students further reading. That they take a cursory look at the RPC.[46] They would be surprised that the RPC offers little guidance about which decisions should be that of the lawyer or that of the client.[47] That can again be used by the teacher to teach the value of regulation moving away from general principles of conduct to narrow explicit rules and regulations, describing explicit minimum standards allowable. Whatever, teaching tools that can be created from the RPC reading assignment are numerous. For example, the teacher can stimulate thinking the flaws conceivable by the ends-means dichotomy; how the fluidity of the concept confuses both lawyer and client as to what falls into the class of ends or means; whether the concept promotes client autonomy;[48] or whether the concept clogs lawyers' view as to what may really matter to the client, etc.[49]

Conclusion

No question about it, students taught to think as lawyers can explain and criticize legal opinion using syllogism acquired as staple diet from the faculties of law. That is fine. Unfortunately, not much of legal practice requires all that. Instead, most lawyers spend their time solving problems. People come to lawyers for them to solve their problems. They do not consult lawyers to read to them abstract law. They want to know how to get out of trouble or not to get into one. We would be failing in our mandate if all we do as teachers is only to train them to "think like a lawyer," when we should be training them to be problem-solvers. Simulation is a

---

Legal Representation and the Next Steps Toward Client Control: Attorney Malpractice for the Failure to Allow the Client to Control Litigation and Pursue Alternatives to Litigation (1990) 47 *Wash. & Lee L. Rev.* 819 (discussing why client should control important decision-making).

[46] Rules of Professional Conduct for Legal Practitioners, 2007.

[47] For comparative analysis on matters of decision-making by clients see, Mark Spiegel, The New Model Rules of Professional Conduct: Lawyer-Client Decision Making and the Role of Rules in Structuring the Lawyer-Client Dialogue [1980] *Am. B. Found. Res. J.* 1003.

[48] The concept of autonomy underlies the ambits of many professional services. For the importance of the concept in medicine, see, Festus Emiri, *Medical Law and Ethics in Nigeria*, Lagos: Malthouse Press, 2012, 299; *Sidaway* v.. *Bethlen Royal Hospital* [1985] AC 871; *Okonkwo* v.. *MDPDT* (1999) 6 NWLR (pt. 786) 1. See also, Feinberg, Autonomy, Sovereignty, and Privacy: Moral Ideals in the Constitution (1983) 58 *Notre Dame L. Rev.* 445.

[49] The stock view that the objective of the client is to win her case is flawed especially in cases where the client may have an economic or psychological reason for engaging the legal process. For example, in Cunningham article tells a story he personally handled for a client (M. Dujon Johnson) who wanted to engage the legal system on the unfair grounds of ethnography arising from a misdemeanour case, alleging that the defendant refused to submit to the pat-down search from police troopers. The defendant who felt the charge was racially motivated simply wanted to show how the American court system, and unfortunately the legal profession, conspire to make and keep the poor voiceless. See Cunningham, above n. 4.

primary pedagogy for teaching them to be problem solvers.[50] Story-simulation gives students the opportunity to reflect on what they have learnt, how they learned it, and so enforces lawyering skills and ethics that are enduring. By learning law through the prism of problem-solving students gain a new understanding of law as they draft documents, negotiate agreements, take depositions, moot practice, etc. and they experience and resolve the professionalism challenges faced by lawyers in practice. This makes it a worthy pedagogy across the curriculum.

Challenges of Simulation

Despite the benefits of simulation to legal education, it has some limitations. They are: (i) simulation and skills courses can be expensive in that they are better fitted for small sections; (ii) it requires law teachers who have cognate practice experience to drive, (in terms of training the students and their evaluation of competent performance) which may be unavailable to the faculty, requiring the hire of additional faculty; (iii) for students to effectively participate, they must possess some minimal background in the doctrine or area of law covered by the simulation classes, so if the exercises implicates other areas of law outside the course syllabus, the teacher must spend some time to do background teaching of the doctrines relevant to the simulation; (iv) when incorporated across curriculum it could constrain time meant for full coverage of substantive law.

These challenges notwithstanding, it is a suggested worthwhile trade-off because it deepens understanding and learning.[51] What is more, the challenges above are surmountable. What is even of interest is the possibility of experimenting with the use of technology to deliver simulation to assuage for the resource, cost, and time pressures challenges posed by in-class simulation.[52] It limitation in this respect being feedback and teacher evaluation.

---

[50] See Myron Moskovitz, Beyond the Case Method: It's Time to Teach with Problems (1992) *J. Legal Educ.* 241 at 245 ("But-you reply-law schools cannot spend their scarce resources teaching students every single skill they will need in law practice-how to bill clients, how to manage an office, how to find the courthouse. True, but problem solving is not like any of these activities. Problem-solving is the single intellectual skill on which all law practice is based."); Edward D. Re, The Causes of Popular Dissatisfaction with the Legal Profession (2012) 68 *St. John's L. Rev.* 85 (discussion why the legal profession should re-access itself in the face of growing public dissatisfaction).

[51] See Robert C. Illig, et. al., Teaching Transactional Skills Through Simulations in Upper Level Courses: Three Exemplars (2009) 9 Transactions 15; Gary A. Munneke, Managing a Law Practice: What You Need to Learn in Law School (2010) 30 Pace L. Rev. 1207.

[52] Stephen M. Johnson, Teaching for Tomorrow: Utilizing Technology to Implement the Reforms of *MacCrate, Carnegie,* and *Best Practices* (2013) 92 *Nebraska L. Rev.* 46 (discussion that since feedback and evaluation are central to simulations, some important parts of the simulation experience cannot be replicated using technology even though technology can play an important role in delivering realistic, rich simulations") at 74.

Johnson provides useful empirical use of technology to deliver simulation by Professor Ira Steven Nathenson worthy of recount.[53] Because of its innovativeness we have chosen to unashamedly related the experience. He creates in his cyber law class websites for fictional companies, assigning his students to represent one of the companies. Each company is concerned about trademark infringement and unlawful cyber activities of the other. As trainer, he plays the role of managing partner for the students' law firm, client, and opposing counsel. Thereafter the students are assigned a series of simulation projects- to investigate the conduct of the opposing company, draft a cease and desist letter with regard to the company's online conduct, and communicate with the opposing party through an e-mail address, an address directed to the professor.

They then meet with the managing partner to report progress, based on which they create case files. Feedback is provided by him through e-mail acting as opposing counsel. Thereafter he provides feedback through written assessment of their case files on the documents and on a score sheet for the files. Aside this skills honing, he uses the responses of the students cease and desist letters to raise ethical issues to teach professional responsibility.

At the end of the online simulation the students deeply understand the underlying cyber law doctrines than other in-class lecture. The experience provides them a rich pedagogical tapestry, permitting them to practice lawyering skills and professionalism such as fact-finding, negotiation, client management, and professional values. All of this facilitated by technology, save the feedback and evaluation provided by the teacher.

---

[53] Stephen M. Johnson, Teaching for Tomorrow: Utilizing Technology to Implement the Reforms of *MacCrate, Carnegie*, and *Best Practices* (2013) 92 *Nebraska L. Rev.* 46 at 74 (relates the experience of Professor Ira Steven Nathenson use of online simulation in his cyber law class at Saint Thomas University School of Law). See Ira Steven Nathenson, Best Practices for the Law of the Horse: Teaching Cyber law and Illuminating Law Through Online Simulations (2012) 28 *Santa Clara Computer & High Tech. L.J.* 657. Karen Barton et al., Authentic Fictions: Simulation, Professionalism and Legal Learning (2007) 14 *Clinical L. Rev.* 143 (discussing computer-assisted simulation designed by Professor Paul Maharg [Glasgow Graduate School of Law], for the course Legal Practice, using a fictional town requiring students to obtain information from online entities and interact with other students and faculty online to buy and sell property, execute estate for deceased clients, institute and defend civil actions).

Chapter 8

Clinical Legal Education

Introduction

Most students enter the law school with little understanding of legal practice. Some may be familiar with television courtroom advocacy as portrayed through popular movies and dramas. That is the much they know. Clinical education is the primary means of training professionals (such as law and medical students) in practical skills. Clinical legal education is a method of teaching that has a social justice dimension. In broad terms, it includes in-house live client clinics, externship, community education projects, simulation courses, skills training courses, and interactive teaching methodology. In its narrow sense, it refers to students' receiving course credit for the combination of their practical work on client's case at the university-based clinic, and their participation in a classroom component or tutorial.[1] This chapter will be devoted to clinical education in the narrow sense, even though it shall tangentially refer as the need may arise to the general understanding of clinical legal education.[2]

Law clinics are called different names in the faculties. Some are referred to as legal aid clinics, law school clinics, university-based law clinics. Generally, they all refer to the law school offices in the university where students work with clients while enrolled in a course for credit. Usually, the clinic is supervised by the lawyers who teach in the clinic. They may be faculty staff hired as clinical law faculty, if it is a faculty with dichotomy of doctrinal and clinical staff. In some other cases, they just be adjunct practitioners experienced in the nuances of legal practice.[3]

---

[1] Peggy Maisel, Sustaining and Expanding Clinical Legal Education in Developing Countries: What We Can Learn from South Africa (2007) 30 *Fordham Int'l. L.J.* 374 at 378. For general discussion on clinical legal education, see, Leah Wortham, Aiding Clinical Education Abroad: What Can Be Gained and the Learning Curve on How to Do So Effectively (2006) 12 *Clinical L. Rev.* 615; Richard J. Wilson, Training for Justice: The Global Reach of Clinical Legal Education (2004) 22 *Penn. St. Int'l. L. Rev.* 42; Symposium, An Overview of Civil Legal Services Delivery Models (2000) 24 *Fordham Int'l. L.J.* 225.

[2] The narrow definition of clinical legal education does not include university or law courses that solely require students to engage in community education activities (street law courses), nor ones that teach legal skills in the classroom such as legal research and writing (skills courses).

[3] Richard J. Wilson, Training for Justice: The Global Reach of Clinical Legal Education (2003-2004) 22 *Penn St. Int'l L. Rev.* 421 (the author provides a brief overview of the development of clinical legal

Clinical education is recommended as a teaching and learning technique congruent with adult learning style.[4]

Clinical legal education expansion is support for many reasons connected with improving teaching and learning and for providing legal assistance to the poor in society.[5] It has been suggested that the expansion of clinical legal

---

education outside of the United States, defines clinical legal education with reference to six components: created by a law school as part of its academic program; students learn experientially by providing legal services or advice to real clients; the students are closely supervised by attorneys–either members of the law faculty or private practitioners who share the pedagogical objectives of the program; clients are from an underserved population; students are prepared by attention to the theories of practice; and students receive academic credit for their work).

[4] Frank S. Bloch, The Andragogical Basis of Clinical Legal Education (1982) 35 *Vand. L. Rev.* 321 (Andragogy, a specially-developed theoretical model for the teaching of adults, has four key elements, all of which support its use as a basis/theory of clinical legal education. The first concept, adults' self-concept as self-directing, ties in with a clinical program's use of learning through client representation and mutual inquiry. Adults expect to learn on their own, to make their own decisions, to live with the consequences, and to learn from their experiences. They do not expect, like children, to be receiving sets for their teacher's wisdom. The second aspect that andragogy attributes to adults is the central role that experience plays in their education. In fact, adults define who they are, based on their experiences. Under the andragogical model, therefore, the best way to teach an adult to be a lawyer is to let the adult experience being a lawyer. The third assumption andragogy makes relative to adult learning is the concept of "developmental tasks." Developmental tasks are those that are necessary to learn when moving from one phase of life to the next. As adults in law school are preparing to enter the phase of being a lawyer, they will have a heightened readiness to learn about being a lawyer. The fourth underlying assumption is that adults are oriented to learn in a problem-solving manner. They want to learn about issues that they are facing or will soon face. They do not want to learn about a subject for use at some unspecified time in the future. Clinical education utilizes all of these aspects to some extent and should be structured to reflect the aspects of andragogy more accurately. The author posits that a "coherent, methodology-based justification for clinical programs does not exist," and that live-client based clinical programs are particularly well-supported by andragogical theory).

[5] Jane H. Aiken, Provocateurs for Justice (2001) 7 *Clin. L. Rev.* (discussion on how clinical legal education offers unique opportunities to inspire law students to commit to justice and how clinicians ought to provoke a desire to do justice in their students); Deborah Maranville, Infusing Passion and Context into the Traditional Law Curriculum Through Experiential Learning (2001) 51 *J. Legal Educ.* 51 (the article argues that traditional legal education is deficient in three significant ways: it fails to nourish the passions and values that directed students to law school, it fails to provide the context for doctrinal learning that both engages students and helps them to learn more effectively, and it fails to assess systematically what is actually happening in the classroom and to provide students with feedback about their progress. The author argues that passion and context are central to effective legal education and that for many students experiential learning is a superior method for generating passion and providing context. The author argues that more experiential learning can and should be introduced into the traditional curriculum in a cost-effective manner and provides a range of concrete suggestions of how the integration can take place both in the first-year curriculum and in upper level courses. Finally, the author suggests that experiential learning methods can provide useful opportunities for feedback to both teachers and students; Jane Harris Aiken, Striving to Teach Justice, Fairness, and Morality (1997) 4 *Clin. L. Rev.* 1 (the article outlines a learning theory that offers a model for teaching about justice through the systematic study of incidents of injustice. The author then describes a clinical experience in which the students encountered injustice in the course of representing clients and analyzes how and why that experience affected the students' sense of justice. Finally, the article examines the ways in which the learning theory and the insights gained from this clinical experience can be applied in other clinical courses as well as in traditional law school courses. It concludes with examples of methods that may make the MacCrate Report's aspiration operational); Jane Aiken & Stephen Wizner, Law as Social Work (2003) 11 *Wash. U. J.L. & Pol'y.* 63 (the article urges clinical teachers to embrace the "social work" aspects of law practice on behalf of low income clients). But cf. Nina W. Tarr, Current Issues in Clinical Legal Education (1993) 37 *How. L.J.* 31 (where the author reviews the ongoing debate about whether the mission of clinical education is to address poverty in a

education is the agent provocateur for the introduction of poverty and development law issues in law curriculum which were generally muted in traditional curriculum steeped in commercial and middle-class interests.[6] In providing access to justice for the disadvantaged in society clinical legal education enhances the values of equality as important ingredient for democracy and good governance. Clinical legal education further improves the quality of legal education in that it provides opportunity for students to learn firsthand lawyering skills such as listening and interviewing clients, negotiation, analyzing cases, drafting documents and court processes, ethical issues that arises in real cases, which are absent from traditional law school curriculum. Outside these visible benefits to effective teaching and learning, clinical education carries with it direct, immediate benefit to law students. To the extent that it resembles law apprenticeship it provides the necessary (in-house, university) experience for disadvantage students to be client-ready for practice on graduation, without needing to seek placement in high-net worth chambers not readily accessible by poor students.[7] For the indigent in society, clinical legal education can be a

---

legal/political manner or to transmit lawyering skills, positing however, that clinical education is not simply a pedagogical method, but is a philosophy about the role of lawyers in our society. The roots of clinical education are in radical or at least liberal reform. The implications of this political orientation, according to the author, must be addressed in issues such as the selection of types of cases, an issue that also raises questions about pedagogical approach and the tension between client needs and student needs. The author argues that when a clinical program focuses on skills training, it does so at the expense of a political orientation. She criticizes pure skills training courses that use simulation technique for failing to expose students to the learning that can only be achieved when students have the kinds of unpredictable and emotionally-challenging experiences that take place through client representation. The second issue is clinical education economics, and the implications of the fact that many law schools have relied on grants, rather than hard funding to support clinics. This structure could result, for example, in a funder's demanding that a clinic engages in litigation even though there is much for students to learn from using other approaches, such as alternative dispute resolution or legislative advocacy. The third issue is the tension between in-house clinics and externship programs and how both have improved through contact and dialogue with the other. Finally, the author addresses the many forms of marginalization to which clinical programs are subject, from the students' perspective and the faculty perspective. The author concludes by describing some of the richness of clinicians' work in the classroom and in scholarship, and surveys briefly some of the trends in clinical theory scholarship. See also, Stephan Anagnost, Promoting Refugee Law as a Means of Challenging the Status Quo at University Level Education in Europe: The Role of the Refugee Law Clinic (2002) 2 *Int'l Clin. Legal Educ.* 38 (the article examines the development of refugee law clinics in the Central European and Baltic States, in providing high quality legal aid to asylum seekers and refugees); Kirsten Edwards, Found! The Lost Lawyer (2001) 70 *Fordham L. Rev.* 37 (the paper discusses the writings of Anthony Kronman and Judge Harry Edwards on the shortcomings of contemporary legal education, particularly at elite law schools, stating that contrary to the solution proposed by Kronman and Edwards – more practical legal scholarship – increased investment in, and celebration of, clinical legal education – has greater potential to promote the attributes of the lawyer-statesman ideal espoused by Kronman: practical wisdom, ethical conduct, and a commitment to pro bono activity).

[6] state a few things about law and development movement. See Peggy Maisel, Sustaining and Expanding Clinical Legal Education in Developing Countries: What We Can Learn from South Africa (2007) 30 *Fordham Int'l. L.J.* 374 at 375.

[7] See example Stephen R. Alton, Mandatory Pre-licensure Legal Internship: A Renewed Plea for Its Implementation in Light of the MacCrate Report (1995) 2 *Texas Wesleyan L. Rev.* 115 (an article written

veritable mechanism for addressing their everyday concerns such as those related to shelter, family matters, and civil rights.[8] While the law school clinics may not be able to address wholly these concerns, they often are the key provider of representation for the poor in this respect, than the traditional lawyer-client setting.[9]

Importance of Law Clinic

The call for clinical legal education is loud. The reason is that clinical education is a significant way to prepare students for the practice of law. Interestingly, the call is not a recent phenomenon. Far back in the early twentieth century, Jerome Frank expressed dissatisfaction with the American Socratic style of legal education for failing to interrogate the core skills students need to enter the legal profession.[10] Recently, the call for law school curricula to pay attention to

---

in response to the MacCrate Report's conclusion that law schools and the practicing bar have a joint responsibility to convey the skills and values identified by the Report as necessary to ensure a minimum level of competence in an attorney, the article advocates a pre-licensure internship requirement, arguing that such a program, if properly administered, could successfully bridge the gap between law school and practice in a way that is consistent with the spirit of the MacCrate Report. In support of this conclusion, the article notes that the MacCrate Report recognizes the differing capacities that the law schools and the practicing bar have to impart specific skills and values to aspiring attorneys, and argues that a jointly run pre-licensure internship program, in which students would be placed in not-for-profit, government, and legal aid practices, would provide a setting in which the skills and values conveyed to a student in law school could be augmented and expanded by being applied in a professional setting, under the supervision of the practicing bar and the law schools). See also, Suellyn Scarnecchia, The Role of Clinical Programs in Legal Education (1998) 77 *Mich. Bar. J.* 674 (the article discusses the clinical programs in Michigan enrich the State Bar, and provides valuable training in legal analysis, practical skills, ethics and professional responsibility, as well as service to the community).

[8] See for example, the Sunday Shoe case. Joseph William Singer, Persuasion (1989) 87 *Mich. L. Rev.* 2442 (The author argues that much of lawyering is persuading parties, juries, and judges to agree with one perspective rather than another. In this article, he explores how one persuades others about the values they should have. To illustrate his problem, he describes a property course in which he taught students about factory closings. While he expected students to identify the unfortunate social costs of closings on the surrounding towns and released employees, he repeatedly met with impersonal doctrinal arguments about managerial prerogatives, freedom of contract, and deference to the legislature. Concerned about the students' professional competence development, he developed a method of creating a relationship between the students and the people affected by factory closings. He constructed a hypothetical in which his law school decided to fail the lowest 33% of first-year students after their first-semester exams in an attempt to protect the public from unprepared lawyers in the future. Faced with similarly desperate and unfair circumstances, the students learned to appreciate the other side of factory closings cases. They felt empathy and connection with the released employees and were able to perceive the imbalance of bargaining power and breach of good faith where they had previously seen only market values. By creating a situation in which the students felt vulnerable and powerless, the author cultivated a relationship between the students and workers, thereby influencing the students' values).

[9] Peggy Maisel, Sustaining and Expanding Clinical Legal Education in Developing Countries: What We Can Learn from South Africa (2007) 30 *Fordham Int'l. L.J.* 374 at 376.

[10] Jerome Frank, A Plea for Lawyer-Schools (1947) 56 *Yale L.J.* 1303 (The article begins with a criticism of the Langdellian method of legal education. It states that as a result of present teaching methods, law students could be likened to future horticulturists who restrict their studies to cutting flowers. Though the article does not propose a return to the old apprenticeship system, the writer makes four specific proposals for the reform of legal education to professionalism, namely: that law school faculty should be drawn from the practicing bar, lawyers with a minimum of five to ten years' experience in varied legal

providing professional experience has been louder. For example, the Nigerian Bar Association (NBA),[11] the American Bar Association (ABA),[12] several reports on legal education share this perspective and recommend that law schools enhance legal education by giving lawyering skills training top priority.[13] Recognizing the

---

practice; that the current case system should be revised to resemble a real case; that students should spend some time in trial courts and in appellate courts; and that law schools should introduce clinical legal education. "The students would learn to observe the true relation between the contents of upper court opinions and the work of practicing lawyers and courts . . . [and] the students would be made to see, among other things, the human side of the administration of justice . . ." After listing some of the specific advantages of a clinic, the article defends the proposition against direct and indirect criticism. To the charge that law school is too short a time in which to also engage in clinical education, the author responds that the bulk of time in law school is wasted by spending the entire three years on "the relatively simple technique of analyzing upper court opinions . . . in a variety of fields." Once the skill of analysis is learned, students are able on their own to apply it to a "variety of subject matters." The author refutes the anti-intellectualism charge, aimed at legal realists and their clinical proposal, by quoting one of his own earlier responses to similar criticism:" [Legal realists] insist that no program for change can be intelligent if it is uninformed." The article next addresses some failings of the trial court system and ways that reform in legal education might ameliorate those failings. The final quarter of the article contains discussions of various phenomena in the legal world); Jerome Frank, Why Not a Clinical Lawyer-School? (1933) 81 *U. Pa. L. Rev.* 907 (The author argues for the development of a clinic in law schools that parallels clinics in medical school. He uses many of the same justifications, such as the argument that nobody would want a doctor who has never operated on someone when they graduated from medical school. The author blames the current law school case method on Christopher Columbus Langdell, the person who instituted the case method at Harvard. While the author admits that there is something to be learned from reading appellate court opinions, he notes that Langdell thought there was nothing to be learned from practical experience. The article contains a short exposition of the weaknesses of the case method – mainly that lawyers and clients are interested in getting a specific judgment from a trial court. Appellate opinions are only partially helpful in getting the desired result. Lawyers must know how to investigate, how to persuade juries and judges that a given set of facts exists, how to draft pleadings, etc. The article concludes with a short description of a law school that incorporates a clinical element).

[11] NBA Task Force

[12] See, ABA, Section of Legal Education and Admission to the Bar, Report and Recommendations of the Task Force on Lawyer Competency: The Role of the Law School, 1979, 17; *ABA Final Report and Recommendations of the Task Force on Professional Competence*, 1983, 11-12; ABA, Section of Legal Education and Admissions to the Bar, Legal Education and Professional Development-An Educational Continuum: Report of the Task Force on Law Schools and the Profession: Narrowing the Gap, 1992, 259-260, 328 (generally referred to as the MacCrate Report); *ABA, Task Force on the Future of Legal Education, Report and Recommendation,* January 2014, 26, available at http://www.americanbar.org/groups/professional_responsibility/taskforceonthefuturelegaled ucation.html, assessed September 23 2015. See also, John S. Elson, Why and How the Practicing Bar Must Rescue American Legal Education from the Misguided Priorities of American Legal Academia (1997) 64 *Tenn. L. Rev.* 1135 (the paper argues that "there are no longer any good reasons to accept the status quo in legal education," urging the leadership of the legal profession to use its considerable authority to compel law schools to change).

[13] See Carnegie Report 2007. The 2007 Carnegie Foundation report on legal education stressed the need for law students to engage in an "apprenticeship of practice" while in law school, contrasting legal education's minimal training with that provided in other professions such as medicine. See the *Best Practice Report* 2007. The Best Practices for Legal Education report argued that it is critical for students to have supervised practice experiences while in law school. Interestingly, several state bars in the United States are pressing for more practice-based training in law school, especially in this era when students are finding it so difficult to market their skills to employers. See for example, Ohio State Bar Association, *Report of the Task Force on Legal Education*, 2009, 4 (call on the Ohio Supreme Court to adopt a rule requiring that a student, prior to taking the bar exam, complete a law clinic or externship in law school or a practice experience through a bar association program that involves law school faculty and the practicing bar); New York State Bar Association, *Report of the Task Force on the Future of the Legal*

importance of experiential legal education, some schools require credit-bearing law clinic or externship as a graduating requirement.[14]

Unfortunately, some teachers are still dismissive of clinical legal education despite its significance in legal education. May be a law students' survey can change their mind. In a ABA survey carried out on young lawyers in the U.S. on how helpful legal education has been to their development as professionals, they rated practice-based experience courses such as clinical courses, legal writing, skills courses, and internship far above traditional doctrinal courses that sadly dominates most of legal education.[15]

Modus Operandi for Law Clinic

Most clinics have a director on permanent employment superintending the programme.[16] She could be drawn from the pool of staff in the faculty or hired for the position outside the pool. Some clinics have support paralegal and legal staff on permanent or adjunct status helping the programme. In some case these latter

---

Profession, 2011, 6. See also, Clinical Legal Educ. Association, Clinical Legal Education Association (CLEA) Comment on ABA accreditation standard, available at http://cleaweb.org/advocacy, accessed September 23 2014. (CLEA, the U.S. largest organization of law professors, petitioned the Council of the ABA Section of Legal Education and Admissions to the Bar to adopt an accreditation standard that requires every J.D. student to complete the equivalent of at least 15 semester credit hours after the first year of law school in practice-based, experiential courses, with at least one course in a law clinic or externship).

[14] For a survey of schools in the U.S. see Karen Tokarz, Antoinette Sedillo Lopez, Peggy Maisel & Robert Seibel, Legal Education at a Crossroads: Innovation, Integration, and Pluralism Required! (2013) 43 *Wash. U. J.L. & Pol'y.* 11 at 45-46 & nn.154-55

[15] National Association of Legal Professionals (NALP) for Legal Career Research and Education and ABA, After the J.D: First Result of a National Study of Legal Careers, 2004, available at http://press.kaptest.com/press-releases/kaplan-bar-review-survey-63-of- law-school-graduates-from-the-class-of-2013-believe-that-law-school-education-can-be-condensed-to-two-years, accessed September 23 2015. See also, NALP & NALP Foundation, 2011 *Survey of Law School Experiential Learning Opportunities and Benefits: Responses from Government and Nonprofit Lawyers,* 2011, 26-27 & 2012, 30; (two studies by the National Association of Legal Career Professionals (NALP) asked lawyers to rate the usefulness of law school experiential learning opportunities in preparing for the practice of law. Lawyers in nonprofit and government legal positions rated law clinics extremely high, with clinics rated 3.8 using a scale of 1 ("not useful at all") to 4 ("very useful") and externships/field placements 3.6, both ahead of skills courses (3.3) and pro bono work (3.2). Law firm associates rated law clinics and externships not quite as high (3.4 out of 4), but still ahead of skills course (3.1) and pro bono work (2.2)). See also, Rebecca Sandefur & Jeffrey Selbin, The Clinic Effect (2009) 16 *Clin. L. Rev.* 57 (observing that new lawyers in the survey "were significantly more likely to say that clinical training was 'extremely helpful' for making the transition to practice than they were to make the same assessment of legal writing training, upper-year lecture courses, course concentrations, pro bono service, the first-year curriculum and legal ethics training") all cited in Robert R. Kuehn, Pricing Clinical Legal Education available at http://ssrn.com/abstract, assessed on September 23 2016.

[16] Margaret Martin Barry, Jon C. Dubin & Peter A. Joy, Clinical Education for This Millennium: The Third Wave, (2000) 7 *Clin. L. Rev.* 1 (This article focuses on the continuing transformation of legal education and the role of clinical legal education in training competent, ethical practitioners, the variety of models for integrating clinical methodology either throughout the curriculum or as a core feature of the curriculum, and how the third wave of clinical legal education can contribute to improving the future of legal education).

categories of staff get salaries or honorarium supplemented by the universities and the clinic centre.[17]

Law clinic in the form of externship is not without its challenges relating to duty of care placed on all the respective actors, the school, field supervisors, externship mentors and the like.[18]

Obstacles to Law Clinic

Beneficial to effective teaching and learning notwithstanding, clinical legal education is not without obstacles. The obstacles to current development of clinical programmes are essential four: (i) funding inadequacy, (ii) resistance from traditionalists in the legal academy, (iii) inadequacy of prerequisite staff experience; (iv) challenges of integration to traditional law school curricula.[19]

(i) Inadequate Funding

Perhaps the biggest obstacle to promoting and sustaining clinical programmes is lack of funding. Clinics receive limited support from their universities and so have to rely on external funding, which by its very nature is transient and unstable. That throws the weight back to the faculty. There is no question about it, clinical education requires money because it is essentially community based pro bono service. As a result, the clinic would have to rely for most of its funding from outside the university. To drive get this would certainly task staff of the programme. The challenge could be assuaged by more university funding support which is unlikely in the face of declining overall university education funding and general education priority summersault being witnessed I Nigeria. Faculties can however make the funding challenge less pressing by changing their academic priorities to transfer currents funds to clinics, an alternative likely to meet with resistance from traditionalists.

---

[17] Philip G. Schrag, Constructing a Clinic (1996) 3 *Clin. L. Rev.* 175 (the article provides a systematic road map to clinic development and design-basic structural questions, how students and teachers will acquire knowledge of the doctrine and practice in the areas of law in which the clinic will work, methods to be employed by teachers, and the possibility of a clinic manual and its contents, addresses practical issues such as planning physical space; locating and use of experts; generating forms and a filing system; building relationships with judges and administrators; and creating an effective system of case transfer and referral for cases that the law school cannot handle. It also examines the classroom component of the clinic, discussing syllabi, class assignments, and lesson plans applicable to a clinical setting).

[18] Kathleen Connolly Butler, Shared Responsibility: The Duty to Legal Externs (2003-4) 106 *W. Va. L. Rev.* 51 (the article explores the potential tort liability of law schools arising out of injuries to students that take place at field placements for legal externships).

[19] Richard J. Wilson, Training for Justice: The Global Reach of Clinical Legal Education (2003-2004) 22 *Penn St. Int'l L. Rev.* 421(the final part of the article discusses some problems being faced in the development of law school clinics, including resistance by traditional faculty or the bar, the service-training dichotomy, and cost); Cynthia Grant Bowman & Mary Beth Lipp, Legal Limbo of the Student Intern: The Responsibility of Colleges and Universities to Protect Student Interns Against Sexual Harassment (2000) 23 *Harv. Women's L. J.* 95 (the article examines the legal liability of colleges and universities for sexual harassment experienced by students in off-site internship placements).

Not to be overlooked is the teaching methodology of clinical legal education. It requires more time and attention of faculty which invariably could stifle other academic activities and programmes. The immediate solution would certain demand hiring of additional faculty. Clinical education requires more faculty than the traditional lecture/seminar format. The same is true of skills courses. They all require more labour intensive to conduct the activities.

Faculties can however make prevailing the funding challenges by adopting strategies for stretching scarce resources in the following ways: (a) by more university funding support for clinical programmes; (b) changing their academic priorities to transfer currents funds to clinics; (c) by hiring law graduates as supervising lawyers at reduced salaries; (d) by sourcing and joining national clinical organizations like NULAI;[20] (e) by harnessing cooperation with the Legal Aid Council and donor agencies funding concerns of access to justice such as International Bridges for Justice, the Open Society Justice Initiative, etc.;[21] (e) by support from the private bar;[22] and (f) schools could restructure their existing curriculum to give each student a faculty-supervised law clinic experience[23] without changing the size of the faculty by merely reassigning teaching responsibilities. In this respect schools can reduce or restructure the wide array of

---

[20] For the successes of the South African association the Association of University Legal Aid Institutions ("AULAI"), see Peggy Maisel, Sustaining and Expanding Clinical Legal Education in Developing Countries: What We Can Learn from South Africa (2007) 30 *Fordham Int'l. L.J.* 374 at 392. See also *Ernest Ojukwu for Nigeria*. For Kenya, see T. O. Ojienda & M. Oduor, Reflections on the Implementation of Clinical Legal Education in Moi University, Kenya (2002) 2 *Int'l. J. Clin. Legal Educ.* 49 (the article examines the challenges faced by Moi University in incorporating clinical legal education into its curriculum and it examines the structure and objectives of the curriculum instituted at Moi, which is focused on promoting social justice and providing instruction in legal doctrine, theory, and practical skills of advocacy such as fact-finding, research, and analogical reasoning. It finds that although the university has succeeded in designing a public interest-oriented curriculum, it needs to better publicize the availability of legal services through its legal aid clinic, grant the clinic greater autonomy regarding the solicitation of funds and the planning of routine operations, promote greater active participation in clinical programs amongst faculty, and increase the level and quality of student instruction prior to their interaction with clients).

[21] Richard J. Wilson, Training for Justice: The Global Reach of Clinical Legal Education (2003-2004) 22 *Penn. St. Int'l. L. Rev.* 421 (the author identifies five international funding sources for law school clinics: The Soros Foundation; The Ford Foundation; the American Bar Association, Central European and Eurasian Law Initiative; the World Bank and other international financial institutions; and the UN High Commissioner for Refugees and Legal Assistance through Refugee Clinics).

[22] For example, the American Bar Association and some state bar association drafted rules mandate members to provide pro bono public interest legal services or make an annual donation to legal aid associations/organizations. To this end the Florida Bar Association proposes to make a rule requiring lawyers to make a donation of $350 for renewal of license to practice. See See Richard W. Painter, Rules Lawyers Play By (2001) 76 *N.Y.U. L. Rev.* 665 at 726-27, cited in Peggy Maisel, Sustaining and Expanding Clinical Legal Education in Developing Countries: What We Can Learn from South Africa (2007) 30 *Fordham Int'l. L.J.* 374 at 397.

[23] Faculty-supervised clinics are programs in which students represent actual clients (individuals or organizations), are supervised by an attorney who is employed by the law school (faculty, adjunct, fellow, staff attorney, etc.), and include a classroom component. See also,

expenditures and course offerings towards more focus on practical training. [24]

(ii)   Lack of Acceptance of Clinical Education

The second obstacle to the promotion and sustenance of clinical legal education comes from its lack of acceptance, especially from the traditional legal academy. Traditionalists think that law is a conservative profession meant to preserve the ideals of liberalism and middle-class philosophy and interests. For those who think like that the liberal nature of legal education is worth sustaining and any step the other direction towards professionalism in training for lawyering skills such as writing, counseling, interviewing, drafting and trial practice, should be left for the vocational stages of legal education or chamber apprenticeship.[25] It is conceivable for them to argue that since as faculty members they succeeded without having clinical experience or undertaking skills courses while at law school, there should be no need to add the extensive component of clinical education to the curriculum. Since this is most likely to be the thinking of senior faculty members usually responsible for hiring new teachers, teachers with a bias for clinics are unlikely to get hired. And if they are lucky to be hired, senior members, using their entrenched advantages could further resist the introduction of clinical and skills components in the curriculum by arguing that too much resources would be devoted to them. What is more, to the extent that clinical and skills components demand less of doctrinal teaching, but rather emphasizing client-readiness, senior faculty who have devoted their careers in extensive expertise doctrinal writing could think legal education a threat to themselves and scholarship. Attention to clinical education could also threaten faculty who show no interest in legal practice, insisting in the very strict separation of the ivory tower from the nuances of legal practice.[26] This explains why faculties that have created law clinics are still reluctant to integrate clinic and skills courses across curriculum in all the law modular law subjects and why a dichotomy is still

---

[24] Robert R. Kuehn, Pricing Clinical Legal Education available at http://ssrn.com/abstract, assessed on September 23, 2016. The author submits that the debate over law school curricula and costs, including discussions about where cuts might be made to reduce expenditures, should focus on the value of certain educational programs, what students need to learn in school to begin the practice of law, and how best it can be taught. If the focus is kept on students and what they should obtain from their professional education, available resources can be allocated to provide a clinical experience for every student without raising tuition. If the will is truly there among law schools and the legal profession to refocus the curriculum of legal education to provide students with more practice-based, clinical coursework, the price of clinical legal education will not impede schools from providing that training for all graduates).

[25] See Solomon Ebobrah, NL&PJ.

[26] A separation between town and gown has its good and harmful sides. See Innovative Legal Market. See also Emily Grant, The Pink Tower Meets the Ivory Tower: Adapting Montessori Teaching Methods for Law School (2014) available at: http://ssrn.com/abstract=2483130, assessed on September 23, 2015 (discussion can incorporate Montessori's ideas to foster a more robust educational environment for law students as they join a profession of life-long self-directed learners).

maintained between doctrinal and clinical faculty.[27]

Admittedly, following the English system of legal education mainly composed of lectures and the bluebook examination with a set curriculum containing numerous required and elective courses has proved inadequate to capture the essence of legal education and transfer the core skills of lawyering. There is therefore a need for change by injecting clinics and skills courses in the curriculum.

Faculties can make less prevailing the resistance by adopting the following strategies: (a) by according clinical faculty members permanent positions in the faculty and encouraging their growth in diverse ways such as promotion prospect to professoriate cadre, access to conference, training and publications, etc.; (b) integrating clinical teachers into regular faculty governance and decision-making such as serving on faculty committees, etc. because by excluding them the faculty misses the difference in perspective they bring on board as teachers who confront and teach the problems of poverty and social justice every day;[28] (c) by increasing resources available to clinics through the formation of national organization for promoting and sustaining clinical legal education such as NUILA. As an organization, NUILA has used its collective bargain power to educate and influence law school decision-makers to include clinics and skills courses in law curriculum;[29] (d) by supporting clinicians to rise to leadership positions where they can influence educational policies; (e) by collaboration with donor agencies, legal aid organizations and the private bar.

---

[27] On how to integrate clinic and skills across the curriculum see, Alice M. Noble-Allgire, Desegregating the Law School Curriculum: How to Integrate More of the Skills and Values Identified by the MacCrate Report into a Doctrinal Course (2002) 3 *Nev. L.J.* 32 (the article discusses how law teachers can integrate the skills and values identified in the MacCrate Report into doctrinal courses that have traditionally not included a lawyering skills component, especially across the legal curriculum. Across the curriculum style is recommended because integrating skills and values into doctrinal courses is beneficial for it leads to enhanced skills and values education because the doctrinal subjects provide context for the teaching of skills and values, which allows students better opportunities for understanding and practice; it is a better way to grasp substantive concepts, while also providing a mechanism in which misunderstandings can be diagnosed; it fosters holistic rather than compartmentalized thinking). See also, Paul Bergman, Reflections on US Clinical Education (2003) 10 *Int'l J. Legal Prof.* 109 (the paper examines two challenges that face clinical legal education-the assumptions that clinical courses should be organized around discrete types of legal problems that affect low income and socially marginalized clients, and that clinical training positively affects students' abilities to practice law. It argues that both assumptions are flawed because the first assumption rests more on faith than analysis and that recent research on education and training suggests the second assumption also may be flawed. The author therefore suggests developing an alternative form of clinical course that exemplifies a 'lawyering skills' approach to training-an approach that limits students' casework experiences largely to the discrete lawyering activities to which a course is devoted, such as interviewing and counseling, with those activities permeating all aspect of the courses).

[28] Peggy Maisel, Sustaining and Expanding Clinical Legal Education in Developing Countries: What We Can Learn from South Africa (2007) 30 *Fordham Int'l. L.J.* 374 at 400.

[29] State how.

(iii) Capacity Issue

One of the serious challenges to maintaining and promoting clinical education has been the issue of capacity of law school faculty to teach clinic courses. Many teachers have no legal practice experience. In fact, they likely choose teaching as getaway to the rigors of practice. Even for those with practice experience, clinic activities steeped in poverty and social justice interests can be challenging because the everyday practice rarely has such subject-matters as regular diet, a situation exacerbated by the fact that the teachers may not themselves have participated in clinical programme as students. They are therefore forced to create clinical programmes and design relevant curriculum to capture the core competencies of lawyering. As clinicians, teachers take on the onerous task of not only conducting the clinic but also in supervising law students to recreate consciousness, reflection and learning from experience. It can be enormous to find and build capacity of faculty as doctrinal teachers, litigators, and supervisors of students.

Again, these challenges can be ameliorated by adopting the following strategies: (a) by collaborating with legal aid agencies and donors such as Ford Foundation, NUILA, Global Alliance for Justice Education (GAJE), etc. faculty capacity can be built to cater for capacity deficiency in clinic activities.

(iv) Balancing Public Service, Teaching and Learning

It is generally recognized that the addition of clinical and skills courses to existing law curriculum can create workload burden for the academy. This is just side of the coin. Students who participate in the clinic may well find it challenging to balance the time they spend listening, counseling, draft processes for indigent clients who use the clinic services with their other faculty/educational studies. The fact that students can do all of that but not participate in trial in courts invariably mean that case workload will fall on teachers.[30] Given that our society has a large segment of the poor would certainly create caseload pressure on clinics. The situation can be made worse if teachers have many students to supervise.

An appropriate balance between public service, teaching and learning can be struck by: (a) allocating more resources to clinical and skills courses and by integrating these components across the curriculum;[31] (b) because clinical

---

[30] The Legal Practitioners Act only permits a person called to bar to conduct proceedings in court. Refer to proceedings pro se as exception. See however the position in the U.S. where limited audience in court proceedings is permitted in some state jurisdictions. See, Stephen R. Alton, Mandatory Pre-licensure Legal Internship: A Renewed Plea for Its Implementation in Light of the MacCrate Report (1995) 2 *Texas Wesleyan L. Rev.* 115; George K. Walker, A Model Rule for Student Practice in the United States Courts (1980) 37 *Wash & Lee L. Rev.* 1101. Because each state in the United States has its own bar admission rules, some have made provision for students' licensure to conduct limited proceeding in courts. See Rules Regulating the Florida Bar, Rule 11-1.4. The U.S. Judicial Conference adopted a model student practice rule in 1979.

[31] Jane Harris Aiken, Striving to Teach Justice, Fairness, and Morality (1997) 4 *Clin. L. Rev.* 1. For example, of an interdisciplinary approach see, Peter W. Salsich, Jr., Interdisciplinary Study in a Clinical Setting

component requires a lower student-faculty ratio, faculty must increase teaching workforce to enhance experiential teaching and learning;[32] (c) some have suggested that it would be helpful to introduce at the lower levels of legal education in the teaching of doctrines and skills doses of poverty and development issues in the curriculum to better acquaint students with upper level clinical courses;[33] (d) cutting down on doctrinal teaching material to create enough room for clinic is recommended;[34] (e) adoption of students' practice rule that permits limited court representation could help fill the gap in legal service delivery for the poor and enhance holistic student experience; (f) allowing students' and teachers clinical specialization can make the experience more productive. The practice would require either students or teacher to work on only one problem area such as shelter, domestic violence, and so can spend more time learning substantive law, skills and values in the special area that are transferable to other types of practice.[35]

(2000) 44 *St. Louis U. L.J.* 949 (discusses the history of an interdisciplinary program at the Washington University School of Architecture and the Saint Louis University School of Law as an experiment to generate feasible solutions to a housing crisis for low- income families as an example of the heuristic/praxis teaching approach).

[32] Robert R. Kuehn, Pricing Clinical Legal Education available at http://ssrn.com/abstract, assessed on September 23 2016. (an article based on empirical study in the U.S. revealing that clinical education is not as expensive as imagined in spite of the higher costs many associate with clinics. Reviewing tuition, curricular and enrollment data from all law schools, it demonstrates that 79% of law schools already have the capacity to provide a clinical experience to every student without adding courses or faculty, although only 18% presently require or guarantee that training. It finds there is no effect on the tuition and fees students pay from requiring or guaranteeing every student a clinical experience and no difference in tuition between schools that already have sufficient capacity to provide a clinical experience to each student and those that do not. It makes the point that providing a clinical experience to every law student has not cost, and need not cost, students more in tuition and is more a question of a school's will to provide that educational experience than of cost).

[33] Peggy Maisel, Sustaining and Expanding Clinical Legal Education in Developing Countries: What We Can Learn from South Africa (2007) 30 *Fordham Int'l. L.J.* 374 at 417. But the suggestion would not be advisable for the style which applies clinical and skills component throughout and across all subjects. See, Alice M. Noble-Allgire, Desegregating the Law School Curriculum: How to Integrate More of the Skills and Values Identified by the MacCrate Report into a Doctrinal Course (2002) 3 *Nev. L.J.* 32 (the article discusses how law teachers can integrate the skills and values identified in the MacCrate Report into doctrinal courses that have traditionally not included a lawyering skills component, especially across the legal curriculum); Paul Bergman, Reflections on US Clinical Education (2003) 10 *Int'l J. Legal Prof.* 109 (the paper examines two challenges that face clinical legal education-the assumptions that clinical courses should be organized around discrete types of legal problems that affect low income and socially marginalized clients, and that clinical training positively affects students' abilities to practice law. It argues that both assumptions are flawed because the first assumption rests more on faith than analysis and that recent research on education and training suggests the second assumption also may be flawed. The author therefore suggests developing an alternative form of clinical course that exemplifies a 'lawyering skills' approach to training-an approach that limits students' casework experiences largely to the discrete lawyering activities to which a course is devoted, such as interviewing and counseling, with those activities permeating all aspect of the courses).

[34] The thinking that cutting down doctrinal teaching in favour of clinics is harmful is unfounded. Refer to article.

[35] Peggy Maisel, Sustaining and Expanding Clinical Legal Education in Developing Countries: What We Can Learn from South Africa (2007) 30 *Fordham Int'l. L.J.* 374 at 418.

Suggested Reform

Clinical legal education currently serves as a valuable tool in developing countries to help promote equal justice for the poor.[36] It is also helping to make traditional legal education more relevant by educating students on the legal needs of the disadvantaged in society while providing them with better preparation in the practical skills and values needed to practice law.

Reflection

An essential part of law clinic and skills courses is the opportunity for students to reflect.[37] Because professionals must and do make several instantaneous decisions from a wealth of their professional experience, reflection must be a necessary ingredient for experiential learning. That is why deliberate reflection is a tool for helping new professionals develop the skills of professional judgment. According to Timothy Casey, "a conscious and deliberate analysis of a lawyering performance can provide the new lawyer with insights into what choices were available, what internal and external factors affected the decision-making process, and what societal forces affected the context of the representation."[38] The ability to reflect provides the new-wig with what has been termed 'a self-improvement algorithm,' which increases her ability to exercise professional judgment in professional context. This is so because reflection forces the professional to increase awareness of factors that affect judgment, such as the social, economic,

---

[36] Lucie E. White, The Transformative Potential of Clinical Legal Education (1997) 35 *Osgoode Hall L.J.* 603 (the article focuses on clinics that are empowerment-focused, community-based clinics both visionary in their goals and down-to-earth in their law practices. The author notes how such clinics have triggered great change, most significantly in creating a new approach to the practices of legal advocacy. Moreover, the article examines the impact such clinics have had, not only on individuals and communities, but also on law schools).

[37] Timothy Casey, Reflective Practice in Legal Education: The Stages of Reflection (2014) 20 *Clin. L. Rev.* 317 (an article that explain reflection, it identifies six stages of reflection, and how to teach reflection as an explicit outcome). See also, Ann Shalleck, Clinical Contexts: Theory and Practice in Law and Supervision (1993) 21 *N.Y.U. Rev. L. & Soc. Change* 109 (the This article highlighting the ways in which the teacher facilitated learning process by encouraging reflection, client-centered representation, and acceptance of responsibility); Angela Olivia Burton, Cultivating Ethical, Socially Responsible Lawyer Judgment: Introducing the Multiple Lawyering Intelligences Paradigm into the Clinical Setting (2004) 11 *Clin. L. Rev.* 15 (the paper explores, in the context of the lawyer's preparation for counseling a client, how conscious attention to the various multiple lawyering intelligences can enhance the quality of both the lawyer's deliberative process and the choices made as a result of that process, and it suggests some ways clinical teachers can use the lawyering intelligences framework to more consciously and deliberately assist students in their development of the divergent, complex, and morally-referenced thinking involved in the exercise of independent professional judgment); Gary Bellow, *On Teaching the Teachers: Some Preliminary Reflections on Clinical Education as a Methodology, in Clinical Education for Law Student,* 1973, 374. The function of clinical teaching is to enlist the motivations, impressions, and relationships of role performance to increase self-reflection, self-consciousness, and to develop a fuller understanding of the legal order. The tensions and conflicts that arise from this method are critical to its purpose.

[38] Timothy Casey, Reflective Practice in Legal Education: The Stages of Reflection (2014) 20 *Clin. L. Rev.* 317 at 319.

cultural, moral values at play in controversies. What it translates to is that the more a new-wig raises the awareness and consciousness of decision-making the more ethical the student becomes. This is why teachers are obligated to teach reflection as a core lawyering skill.

Cognitive science reveals that reflection often travels at the same level as student's cognitive development. In effect, as a student travels the road from objectivist to a subjective, relativistic stance and ultimately to a contextual, constructive perspective of knowledge, so too does the student's reflection track a similar trajectory. Increasingly, epistemic cognitive studies reveal that the way a person perceives knowledge or reality affects the way the person acquires and uses knowledge.[39]

Reflection is the synthesizing of intentional thoughts and specific action in a professional context. It is deep thinking with the purpose of application in situations in which material is unstructured or uncertain and where there is no obvious solution.

Recognizing the trajectory track of reflection can then be used by the teacher to deepen reflection of students. At the objective learning stage, the teacher would need to ask the student to compare her performance to the standard of professional competence by asking for example, 'what would a competent lawyer faced with the fats do? Did you do so? etc. The goal at this state of learning focuses on professional standard of competence. The stage squares well with lawyering performance related to legal research assignment where the student is required to find a certain answer. An IRAC formulation is to be expected. However, more than this would be required to grow students in reflection from the objective to the subjective.

To achieve this the teacher could ask the student what her subjective standard would consider competent performance. This simple thrust away from the objective triggers reflection of an individual professional identity for the internalization of professional duty.

The stage is now set to interrogate subjective relativism. The teacher can ask the student to now identify different, equally successful ways to accomplish the lawyering performance. As they learn multiple sets of correct answers, the teacher could ask the student to identify means she could use to achieve the same end. By identifying the routes to the goal, the student discovers that she can make professional choices in performance. It is suggested that client interview and video

---

[39] Barbara Hofer, Personal Epistemology as a Psychological and Educational Construct: An Introduction, in Barbara Hofer & Paul Pintrich, eds., *Personal Epistemology: The* Psychology *of Beliefs About Knowledge and Knowing*, 2004. See also, Barbara Hofer, Personal Epistemology Research: Implications for Learning and Teaching (2001) 13 *J. Educ. Psychol. Rev.* 353, both cited in Timothy Casey, Reflective Practice in Legal Education: The Stages of Reflection (2014) 20 *Clin. L. Rev.* 317 at 321.

recorded performance of other students' performance of specific task can be ideal learning technique to teach relativism in performance.[40]

Contextual stage three interrogates the "why" of decision-making in reflective practice. By asking why the student makes a specific choice as against others she looks rather inward for reason, which is a product of preferences, experiences, biases and characteristics. The student is thus helped to become more self-aware, recognizing that these are things not simply 'not-out-there' as it were, that affect lawyering performance. The realist perspective creates consciousness and awareness that personal traits and experiences affect lawyering in intangible ways.

At the constructive perspective to learning and reflection, the focus shifts away from the internal configuration of to the external-awareness of the preferences, biases, experiences and characteristics of the other people involved in lawyering performance. These legal actors could be clients, judges, third parties and the like. The stage enacts much of what law and economics scholars would call the 'game-theory.' Decision-making in lawyering reflects the personal traits and experiences the other side brings on board. For example, in a negotiation the student would find out that her competitive attitude would not result in an amicable settlement if the other side too has same negotiating style. At this stage, it would also be appropriate the dynamics of politics, economics, and social realities that shape law and professional performance, and they can also be useful signpost for judging competence.

All of these stages recreate lawyering awareness that enhance reflective practice. Objectivism helps our student to identify competent performance. Relativism identifies different ways to achieve client's goal. Contextualism identifies her own preferences while constructionism identifies the preferences of others. As the student reviews her performance in the matrix of all of these her lawyering performance improves and is shaped by intrinsic and extrinsic factors enhances decision-making.

Journaling can be a good way to review students' reflection.[41]

Simulation and Law Clinic

Some commentators think that it is unhelpful to distinguish between law clinic and simulation.[42][43] [44]

---

[40] Timothy Casey, Reflective Practice in Legal Education: The Stages of Reflection (2014) 20 *Clin. L. Rev.* 317 at 339.

[41] J. P. Ogilvy, The Use of Journals in Legal Education: A Tool for Reflection (1996) 3 *Clin. L. Rev.* 55 (the article explores the use of an academic journal in an instructional setting, explaining its benefits).

[42] Deborah Maranville, Passion, Context, and Lawyering Skills: Choosing Among Simulated and Real Clinical Experiences (2000) 7 *Clin. L. Rev.* 123 (the article, the author argues that the common typology that divides clinical courses into simulation course, live-client clinics, and externships has become more

"Simulation courses are those courses in which a substantial portion of the instruction is accomplished through the use of role playing or drafting exercises, e.g., trial advocacy, corporate planning and drafting, negotiations, and estate planning and drafting."

---

misleading than helpful, "masking both differences within categories and similarities among them." In order to take the next steps in transforming the law school curriculum, the author argues that we should abandon this typology and focus instead on three primary achievements of clinical methodologies: generating passion within students; providing context for their learning; and teaching lawyering skills. The article argues three points. First, relying solely on simulation-based experiences prior to the third year of law school neglects the passion dimension of legal education. Second, relatively unsupervised externships (or paid work experiences) can play a useful role in providing crucially important context for doctrinal learning, although they are not the most effective approach to teaching lawyering skills. Third, clinicians should aspire to integrate clinical experiences into the curriculum during the first and second years of law school in simplified forms. The article concludes with a proposed ideal curriculum).

[43] David A. Binder & Paul Bergman, Taking Lawyering Skills Training Seriously (2003) 10 *Clin. L. Rev.* 191 (the paper distinguishes between case-centered and skill-centered clinical programs, arguing that case-centered clinical programs are less helpful in transferring lawyering skills learning from law school to practice).

[44] Paul Bergman, Reflections on US Clinical Education (2003) 10 *Int'l J. Legal Prof.* 109 (the paper examines two challenges that face clinical legal education-the assumptions that clinical courses should be organized around discrete types of legal problems that affect low income and socially marginalized clients, and that clinical training positively affects students' abilities to practice law. It argues that both assumptions are flawed because the first assumption rests more on faith than analysis and that recent research on education and training suggests the second assumption also may be flawed. The author therefore suggests developing an alternative form of clinical course that exemplifies a 'lawyering skills' approach to training-an approach that limits students' casework experiences largely to the discrete lawyering activities to which a course is devoted, such as interviewing and counseling, with those activities permeating all aspect of the courses).

Chapter 9

Use of Visuals and Technology

Introduction

The message from best practice is that law schools need to reform legal education to provide more focus on training students in professionalism and practical skills.[1] The nature of legal practice and the job market today gives technology a central role in the reform of legal education. It would therefore be strange for a law classroom to look significantly the same as it was twenty years ago. Today's classroom should look hi-tech because e-learning and other instructional methods that focus on developing skills will be more prevalent. Technology itself has become a core skill for effective law practice. It is thus imperative that legal education captures this component which will likely shape the structure of present curriculum. For instance, law teachers will likely incorporate more formative assessment into their courses to be facilitated by technology. Instructional models and materials changes are also envisaged.[2]

According to Johnson technology must play a pivotal role in legal education because: "(i) it provides a vital way to connect with the students from Generations X and Y that dominate the student body at most law schools; (ii) appropriate use of technology can relieve economic pressures in implementing these reforms; (iii) technology can facilitate access to new learning experiences for all students, regardless of disabilities or learning styles; and (iv) technology is itself a skill that must be mastered in order to practice law in the twenty-first century."[3]

---

[1] Carnegie Best Practice etc.

[2] Stephen M. Johnson, Teaching for Tomorrow: Utilizing Technology to Implement the Reforms of *MacCrate, Carnegie*, and *Best Practices* (2013) 92 *Nebraska L. Rev.* 46.

[3] Stephen M. Johnson, Teaching for Tomorrow: Utilizing Technology to Implement the Reforms of *MacCrate, Carnegie*, and *Best Practices* (2013) 92 *Nebraska L. Rev.* 46 at 53; "[L]egal educators [who neglect technology in the classroom] are generally falling behind the legal profession itself. Modern trial lawyers regularly use display technology, such as computer animations, videotaped depositions, and PowerPoint presentations, to 'teach' and persuade juries, judges, and colleagues in a very effective way." Fred Galves, Will Video Kill the Radio Star? Visual Learning and the Use of Display Technology in the Law School Classroom (2004) *U. Ill. J.L. Tech. & Pol'y.* 195 at 195-96 (discussing "visually enhanced communication in the practice of law).

It is not the thinking (for now) that technology will replace the traditional law school classroom, but it must play an integral role in the implementation of new teaching methods and means of assessment required for the transformation of legal education. Many students now use laptops and other forms of computer and are generally e-learning friendly.[4]

Learning is enhanced and reinforced when verbal communication is combined with visual. Visual includes but is not limited to pictures, PowerPoint (PP) presentation, handouts, blackboard, flipchart, slides, videos and computer. Visual tools are devices that allow teachers to engage students through their sense of sight.[5] In this sense it is wider than technology known more as descriptive of computer and allied information technology. Both however are being discussed in one chapter because they shade into one another.

Communication through the ear and also through the eyes (sight) increase the ability of an audience to grasp and retain information. The reason isn't farfetched. Objects that appeal to the eyes get quickly transmitted to the senses and mind, which ultimately triggers emotive responses. Cognitivists tell us that messages communicated through the eyes in for of visuals or graphics stick faster and remain remembered more that text-based or ear-based communication.[6] Visual tools help create schemata. For example, graphics are visual aids the help create cognitive connection. By nature, objects that catch eye attention engage the mind easily.

Generally, visual tools can be divided into two categories according to their primary use; those useful for presenting graphics and those use to view performance. The former pigeonholes visuals like slides, flipcharts, blackboards, handouts, and overhead transparencies. The latter category includes films, videos, and the Internet.

The use of technology for legal education is not widespread in Nigeria. Though most faculties now have e-learning libraries, thanks to NUC-CLE-NBA accreditation, there is minimal use of them in delivery of legal instruction. Online and computer-based legal education conducted through a combination of

---

4

5 Gerald F. Hess & Steven Friedland, *Techniques for Teaching Law,* North Carolina: Durham: Carolina Academic Press, 1999, 81.

6 Johnson & Robbins, states that scientific and social research reveal that "the general population is approximately 65 percent visual in learning and communication styles." Johnson & Robbins, above n. 1, 58. Some research suggest that much of the brain cortex region is devoted to imagery and that image processing is the main brain function than words. See Lucile A. Jewel, Through a Glass Darkly: Using Brain Science and Visual Rhetoric to Gain a Professional Perspective on Visual Advocacy (2010) 19 *S. Cal. Interdisc. L.J.* 237. Steve Johnson & Ruth A. Robbins, Art-Iculating the Analysis: Systemizing the Decision to Use Visuals as Legal Reasoning (2015) 20 *J. Leg. Writing* 57. Ellie Margolis, Is the Medium the Message? Unleashing the Power of E-Communication in the Twenty-First Century (2015) 12 *Leg. Comm. & Rhetoric: JALWD* 1. See generally, David I.C. Thomson, *Law School 2.0: Legal Education for a Digital Age,* LexisNexis, 2009.

software and hardware, and delivery of online content through the internet is rare phenomena in most faculties.[7] In fact, the CLE is known to resist online learning techniques and distance education methodologies.[8] It would appear that the oldest visual aid in learning is writing on the blackboard.[9] Blackboard visual enjoys the virtues of spontaneity and flexibility. The teacher could in one go get to the board and write and she would not be constrained in deleting or making additions if thought necessary. But we all know what headache students can go through if a teacher's writing were terrible. Even at that, chalk script can pose visibility challenges, especially to those at a distance. What is more, the blackboard arrangement can particular be time-consuming to write extensive statements or quotes, often referred in legal education. It is therefore not surprising that many faculties are discarding the blackboard for some other forms of visual.

Use of Visual Tools

Teachers who use visuals, especially in the form of graphs and diagrams admit that they are rich tools helping students see the components of rules or situations in a course.

Types of Teaching Technology

There is no question about it technology is here to stay and will continue to inform and reform legal education and service delivery in law.[10]

1. PowerPoint and Videos

PP and the flip-chart board are widely now used as substitute for the blackboard. PP however does not enjoy the advantages of spontaneity and flexibility, but has the advantage of clarity, visibility and easy graphic and pictorial ability.[11]

---

[7] There is however global recognition of e-legal education in the form of computer, internet and distant education. See Peter B. Maggs & Thomas D. Morgan, Computer-Based Legal Education at the University of Illinois: A Report of Two Years' Experience (1975-1976) 27 *J. Leg. Educ.* 138; Alan Davidson, Electronic Legal Education (2003) 2 *J. Commonwealth L. & Leg. Educ.* 16.

[8] Refer to CLE position on National Open University of Nigeria. State that all of this would be past if the CLE were to transform to a bar exam body in line with global best practices.

[9] Howard E. Katz & Kevin F. O'Neil, *Strategies and Techniques of Law School Teaching*, New York: Aspen Pub. 2009, 58.

[10] Richard Susskind, The End of Lawyers? Rethinking the Nature of Legal Services, 2009; Thomas D. Morgan, The Vanishing American Lawyer, 2010; David I.C. Thomson, Law School 2.0: Legal Education for Digital Age, 2009; Michele R. Pistone & John J. Hoeffner, No Path But One: Law School Survival in an Age of Disruptive Technology (2013) 59 *Wayne L. Rev.* 193

[11] Recognizing these advantages and its ability to humanize legal reasoning, it is not surprising that there is a growing call to persuade adjudicator through visuals. See for example, Richard A. Posner, Judicial Opinions and Appellate Advocacy in Federal Courts-One Judge's View (2013) 51 *Duq. L. Rev.* 3 ay 23, cited in Johnson & Robbins, above n.1 at 61. The legal practitioners and the academy appears poised to catch on the call for visual communication. See Elizabeth Porter, Taking Images Seriously (2014) 114 *Colum. L. Rev.* 1694; Adam L. Rosman, Visualizing the Law: Using Charts, Diagrams, and Other Images

Additionally, a hyperlink can be inserted on a PP slide which will transport a class to a particular website. For example, it is possible with the hyperlink to jump from a PP slide directly to say the website of a court to show a class how trials are conducted in a court when hocked to the website. Because PP highlights key points of lecture it makes it easier for students to form accurate and complete lecture notes.[12]

Aside PP, teachers have found it helpful to deploy videos and DVDs as teaching tools. For example, films on trial advocacy, excerpts from documentaries can be used to recreate consciousness in ways difficult to do by sheer verbal communication.[13] Care must however be taken to comply with relevant copyright regulation by the teacher.

Video vignettes could be skillfully used to bring cases, disputes, and legal issues, including issues of professionalism, to life in ways that are impossible in text alone. Video could be used to help students understand the facts of a case or a dispute, the relationships of parties involved in disputes, and the policy reasons in support of various resolutions of disputes.[14]

2. Class Web Page

It is expected that all law students and teacher should be familiar and conversant with the use of the Internet. Students university matriculation exams are usually conducted using JAMB websites. Teachers are expected to be avid researchers using e-learning tools. So, all in the teaching and learning square ought to be comfortable with obtaining information from the Internet.

Developing a webpage for a course by the teacher for purpose of academic interaction with the class carries numerous advantages, namely: (i) it provides an efficient communication means with the class much more than any synopsis or lesson plan; (ii) in today's digital age where young people are addicted to computer gadgets rather than paper, e-communication enjoys special attraction of affordability and availability to more students; (iii) e-communication carries with it the advantages of flexibility, spontaneity and convenience not constrain by

---

to Improve Legal Brief (2013) 63 *J. Leg. Educ.* 70. See also, Persuasion Litigation Blog at http://www.persuasivelitigator.com.

[12] See on how to create effective PP. Some teachers give the PP after lecture to the class to more fully complete notes, thereby making up for what is lost in note taking during lecture. But it is best to post the PP slides on a password-protected Web page. This can relieve students of the stress of note taking during lecture, thus creating a better environment for students to concentrate during lecture hours.

[13] Paul Wangerin, Technology in the Service of Tradition: Electronic Lectures and Live-Class Teaching (2003) *J. Leg. Educ.* 213 (discusses the effectiveness of technology lass over live-class); Robert E. Oliphant, Using Hi-Tech Tools in a Traditional Classroom Environment: A Two-Semester Experiment (2002-2003) 9 *Rich. J.L. & Tech.* 5.; Richard Warner et al., Teaching Law With Computers (1998) 24 *Rutgers Computer & Tech. L.J.* 101.

[14] Stephen M. Johnson, Teaching for Tomorrow: Utilizing Technology to Implement the Reforms of *MacCrate, Carnegie*, and *Best Practices* (2013) 92 *Nebraska L. Rev.* 46 at 78.

space and time; (iv) free the teacher's consulting hours with students, because with the webpage in place students will rarely bother the teacher with administrative questions; (v) promotes easy delivery of course materials while expanding teaching material package; (vi) serves as repository of academic materials; (vi) helps the teacher to respond to varying student learning styles, as it helps the crop of students who learn more comfortably in electronic environment; (vii) and is an inexpensive method of delivering course materials.

A course webpage should be designed to be functional, not complex for navigation. Its menu should consist of items like, syllabus, lesson plan, synopsis, general, etc.-all functioning as hyperlinks. If permitted and available the hyperlink should include a menu link to other websites like that of the courts. Its design should admit post of Microsoft Word, PDF files, PowerPoint presentation, and other modern formats. [15]

Much as technical assistance may be needed to maintain the page, the teacher could use software that facilitates direct, hands-on control, such as TWEN,[16] Blackboard,[17] ExamSoft,[18] Electronic BlueBook,[19] Extegrity[20] or Contribute,[21] to edit or update the webpage and to streamline administration and grading.[22]

3. E-Course Book and Learning Materials

With focus on technology as central to legal education, faculties will have to adapt instructional materials that designed with goals of engaging law students in this age of technology. E-course books are beginning to make the debut, such as Lexis series of skills and values course books.[23] Other publishers are doing the same. Much as these efforts are commendable, they fail to embrace technology fully because many of these materials are simply digitized versions of hardcopy books. They simply fail to engage students with materials that are designed to cater to students learning styles and preferences and their facility with technology because they are best evolutionary of technology rather than being revolutionary.[24]

---

[15] Katz & O'Neil, above n. 4, 60.

[16] See Twen Resources, Thomas Reuters Westlaw, https://lawschool.westlaw.com/shared/signon10.asp?path=%2ftwen%2fdefault.aspx (last visited March 1, 2017).

[17] See Blackboard, http://www.blackboard.com/ (last visited March 1, 20017).

[18] See ExamSoft Worldwide, http://www.examsoft.com/main/index.php (last visited March 1, 2017).

[19] See EBB Electronic Bluebook, Computest, http://electronicbluebook.com/ (last visited March 1, 2017).

[20] See Exam 4 Exam Software, Extegrity, http://www.exam4.com/ (last visited March 1, 2017).

[21]

[22] Katz & O'Neil, above n. 4, 60. See also, web management tools at http/www.lawschool.westlaw.com; http//www.blackboard.com; http/www.www.adobe.com/products/contribute.

[23] See About the Skills & Values Series, LexisNexis, http://www.discoveryskills. com/aboutsv.htm (last visited September 23, 2016).

[24] Stephen M. Johnson, Teaching for Tomorrow: Utilizing Technology to Implement the Reforms of *MacCrate, Carnegie,* and *Best Practices* (2013) 92 Nebraska L. Rev. 46.

Technology and Survival of Law School

Whether we like it or not, technology for law schools have its good and adverse side. Not to be ignored is the fact that technology can drive faculties out of business as it can also do to legal service delivery.[25] The challenge is heightened by the fact that internet competition doesn't just emerge as competitors, they have demonstrable ability to change the rules governing what takes place in the field of competition. It is foolhardy not to notice the cost advantages of distance learning and that as distance learning techniques and technology improves, distance learning would become commonplace, and that the regulatory moat protecting law schools will not vanish. Present teaching pedagogy of law schools rooted in analytical and doctrinal training increasingly makes law schools venerable to technology takeover because the course content and teaching methodology could effectively be replicated online. Law school traditional pedagogy is less prevailing argument for it being insulated from internet competition.

To use the words of Pistone and Hoeffner, "law schools have the luxury of having a choice—which may remain available only a short time—as to whether, in the age of the Internet, they want to become more like barbers or stay, vis-a-vis their vulnerability to Internet competition, like traditional booksellers."[26]

Barbers need not fear internet competition. Their nightmares don't come from internet. Bookstores and newspaper companies have not been lucky. The majesty of law, especially legal education may be next. In the face of this invading army, how should law schools and the legal academy prepare to meet with the challenges? What can faculties do to the threat of extinction from online technology competition?

Piston and Hoeffner provides five tips for preparation.[27] They are:

(i) No uninformed Denial

Law teacher must not respond with uninformed denial of the challenges internet poses to them. The advice, is that at the very least, we should not dismiss the potential for change without knowing what arguments are being made by those who believe the law school status quo will not endure. Teachers are advised to read relevant text on internet competition with traditional legal services and education.[28] These works will reveal to teachers how networked and connected

---

[25] Richard Susskind, The End of Lawyers? Rethinking the Nature of Legal Services, 2009; Thomas D. Morgan, The Vanishing American Lawyer, 2010; David I.C. Thomson, Law School 2.0: Legal Education for Digital Age, 2009; Michele R. Pistone & John J. Hoeffner, No Path But One: Law School Survival in an Age of Disruptive Technology (2013) 59 *Wayne L. Rev.* 193

[26] Hoeffner, above n. 25 at 201.

[27] Ibid at 228.

[28] Richard Susskind, The End of Lawyers? Rethinking the Nature of Legal Services, 2009; Thomas D. Morgan, *The Vanishing American Lawyer,* 2010; David I.C. Thomson, *Law School 2.0: Legal Education for Digital Age,* 2009; Michele R. Pistone & John J. Hoeffner, No Path But One: Law School Survival in an

lives affect the way we approach learning. This could spur teachers to try hands-on with classroom technology such as flipped learning-a technique that allows the blending of online lectures with in-class instruction. By migrating lectures to the web, flipped learning can free face-to-face class time for active learning,[29] simulation, clinic, drafting, role-play, assessment of performance and the like. Adaptive learning could be added as a technology that helps the teacher to know what a student knows and then adapt the content taught to knowledge level of student.

(ii) Understand that Past Performance Will Not Provide Moat Protection

It is important for law schools to avoid reliance on their societal contribution as reason why there should be moat protection to change. What matters to people is likely going to be costs efficiency and convenience. That law schools did contribute to legal education will not matter in the competition market.

(iii) Experimental Response

Law schools must raise the quality of legal education by responding experimentally to the invading changes. The greatest vulnerabilities are noticeable in high cost of legal education and a failure to take a broader and deeper approach to practical training. This can be remedied by educational initiatives that drive down costs and introduce practical components difficult for internet learning competitors. For example, they can take the initiative to experiment on online learning models to drive down costs, rolling-over the savings to improve active, practical training. It is suggested that a failure to act on both fronts will maximize the threat that stems from the cheaper costs of alternative model of legal

---

Age of Disruptive Technology (2013) 59 *Wayne L. Rev.* 193; Clayton M. Christensen, Michael B. Horn, Louis Caldera & Louis Soares, Disrupting College: How Disruptive Innovation Can Deliver Quality and Affordability, CTR. for AM. Progress & Innosight Inst. 2011, available at http://www.americanprogress.org/issues/2011/02/pdf/disruoting-college.pdf. Accessed March 10, 2016.

[29] The "flipped" format does not replace face-to- face classes with online instruction; instead, it is intended to free up class time for activities other than lecture." Gerald F. Hess, *Blended Courses in Law School: The Best of Online and Face-to-Face Learning?* (2013) 45 *McGeorge L. Rev.* 51, 56; Catherine A. Lemmer, A View from the Flip Side: Using the "Inverted Classroom" To Enhance the Legal Information Literacy of the International LL.M. Student (2013) 105 *Law Libr. J.* 461; Nancy B. Rapoport, Rethinking U.S. Legal Education: No More "Same Old, Same Old (2013) 45 *Conn. L. Rev.* 1409; Laurel E. Davis et al., Teaching Advanced Legal Research in a Flipped Classroom (2013) 22 (1) *Persp: Teaching Legal Res. & Writing* 13; Todd E. Pettys, The Analytic Classroom (2012) 60 Buff. L. Rev. 1255; Joseph A. Rosenberg, Confronting Clichйs in Online Instruction: Using a Hybrid Model to Teach Lawyering Skills (2008) 12 *Smu Sci. & Tech. L. Rev.* 19 at 33 ("As the presence of technology becomes increasingly ubiquitous and user-friendly, and the lives of our students are inextricably linked with technology, we should embrace the potential of online learning to enhance the quality of our teaching, the learning experience of our students, and most importantly, how effectively we prepare students for the challenge of lawyering in the twenty-first century)." See also David Thomson, Shorten Law School, but Keep the Third Year, Law School 2.0 (Oct. 4, 2013), http://www.lawschool2.org/ls2/2013/10/shorten-law-school-but-keep-the-third-year.html (suggesting significantly reengineering the first year of law school to put most of it online).

education.[30]

(iv) Act with a Sense of Urgency

Law institutes are warned not to display complacency, but to act with a sense of urgency. They should not wait for the race to catch up with them because it is easier to make changes from a position of strength rather than a position of weakness. Acting from the vintage of strength allows the academy to take experimental risk of finding cheaper and more convenient ways to structure learning, survive the (more) mistakes, drive better bargains with outside entities, choice of acting whether on long or short-term interest, right-size employment, etc. if we don't want to be caught pants-down.

(v) Practical Legal Education

Faculties and the academy must begin to prepare by moving the regulated norm in legal education to a place where online schools cannot follow, such as extensive teaching of the many practical lawyering skills that require to be taught effectively, face-to-face, in-person interactions.[31]

Progress along the lines above will allow existing law schools to prosper in the years to come. Time is ticking fast and late movers will find that complacency does not pay. Many entities thought impregnable to technology are now extinct. Given that current technology can deliver on efficient cost and convenience of legal education creates the possibility that law school cannot remain an exception to technological imperative to adapt or die. The handwriting is very visible to the sighted.

---

[30] Michele R. Pistone & John J. Hoeffner, No Path but One: Law School Survival in an Age of Disruptive Technology (2013) 59 *Wayne L. Rev.* 193 at 245.

[31] Michele R. Pistone & John J. Hoeffner, No Path but One: Law School Survival in an Age of Disruptive Technology (2013) 59 *Wayne L. Rev.* 193 at 202.

Chapter 10

Teaching Legal Writing Skills

Introduction

Legal writing demand lawyers to evaluate the strength of their client's case and effectively communicate it by keeping focus on three basic elements, the who, the why and the how. As a form of writing it is serious business, its heightened importance deriving from the critical impact it can have on the lives and destinies of the people who are the subject of it. Because legal writing is a lawyer must possess, faculties of law give it its deserved importance. Usually, it forms part of the first lessons students receive in a legal method class on admission. One of the things they are quickly taught is to start 'think like a lawyer.' Thinking as a lawyer is often associated with students becoming familiar with the organizational schemata known as *IRAC*, suggested to helps them think and write logical. While this chapter recognizes that the *IRAC* structure can be helpful in imposing a logical grammar for lawyers to understand themselves and explain law to outsiders, it disagrees with it being used as the paradigm and the primary method for organizing writing because it is an approach that funnels human disputes into a single rule-based approach leaving little or no room for recognizing the complexities of human interaction which generate disputes. The chapter therefore seeks to open legal analysis and reasoning beyond rigid rule-based rule in a manner which admits alternative analysis in the light of social realities, by encouraging the profession, especially teachers of legal method and legal writing to reassess the foundation of *IRAC*, ceasing to cling to it as paradigm for successful legal and brief writing. It concludes by urging that *IRAC* and its *cousins* should be treated as illustrative of basic framework for legal reasoning and analysis in a manner that admits of other styles incorporating analysis that melds facts and experience with legal rules.

A survey of recruiters of fresh lawyers in the United States reveals that legal writing deficiency is one of the five basic skills lacking in new lawyers.[1] This

---

Oghenemaro Festus Emiri is a Professor of Jurisprudence. He practices with *LexFori* Partners, Calabar, Cross River State of Nigeria. His major interest is Meta-theory, Legal Remedies, Bar Practice & Legal Education (ofemiri@yahoo.co.uk); Dr. Ayuba Giwa, Senior Lecturer, Delta State University,

observation is also representative of the situation in Nigeria. In our country concerns have been expressed by the bar and bench about the competence and character of "new wigs," especially their communication skills. This is particularly worrisome considering that lawyers are constantly required to communicate with others either in the form of memorandum or processes connected with resolution of disputes. That being so, lawyers are expected to deploy persuasive writing to convince deciding authorities to resolve disputes in favour of their clients. Legal writing is therefore a form of writing which demands lawyers to evaluate the strength of their client's case and effectively communicate it, focusing on the three basic elements of *who, why* and *how.*[2] The "who" being the audience, the "why" representing the purpose of communication, and the "how" being the manner or style of writing. It is serious business, its heightened importance deriving from the critical impact the communication can have on the lives and destinies of the people who are the subject of it.[3]

Recognizing the importance of legal writing as a core skill, faculties of law give it its deserved importance. Usually, it forma part of the first lessons students receive in a legal method class on admission.[4] One of the things they are quickly taught is to start 'thinking like a lawyer.' Thinking as a lawyer is often associated with students becoming familiar with the organizational schemata known as *IRAC.* It is said that analysis and reasoning using the schemata helps then to think and write logical.[5] The importance of *IRAC* is elevated to a paradigm for analysis, reasoning and writing, further reified by teachers telling them that good grades in law are entailed with an ability to master the lawyers' scientific way of reasoning: the *IRAC* schemata for organizing legal analysis and reasoning. The students naturally thus settle for IRAC as key to success in the legal profession.[6]

IRAC (Issue, Rule, Application, and Conclusion) constitutes the building block for exams and writing in the faculties of law, snowballing eventually into the legal profession. Students are generally happy to master *IRAC* because it allows

---

Abraka, Nigeria (ayubagiwa@gmail.com) & Jonathan Ehusani, Faculty of Law, University of Abuja, Abuja. His interest is Human Rights and Writing (ehusanij@yahoo.com).

[1] Bryant G. Garth & Joanne Martin, Law School and the Construction of Competence (1993) 43 *J. Legal Educ.* 469. Cite the US survey. For the position in Nigeria, see Augustine Alegeh, in Olanrewaju Onadeko, et al., *Legal Education in Nigeria:* Challenges and Next Steps, Abuja: CLE, 151

[2] Teresa J. Reid Rambo & Leanne Pflaum, *Legal Writing by Design: A Guide to Great Briefs and Memo,* 2nd ed. NC, Durham: Carolina Acad. Press, 2013, xiii.

[3] Rambo & Pflaum, above n. 2 at xii.

[4] Legal method is a core course under the BMAS scheme and it is suggested in the guideline as a pre-law core subject. See BMAS Guide.

[5] Garth & Martin, above n. 1. Cite other articles on core skills demanded of lawyers.

[6] The precise origin of IRAC is largely unknown, but it as been suggested that it likely originated as a simple mnemonic for teaching legal analysis. It certainly was not intended as an organizational paradigm for legal writing. See Laura P. Graham, Why-RAC? Revisiting the Traditional Paradigm for Writing About Legal Analysis (2015) 63 *Kansas L. Rev.* 681 at 706.

them to reduce complexities of the social world, which generates controversies into simple, manageable legal formula and equation. They are proud to tell other not so fortunate to gain law admission about their new organizational tool that can be logically deployed to even every day analysis of events in the social world. The paradigm they reason enables them to seamlessly join the elite group of learned people. This is what translates *IRAC* to become the signature pedagogy for legal analysis and reasoning.[7] Over time this practice of reasoning and writing fossilizes.

IRAC is extolled by the profession for its deductive reasoning potential, reasoning from the major to minor premise through syllogism. Reasoning in syllogism proceeds from the major premise, such as, "All humans are mortal," to the minor premise, "Socrates is a human," therefore making the conclusion logically correct: "Therefore Socrates is mortal." Transposed to *IRAC*, having framed the issue as question for determination, the rule requires stating the broad statement of general applicability "All humans are mortal," as representing the *R* (rule). It is from this that the minor premise is constructed. The minor premise or narrow statement of particular applicability, "Socrates is a human," translates to *A* (applicability of the rule to facts). A combination of both premises makes "Therefore Socrates is mortal," the *C* (conclusion) logically correct.[8] So you can see why lawyers extol the rule. It is stepped in deduction reasoning by syllogism, which closes on a science of reasoning and analysis associated with common sense and comprehension.[9] What is more, members of the legal community think that

---

[7] Abiola O. Sanni, ed., *Introduction to Nigerian Legal Method*, Ile-Ife: Kuntel Pub. 1999, 54. Generally, Nigerian universities teach writing as part of the subject legal method and research methodology. Legal writing as a distinct course in the curriculum is however taught in U.S. as a distinct subject. See generally, Tracy Turner, Flexible IRAC: A Best Practice Guide (2015) 20 J. Legal Writing Inst. 233; The IRAC Formula, http://www.lawnerds.com/guide/irac.html (visited) and courses in legal writing. The US has courses in legal writing in many of its universities. The first legal writing conference was held in 1984 and the Legal Writing Institute was established in 1986. Since then the Institute has established the journal of the Legal Writing Institute. Noteworthy, some teachers of legal writing advice that writing should begin with conclusion not issue, especially for persuasive writing, arguing that such a pattern follow more the way human ground meaning from experience. See Tracy Turner, Finding Consensus in Legal Writing Discourse Regarding Organizational Structure: A Review and Analysis of the Use of IRAC and its Progenies (2012) 9 *Legal Comm. & Rhetoric: JALWD* 351 at 359; Harold A. Lloyd, Plane Meaning and Thought: Real-World Semantics and Fictions of Originalism (2015) 24 *Southern Cal. Interdisciplinary L. J.* 657 ("judges, lawyers, and clients want to begin with conclusion. Unlike readers of mystery novels, judges, lawyers, and clients do not consider matters spoiled if they get the ending first ... These audience demands therefore require that IRAC be modified to begin with a conclusion." Id 673). See also Harold A. Lloyd, Crushing Animals and Crushing Funerals: The Semiotics of Free Expression (2012) 12 *First Amend. L. Rev.* 237.

[8] James A. Gardner, Legal Argument: The Structure and Language of Effective Advocacy, 2nd ed., 1999.

[9] Anita Schnee, Logical Reasoning "Obviously" (1997) 3 *J. Legal Writing Inst.* 105; Kristen K. Robbins, Paradigm Lost: Recapturing Rhetoric to Validate Legal Reasoning (2003) 27 *VT L. Rev.* 483; Tracy Turner, Finding Consensus in Legal Writing Discourse Regarding Organizational Structure: A Review and Analysis of the Use of IRAC and its Progenies (2012) 9 *Legal Comm. & Rhetoric: JALWD* 351.

this form of syllogistic reasoning is best suited for the profession that professes to adjudicate controversies without bias.

But not all of us are fans of this organizational schemata. While we recognize that the *IRAC* structure can be helpful in imposing a logical grammar for lawyers to understand themselves and explain law to outsiders, we disagree with it being used as the paradigm and the primary method for organizing writing.[10] Often, any simplistic method of synthesizing the complex to manageable comprehension can be *Procrustean*, masking subtleties and peculiarities not overt to the mind. That is why some of us suggest that students should not see analysis of human disputes from a single rule-based approach leaving little or no room for recognizing complicated and hard cases requiring a multidisciplinary approach to problem-solving.[11] This chapter therefore seeks to open legal analysis and reasoning beyond rigid rule-based rule in a manner, which admits alternative analysis in the light of historical, political, and economic contexts. We encourage the profession, especially teachers of legal method and legal writing to reassess the foundation of IRAC, by ceasing to cling to it as paradigm for successful legal and brief writing. We rather urge that the rule and its *cousins* should be treated as illustrative of basic framework for legal reasoning and analysis in a manner that admits of other styles incorporating analysis that melds facts and experience with legal rules.[12]

In Part II of this chapter, we examine the limitations and sometimes-harmful effects of *IRAC* to writing skills in stratifying analysis under the single *IRAC* jacket. We navigate this part essentially using the 1995 Washington Report of legal writing teachers conference as reference. Part III reviews why the legal profession, especially teachers, continues to cling to *IRAC* as signatory pedagogy for writing despite its recognized limitations and criticisms, by suggesting that the paradigm aligns with logic and the general Socratic pedagogy of law school training. Part IV,

---

[10] For example, even though some commentators think that IRAC is a basic way of organizing winning briefs, they urge the use of narrative style for making brief persuasive. See Karin Ciano, A Briefreader's Guide to Brief-writing, Fed. Law., Jan-Feb. 2012, at 43, cited in Diane B. Kraft, CREAC in the Real World (2015) 63 *Clev. St. L. Rev.* 567 at 573 n. 36.

[11] Clyde H. Hamilton, Effective Appellate Brief Writing (1999) 50 *S.C. L. Rev.* 581 at 587 (commentator did not include the IRAC method in the list of factors that make a good brief); Jane K. Gionfriddo et al., A Methodology for Mentoring Writing in Law Practice: Using Textual Clues to Provide Effective and Efficient Feedback (2009) 27 *Quinnipiac L. Rev.* 171.

[12] Legal writing teachers have suggested a range of IRAC cousins to include acronym like CREAC (conclusion, rule, explanation of rule, analysis and conclusion), CRAC (conclusion, rule, analysis and conclusion); CRExAC (conclusion, rule of law, explanation of rule, application of facts to the rules and connection-conclusion); RIRAC (reference, issue(s), rule(s), application, and conclusion) etc. See also, Phillip C. Kissam, The Decline of Law School Professionalism (1986) 134 *U. Pa. L. Rev.* 251 ("the study and practice of law would be improved by a more contextual approach that places a greater emphasis on both the application of law to concrete situations and the understanding of how law serves or fails to serve conflicting social values. This approach would improve professional education by initiating future practitioners into the uncertainties, complexities and value conflict of the 'practice situation.'") Id at 254.

reveals that *IRAC* isn't really a style extolled by the legal profession because good judicial opinions and brief writing follows a pattern which centralizes facts rather than the *IRAC* rule-based form. The point is deepened by an illustrative example of both writing forms in the real world to enable the reader appreciate that good writing need not be located within the *IRAC* square to qualify as good. Part V, reveals that good brief writing and judicial opinion are generally non-*IRACian*, because judges and brief writers seek to persuade like ancient rhetoricians through the three triangular paths of logo, pathos and ethos. It is followed in Part VI, by comparing the *IRAC* and non-*IRAC* structure for writing and persuasion. Using illustrative examples drawn from the basic components of lawyering-transactional lawyering, regulatory practice and litigation, it shows how non-*IRACian* style, incorporating narrative elements further the client's theory of the case better than the IRAC structure. It essentially examines the implication of how non-*IRAC* writing can expand and open otherwise closed doors for robust legal reasoning and analysis. Part VII, suggest ways and means writing teachers can teach the subject using flexible organizational techniques to produce future great brief or judicial opinion writers. It includes empirical examples of how some teachers have helped their students to develop analytical minds that transcends the simplistic, dogmatic and rule-centered *IRAC* structure. The conclusion is modest. While admitting that *IRAC* can be a good learning formula for starters, teachers must help their students outgrow the template remembering that *IRAC* conceived primarily as an analytical tool must not be converted into a writing formula that stupefies reasoning in society.

II. Limitations of the IRAC Method

Since the emergence of legal writing as a discipline, writing teachers have been critical of the use of *IRAC* as template for writing for two basic reasons: the limitation of the rule as a tool for analyzing complexities in law and for the suffocating influence it can exert on the architecture of legal reasoning.[13] It is

---

[13] For general reading on a critique of the IRAC paradigm for legal writing, see, Terri LeClercq, The Success-And Failure-of IRAC (1987) 50 *Tex. B.J.* 222; Jane K. Gionfriddo, Dangerous! Our Focus Should Be Analysis, Not Formulas Like IRAC, The Second Draft Nov. 1995 of the Legal Writing Institute, Tacoma, Wash, at 2; Wilson R. Huhn, Teaching Legal Analysis Using a Pluralistic Model of Law (2000-2001) 36 *Gonz. L. Rev.* 433; Helen A. Anderson, Changing Fashion in Advocacy: 100 Years of Brief-Writing Advice (2010) 11 *J. App. Prac. & Process* 1 (judges expect legal analysis to go beyond atomistic logic); Christine M. Venter, Analyze This: Using Taxonomies to "Scaffold" Students' Legal Thinking and Writing Skills (2006) 57 *Mercer L. Rev.* 621; Jennifer Sheppard, Once Upon a Time, Happily Ever After, and in a Galaxy Far, Far Away: Using Narrative to Fill the Cognitive Gap Left by Overreliance on Pure Logic in Appellate Briefs and Motion Memoranda (2009) 46 *Willamette L. Rev.* 255;; Kristen K. Robbins-Tiscione, A Call to Combine Rhetorical Theory and Practice in the Legal Writing Classroom (2011) 50 *Washburn L.J.* 319; Soma R. Kedia, Redirecting the Scope of First-Year Writing Courses: Towards a New Paradigm of Teaching Legal Writing (2010) 87 *U. Det. Mercy L. Rev.* 147; George D. Gopen, IRAC, REA, Where We Are Now, and Where We Should Be Going in the Teaching of Legal Writing (2011) 17 *J. Legal Writing Inst.* xvii (keynote address at Capital Area Legal Writing Conference, Feb. 26, 2011- "there is not

reasoned that a straight-jacket rule-based tool can fossilizes students reasoning, preventing them from the flexibility and creativity legal analysis requires.

This is what prompted legal writing teachers in 1995 to make topical an examination of the advantages and disadvantages of *IRAC* at the Legal Writing Institute conference in Washington.[14] The Report issued after the conference indicated clearly that writing professors acknowledge the value of *IRAC,* but are split on the danger of using it without flexibility.[15] One group think the template truncates and restricts the architecture of legal reasoning, while the other urges for its usefulness as standard template for legal analysis with certain modification.[16] We shall navigate the criticism of the rule essentially from the Second Draft, the report issued at the conclusion of the 1995 deliberations.

Critique of the *IRAC* Template
1. *Issue (I)*
There is no question about it. Before a student formulates the "I" she must have done some preliminary analysis. This is to be expected. If asked what "I" is of *IRAC* in a fact scenario where say C is knocked down his bicycle by D, a driver on the highway, she can only formulate the issue from preconceived knowledge of the question (Q), the entire relevant facts and rules (fr) and the relevant facts and rules (FR) governing the formulation of "I." in truth, "I" is only formulated when the student has done all the research and analysis of the controversy and is ready to report a conclusion.[17]

---

and cannot be a single structure that is the right answer to the question of how argumentative thought is best conveyed from the mind of a writer to the mind of a reader. ... These organizational structures [CRAC, CREAC, MIRAT, IDAR, ILAC, TREACC, CruPAC, ISAAC, CRRACC, BARAC etc.] are both necessary and dangerous, both supporting and defeating. As with any good idea or good invention, they can all be used for harm as well as good," id xviii); Laura P. Graham, Why-RAC? Revisiting the Traditional Paradigm for Writing About Legal Analysis (2015) 63 *Kansas L. Rev.* 681. But cf. generally, Lurene Contento, Demystifying IRAC and Its Kin: Giving Students the Basic to Write "Like a Lawyer," *The Second Draft*, Nov. 1995 of the Legal Writing Institute, Tacoma, Wash; Tracy Turner, Flexible IRAC: A Best Practice Guide (2015) 20 *J. Legal Writing Inst.* 233 (recommends the syllogistic IRAC reasoning, while suggesting the best guide for teachers use of the rule, such as the one-sequence IRAC; the alternating IRAC; IRAC by paragraph; the IRAC sentence; and the narrative add-ons which mixes facts into the "I" of IRAC).

[14] See generally The Value of IRAC, *The Second Draft* (Legal Writing Institute, Tacoma, Washington, Nov. 1995).

[15] Above n. 14 at 1.

[16] For critique of the rule see, Jane K. Gionfriddo, Dangerous! Our Focus Should Be Analysis, Not Formulas Like IRAC, *The Second Draft* Nov. 1995 of the Legal Writing Institute, Tacoma, Wash, at 2. For flexibility of the rule see, Tracy Turner, Flexible IRAC: A Best Practice Guide (2015) 20 *J. Legal Writing Inst.* 233.

[17] Framing the issue as a thesis however has its attraction, e.g. "the defendant will be liable for negligence because the defective product manufactured by the defendant caused the plaintiff injury." See Michael D. Murray, Classical Rhetoric, Explanatory Synthesis and the TREAT Paradigm (Univ. Ill. L. & Econ. Working Paper No. 75, 2007), available at http://works.bepress.com/michael_murray/9 ("Presenting the thesis on the issue first brings to the front the most important part of the discussion: the answer to the legal question posed by the issue. Readers of all types-judges and law clerks, ... -will appreciate not having to wait for the answer.")

So in this fact scenario, the student has to draw on "what question arise here." She recognizes that the frame is one within the bracket of accident. Next, she proceeds to reflect on the possible relevant facts and rules. Reflection on facts would require her to know the nature of the highway, whether it is a busy one, whether the driver skidded off his own section of the road etc. Reflection on relevant rules possibly informs her that it is a matter connected with either (criminal) dangerous driving or (tortious) liability in negligence. Finally, she uses the relevant facts and rules to plot what will resemble a prima facie conclusion, which she calls issue. That being so, *IRAC* must account for these preliminary matters that enter the cognitive mind in formulating the "I," presently omitted in the *IRAC* template. This explains why one contributor to the Report suggested that there is the need to expand *IRAC* into an acryomn like '(QfrFR)+IRAC,' if it must retain its explanatory power as an accurate formula for organizing legal analysis.[18]

Implicit in this (that preliminary analysis is what triggers the "I"), it follows that legal analysis stands on its head, upside down, because, the "I" is itself at worse an answer (conclusion). As one commentator puts it "assuming that "I" correctly understand . . . the legal problem solving process, then analysis of a question raised by a legal problem should begin with the answer to that question."[19]

2. Rule

What is meant by "R" in the IRAC template can be problematic for many reasons. Rules are not objects out there in the world for capture. In legal analysis, they can just be in a state of flux. Identifying them is not as simple as the *IRAC* formula would have us think. For example, a system that function at the level of facts, such as inductive common law would likely make fundamental distinction between types of persons and things and words used in legislation.[20] That being so, a court decision such as in *Donoghue v. Stevenson*[21] concerning injury caused by a defective bottle of ginger beer containing decomposed snail, may not necessarily apply to other defective products. So formulating the rule emerging from the case

---

[18] Dennis R. Honabach, IRAC or (QfrFR)+IRAC, *The Second Draft* (Legal Writing Institute, Tacoma, Washington, Nov. 1995, 8.

[19] Kim Cauthorn, Keep on TRRACING, *The Second Draft* (Legal Writing Institute, Tacoma, Washington, Nov. 1995, 4. The learned scholar recommend that rather than retain the IRAC acronym, it should be replaced the "I" with "T" (for thesis). See id at 5; Laura P. Graham, above n. 6. See also Tracy Turner, Finding Consensus in Legal Writing Discourse Regarding Organizational Structure: A Review and Analysis of the Use of IRAC and its Progenies (2012) 9 *Legal Comm. & Rhetoric: JALWD* 351 at 359 (survey of writing whether legal writing should start with issue or conclusion). But cf. Tracy Turner, Flexible IRAC: A Best Practice Guide (2015) 20 *J. Legal Writing Inst.* 233 n. 2 (where the learned writer states that in her paper she treats "issue as synonymous with thesis or conclusion."

[20] Geoffrey Samuel, *Law of Obligations and Legal Remedies,* 2nd ed., London: Cavendish Pub., 2001.

[21] [1932] AC 562 (HL)

could be problematic. Would we for instance, reason that the rule would apply or be relevant for damages inflicted by say a defective wall or damages caused by an old tree, even though all these items can be properly described as "things." Difficult to say with certainty.

That explains why even four years after the invention of the negligence rule in *Donoghue* it was unclear if the injury caused by the defective bottle of ginger could be extended to injury caused by a defective pair of underpants. Not surprising counsel for the defendant in *Grant v. Australia Knitting Mills Ltd,*[22] argued that a rule fashioned for ginger beer bottle should not apply to an article of clothing because beer and clothing are different objects. Though the Privy Council rejected the argument, it does not detract from the fact that a system that operates at the level of facts is bound to draw distinction between "things" and "persons," and so a rule may just well mean many things to different persons depending on how they construct the relevant ratio emerging from given facts. What the rule of negligence is from *Donoghue v Stevenson* is therefore a matter of fitting the facts to law. It is plausible to construct several rules from the case. That why it was not illogical for defendant to argue in *Australian Knitting* that the *Donoghue* ratio did not apply to the set of facts in the instant case.

While the *IRAC* "R" represents the general premise in the deductive reasoning paradigm, it could admit of fact specific examples about how the premise is constructed. That explains the basis for which the defense constructed *Donoghue* in the new fact-situation in the *Australian Knitting* case. This is understandable, especially in the context that common lawyers reason inductively.[23] That being so, the acronym "R" can be divided into two parts-the general rule and the precedent (which decides the facts-specify application to the abstract rule). That is the only way the defense argument (though dismissed by the court) in the *Australian Knitting* could count as valid analysis, though overruled by the Privy Council. Some commentators have therefore suggested that "R" should be rather replaced and represented as "GP," "G" being the general rule and "P" the precedent that decides specific facts situation. Such a stance will convert *IRAC* to *IGPAC.*[24] The rule states the law that governs the legal issue. But rule explanation presents principles of interpretation derived from case and

---

[22][1936] AC 85

[23] Geoffrey Samuel, above n. 20. In fact, one hallmark of the common law legal system is that it is under theorised, in the sense that a court decision is not an instantiation of an explicit theory for resolving similar matters. Cass R. Sunstein, Incomplete Theorised Arguments (1995) 108 *Harv. L. Rev.* 1733. (discussion that because the incremental work of judges is accomplished by merely fitting new facts into existing precedent without necessarily articulating broad theory in the area that is in issue or dispute, the implication of this is that gaps are left unfilled until presented by facts pattern that demand gap-filling decisions).

[24] See Barbara Blumenfeld, Why IRAC Should Be IGPAC, *The Second Draft* (Legal Writing Institute, Tacoma, Washington, Nov. 1995, 3; Laura P. Graham, above n. 6.

secondary authorities to show how a rule or sub-rule applies in actual situation. Both are simply referred to as rule in *IRAC*, when they in fact, implicate different types of analysis. The later involves using inductive reasoning to derive genus principles of how a rule is to be interpreted and applied. These principles derive from factual elements, policies, or themes found in the cases and other authorities that are relevant to the interpretation of the rule. To therefore refer to both as one, as "R" does in the *IRAC* paradigm is misleading.

Furthermore, it must be recognized that "R" can make a difference on how students write. Because they think that "R" is always determinate, they are given to linear analysis of the "R" which they mathematically apply to arrive at a legal answer. But legal educators know that this kind of modular reasoning does not properly align with the intellectual development of students. No sooner after being taught *IRAC*, they see "R" from the perspective of dualism-right/wrong, true/false, good/bad etc. At this elementary stage, they can see the "R" as clear as sun in midday. But as they progress in learning they get transformed to the multiplicity stage, where they see the "R" as "R" or unknown. They realize that it is important to know *how* to think rather than *what* they think.[25] They progress from multiplicity to contextual relativism, where they gradually sees for the first time that they too can be a legitimate source of knowledge and that former knowledge-iconoclasts, such as their teachers, who analyse statute, case-law and legal texts to them are also fellow knowledge/truth-seekers, who likely possess more experience in the adventure. At this stage of their development, they begin to recognise that "R" is principle of law on which they can evaluate arguments in any given setting, and that the principle or "R" in a case is facts, precedent, and policy synthesis, not a determinate given. So "R" may not just be something out in the world capable of summarising in one way and one way only. It can be susceptible to different analysis.

It is no wonder therefore that a theoretical level some contributors think that the *IRAC* rule stupefies reasoning and analysis. They critique the "R" for encouraging students to assume that there is a rule clearly set forth by the facts so that all they need to do is apply the rule to get right answers in law, when in truth analysis requires making the difficult choice of choosing between competing and sometimes conflicting rules. Thus, to the extent that teachers use *IRAC*, it encourages students to keep a narrow perspective of law, when indeed writing ought to encourage evaluation of competing rules-a necessary skill for lawyers.[26]

---

[25] Gerald F. Hess & Steven Friedland, *Techniques for Teaching Law*, Durham, North Carolina, Caroline Academic Press, 1999, 7. See also Paula Lustbader, Construction Sites, Building Types, and Bridging Gaps: A Cognitive Theory of the Learning Progression of Law Students (1997) 33 *Willamette L. Rev.* 317.

[26] Laura P. Graham, above n. 6 at 684; Marion W. Benfield, Jr., Thoughts on IRAC, The *Second Draft* (Legal Writing Institute, Tacoma, Washington, Nov. 1995, 17. According to Ronald Dworkin in *Taking*

Although a sceptic position to reasoning, some commentator even disputes the proposition that there is anything clearly marked as rules, to warrant an "R" within the paradigm. They question whether judicial decisions are founded on rules. Maintaining such a stance for instance, Sinclair posits that there are many ways rules can be formulated to fit an opinion, none of which can lay validity to superiority.[27] The learned writer presses the point by an analogy. Assuming ordinary people can read and understand cases and distil rules therefrom, he states that lawyers would be amazed at the different interpretations they will put on cases. Perhaps corroborative of his position is the thinking that lawyers do not extract rules from a single case but rather from a series of them. That being so, a science of law which constructs a principle from them should be seen as a process of synthesizing, which ordinarily admits of rule pluralism.[28]

3. Application (A)

The "A" is justified in *IRAC* as rooted in deductive syllogism. This form of reasoning that relies of the certainty of the major and minor premises is said to yield truth about the conclusion. If that were the case, then our "A" would certainly be problematic in yielding truth value using the *IRAC* rule. Teachers agree at a minimum that if the issues are even correctly framed, in the application section, students may not agree as to how the rules sit with the facts application. For instance, while students may agree that a given rule prohibits say murder (major premise), they are bound to defer on whether doctor assisted suicide or euthanasia should be classed as murder (minor premise). That being the case, it is hard to justify the certainty of conclusion, a position which implicates appeal to syllogism as bases for justifying *IRAC.* So in the theoretic sense, *IRAC* is less prevailing as deductive reasoning. The scope of ambiguity in the "A" weakens the algorithmic of *IRAC* transforming legal analysis into a model fit for enthymeme. There are no clear major and minor premise. Therefore, legal conclusion is stepped in enthymeme, mere probabilities of truth. Nothing more.[29]

Rights Seriously, 2nd ed. Cambridge, 1978, p. 23, legal norms are in two categories-rules and principles. While the former are applicable in an all-or-nothing fashion, the later are best described as value-maximising norms, i.e. they aim at promoting certain legal values. It is therefore not surprising why common lawyers trained in Anglo-American legal system would treat a statute as not intended to introduce new legal principles.

[27] Michael Sinclair, What is the "R" in IRAC (2003) 19 *N.Y.L. Sch. J. Hum. Rts.* 87.

[28] Murray, above n. 17.

[29] Logicians generally recognise two logical structure for argument: the deductive and inductive. The deductive comprises of syllogism and enthymeme. The latter is more suited for legal arguments. See basic book in Philosophy. See also Murray, above n. 17 ("Given the uncertainties of the law, where legal rules are constructed from multiple controlling authorities and, in certain instances, colored by persuasive authorities, and where facts might be uncertain or subject to multiple credible interpretations, the model of enthymeme with its anticipation of uncertainty, is the better model. Aristotle recognizes that in legal discourse (continuous discourse), the enthymeme is preferred)."

If that puts legal analysis in the mould of enthymeme, then legal analysis is inductive reasoning (reasoning by analogy) pretending to be scientific deductive reasoning.[30]   What this tells us is that the "A" is not simply an analysis of facts tied to some absolute correct rules. Legal writing is therefore contextual and expansive to a large extent which includes not just analysis but also counter-analysis and policy analysis.

4. Conclusion (C)

The "C" is actually the beginning point. Legal writing begins with it, then move backwards from there. When faced with legal questions, lawyers instinctively first reach a conclusion and thereafter try to make the analysis fit.[31] But the *IRAC* rule as against the customary instinctiveness. It encourages suspending conclusion in pretence of promoting the objective character of law, especially in adjudication.

That notwithstanding, the "C" component has a way of stupefying reasoning in that it tends to make students think that deductive reasoning must produce right answers and conclusions. According to Seymour, "when *IRACian* students make up their mind how the law applies to the facts, they can undervalue opposing views. *IRAC* pushes students towards answers rather than arguments. *IRAC* is sleek and efficient, once issue emerges, conclusion ever beckons."[32]

These are some of the critique of the *IRAC* paradigm, which triggers suggestion for revisiting it as a writing style.

---

[30] Cass R. Sunstein, On Analogical Reasoning (1993) 106 *Harv. L.R.* 741 at 747; Burton, *An Introduction to Law and Legal Reasoning*, Boston & Toronto, 1985. Reasoning by analogy constitutes the most familiar form of legal reasoning in the common law legal system. It general proceeds based on a theory of probabilities. For example, it goes like this: I have a Honda car that is fuel efficient, so I assume that your Honda would also be fuel efficient. The logical structure is simple: (i) A has characteristic Y; (ii) B shares that characteristic; (iii) A also has characteristic Z; (iv) Because A and B share characteristic Y, we conclude what isn't known, that B shares characteristic Z as well. This form of reasoning pervades daily life and law. This reasoning does not guarantee truth about conclusions. It focuses on the particulars, and is developed from concrete controversies. It is a bottom-top thinking because ideas are developed from details. Principles are created which operates at a low or intermediate level of abstraction. For instance, when we say the state cannot ban civil demonstration, we invariably are implying that the state has no constitutional power to prevent lawful assembly and association without showing that in the instant case such demonstration poses imminent and clear harm. This is a principle, and it does involve a certain degree of abstraction from the particular case (legitimacy of civil demonstration), but it does not entail any high-level theory about the purpose of the free assembly and association provision of the Constitution or what is considered the proper relation between the citizen and state.

[31] Kristen K. Robbins-Tiscione, *Rhetoric for Legal Writers: The Theory and Practice of Analysis and Persuasion,* 2009. According to Justice Holmes, the common law court decides a case first and determines the principles afterwards. Oliver W. Holmes, Jr., Codes and the Arrangement of Law (1870) 5 *Am. L. Rev.* 1 reprinted in (1931) 44 *Harv. L. Rev.* 725. But that hardly be the factual position, because legal reasoning must somehow be raised from some rough commitment to principles (values) that form the underlying basis for fitting facts.

[32] Thomas H. Seymour, Between IRAC and a Hard Place, *The Second Draft* (Legal Writing Institute, Tacoma, Washington, Nov. 1995) 14.

III. Why Teachers Continue to Cling to *IRAC*

Despite recognizing the limitations of the *IRAC* template, some writing teachers cling to it because of the thinking that deductive reasoning (one that moves from the general to the particular) is good basis for legal analysis in reducing complex to the simple.[33] Relying on deductive syllogism, a number of other versions of the rule-based *IRAC* paradigm have been invented. They include acronym like *CREAC* and many others.[34] Some have suggested other *IRAC* acronyms to fill the gaps of deficiency of *IRAC* to better capture the supposed different methods of analysis in law. As revealed in the preceding section this have sometimes led legal writing teachers to suggest acronyms like '(QfrFR)+I*RAC*,' *IGPAC, CREAC, TREAT, CREXAC, CRAC, CRuPAC,* and other similar formulations to better capture the multifaceted dimensions legal writing requires.[35] All of these *IRAC* cousins, like its progeny are rooted in the philosophy that it is best to teach students to reason as syllogistically as possible, and that a rule-based approach enables law to remain an autonomous discipline, divorced from mundane bias. It is the general thinking that anything short of *IRAC* syllogism implicates enthymeme; a thing lawyers' must avoid in keeping law the envy of other disciplines.[36] The beauty of the paradigm and its cousins is extolled for its capacity to project argumentation within scientific boundaries to produce logically accepted conclusions.

But herein lurks the danger of the so-called scientific analysis. Following deductive syllogism, the first task is to frame the general rule before applying it to the facts. We must first begin with "All humans are mortal." The facts, "Socrates is a human," is therefore made relevant only as defined by the rule. The paradigm does not permit placing the facts before the rule. So the facts relevant are simply those conscripted by the rule. One scholar captures this way: "no paradigm recognizes a place for inclusion of facts within the analysis-other than the limited facts that may be part of the initial conclusion-before the rule is stated and explained, much like no effective syllogism puts the minor premise before the

---

[33] James A. Gardner, *Legal Argument: The Structure and Language of Effective Advocacy,* 1st ed., 1993, 6; Teresa J. Reid Rambo & Leanne J. Pflaum, above n. 2; Anita Schnee, above n. 9.

[34] See Gopen, above n. 13.

[35] See for example Richard K. Neumann, Jr., *Legal Reasoning and Legal Writing: Structure, Strategy and Style,* 5th ed., Aspen Pub., 2005; Charles R. Calleros, *Legal Method and Writing,* 5th ed., Aspen Pub, 2006; Michael D. Murray & Christy H. DeSanctis, *Legal Research and Writing,* Found Press, 2006, 95-112; Mary B. Beazley, *A Practical Guide to Appellate Advocacy,* 2nd ed., Aspen Pub, 2006, 61-76; Brian Foley &Ruth A. Robbins, Fiction 101: A Primer for Lawyers on How to Use Fiction Writing Techniques to Write Persuasive Facts Section (2001) 32 *Rutgers L.J.* 459 at 462.

[36] For the difference between syllogism and enthymeme and the supposed preference of the former to the latter, see Robbins-Tiscione, above n. 31; Linda L. Berger, Studying and Teaching "Law as Rhetoric": A Place to Stand (2010) 16 *J. Legal Writing Inst.* 3 at 50; Kraft, above n. 10.

major premise."[37] That being so, the minor premise is confined to the structure only permitted by the major premise. Only facts within the confines of the framed question (issue) for determination can get ventilated.

For those of us who subscribe to the thinking that law must account for peoples' experience and reality, syllogism must be construed expansive. After all, there are two generally permitted logical structure for argumentation-deductive and inductive reasoning. Even at that, deductive reasoning admits of syllogism and enthymeme. Both syllogism and enthymeme begin with major premise, followed by the minor premise. The difference between them being that in the former both premise (major and minor) are absolute certainty, making the conclusion an absolute, unrefutably truth. This kind of reasoning should be a suspect candidate in legal analysis. No one can seriously doubt that legal rules constructed from multiple sources, colored by persuasive authorities, in context of facts indeterminacy should be a candidate for enthymeme. In fact, even Aristotle recognizing the indeterminate nature of law and facts in legal disputes was of the view that enthymeme constitutes a better model for legal reasoning.[38] In enthymeme, a highly probable legal principle is applied to the specific facts of the case to produce a highly probably conclusion. This explains how law works in the real world as we know it.

But adherents of *IRAC* just remain glued to it standard pedagogy for analysis. While some admit that it imposes an architectural restrain of the edifice of legal reasoning they are reluctance to discard it because it adherents argue (may be rightly so) that the organizational paradigm is useful to teach starters the rudiments of legal analysis, especially in helping them grasp doctrinal analysis, thinking as a lawyer.[39]

---

[37] Kraft, above n. 10.

[38] Murray, above n. 17; Aristotle, *The Rhetoric*, Book 1, ch. 1 at 1355; Book 1, ch. 2 at 1356.

[39] It is recognized that legal training involves doctrine, skills and ethics. See tilt towards professionalism in Reports. William M. Sullivan, et al. eds. *Carnegie Fund for the Advancement of Teaching, Educating Lawyers: Preparation for the Profession of Law*, 2007 (hereinafter called the *Carnegie Report*) Foundation for the Advancement of Teaching, Preparation for the Professions Program (PPP) 2007, Legal Education Report based on a survey of more than two hundred law faculties (schools) in the US and Canada in 1999; H.R. Cort & J.L. Sammons, The Search for Good Lawyering: A Concept and Model for Lawyering Competencies (1980) 29 *Cleveland State L. Rev.* 397; James R. Maxeiner, Educating Lawyers Now and Then: Two Carnegie Critiques of the Common Law and Case Method (2007) 35 *International J. Leg. Info.* 1; John B. Garvey & Anne F. Zinkin, Making Law Students Client-Ready: A New Model in Legal Education (2009) 1 *Duke Forum Law & Soc. Change* 101; Karen Tokarz, et al, Legal Education at a Crossroad: Innovation, Integration, and Pluralism Required (2014) 43 *Washington Univ. J Law & Policy* 11. See also Robert MacCrate in forward to *Best Practices* said: "The central message in both Best Practices and in the contemporaneous Carnegie Report is that law schools should broaden the range of lessons they teach, reducing doctrinal education that uses the Socratic dialogue and case method: integrate the teaching of knowledge, skills and values, and not treat them as separate subjects in separate courses: and give greater attention to instruction in professionalism." Roy Stuckey et. al., *Best Practices for Legal Education: A Vision and a Roadmap*, 2007 (hereinafter called *Best Practices*) and generally,

Recognizing the place of legal writing in the law academy, writing professors in the United States in 1984 organized a writing conference, which led to the establishment of the Legal Writing Institute in 1986. The goal of the Institute has been to encourage a broader understanding of legal writing and the teaching of it. To further the goal, the Institute established the Journal of Legal Writing Institute in 1988 to showcase the developing discipline of legal writing.[40] Since emerging as a discipline, writing teachers have been critical of the use of *IRAC* as template for two basic reasons: the limitation of the rule as a tool for analyzing complexities in law and for its suffocating influence it can exert on the architecture of legal reasoning.[41]

While many agree that deductive syllogism is a useful way for organizing legal analysis and that it is signature template for writing, legal writing teachers and the profession demands re-assessment of the paradigm to make lawyering robust by giving attention to pluralistic and multidisciplinary reasoning not rooted in rule-based analysis. Strong critics of *IRAC* have been storytelling teacher, who argue that *IRAC* banishes from courts the real forces that generate disputes between parties.[42]

Association of American Law School, Conference on the Future of Law School Curriculum: Brochure (Seattle, 2011).

[40] See webpage of the Institute. For a history of legal writing as a discipline see Mary S. Lawrence, The Legal Writing Institute the Beginning: Extraordinary Vision, Extraordinary Accomplishment (2005) 11 *Legal Writing* 213.

[41] For general reading on a critique of the IRAC paradigm for legal writing, see, Terri LeClercq, The Success-And Failure-of IRAC (1987) 50 *Tex. B.J.* 222; Jane K. Gionfriddo, Dangerous! Our Focus Should Be Analysis, Not Formulas Like IRAC, The Second Draft Nov. 1995 of the Legal Writing Institute, Tacoma, Wash, at 2; Wilson R. Huhn, Teaching Legal Analysis Using a Pluralistic Model of Law (2000-2001) 36 *Gonz. L. Rev.* 433; Christine M. Venter, Analyze This: Using Taxonomies to "Scaffold" Students' Legal Thinking and Writing Skills (2006) 57 *Mercer L. Rev.* 621; Kristen K. Robbins-Tiscione, A Call to Combine Rhetorical Theory and Practice in the Legal Writing Classroom (2011) 50 *Washburn L.J.* 319; Kedia, above n. 13; Jennifer Sheppard, Once Upon a Time, Happily Ever After, and in a Galaxy Far, Far Away: Using Narrative to Fill the Cognitive Gap Left by Overreliance on Pure Logic in Appellate Briefs and Motion Memoranda (2009) 46 *Willamette L. Rev.* 255; Helen A. Anderson, Changing Fashion in Advocacy: 100 Years of Brief-Writing Advice (2010) 11 *J. App. Prac. & Process* 1 (judges expect legal analysis to go beyond atomistic logic); George D. Gopen, IRAC, REA, Where We Are Now, and Where We Should Be Going in the Teaching of Legal Writing (2011) 17 *J. Legal Writing Inst.* xvii (keynote address at Capital Area Legal Writing Conference, Feb. 26, 2011- "there is not and cannot be a single structure that is the right answer to the question of how argumentative thought is best conveyed from the mind of a writer to the mind of a reader. ... These organizational structures [CRAC, CREAC, MIRAT, IDAR, ILAC, TREACC, CruPAC, ISAAC, CRRACC, BARAC etc.] are both necessary and dangerous, both supporting and defeating. As with any good idea or good invention, they can all be used for harm as well as good," id xviii);; Laura P. Graham, Why-RAC? Revisiting the Traditional Paradigm for Writing About Legal Analysis (2015) 63 *Kansas L. Rev.* 681. But cf. generally, Tracy Turner, Flexible IRAC: A Best Practice Guide (2015) 20 *J. Legal Writing Inst.* 233 (recommends the syllogistic IRAC reasoning, while suggesting the best guide for teachers use of the rule, such as the one-sequence IRAC; the alternating IRAC; IRAC by paragraph; the IRAC sentence; and the narrative add-ons which mixes facts into the "I" of IRAC); Lurene Contento, Demystifying IRAC and Its Kin: Giving Students the Basic to Write "Like a Lawyer," *The Second Draft*, Nov. 1995 of the Legal Writing Institute, Tacoma, Wash.

[42] Kenneth D. Chestek, Judging by the Numbers: An Empirical Study of the Power of Story (2010) 7 *J. Ass'n.* Legal *Writing Directors* 1 (study found that judges were more persuaded by narrative briefs than

Because *IRAC* does not teach students who would become members of the legal profession flexibility and creativity in their analysis, writing teachers have been concerned about how they can collectively improve the writing skills of students. in 1995 for instance, they gathered in Washington to examine the advantages and disadvantages of the *IRAC* template.[43] Their Report revealed that writing professors generally acknowledge the value of IRAC rule but are split on the danger of using *IRAC* without flexibility.[44] One group think the template truncates and restricts the architecture of legal reasoning, while the other urge for its continuing use with modification to make it amenable to different types of analysis as the facts of a case admits.[45]

A survey of teaching methodology in Nigeria however indicates that despite the criticism of *IRAC* it remains the dominant pedagogy in faculties of law, and even brief writing.[46] The reason is not farfetched. One scholar suggests that this is because "there are not many alternatives from which to choose" given legal writing's fairly recent emergence as part of the law school curriculum.[47] The emergence of law clinics in many faculties is however indicative that legal writing is here to stay and that a review of *IRAC* as a writing style is in the wings.

IV. IRAC and the Legal Profession

It is plausible to reason that if *IRAC* exhibits all the flaws said to attach to it as a writing style and yet teachers still cling to it, then it must be in part because practicing lawyers also use a similar thought thread in writing briefs. But it is not true. The most daunting criticism of *IRAC* does not really emerge from the legal academy and legal writing teachers, but it comes from legal practitioners and judges who call for better writing.[48] Complain by judges and senior lawyers over the writing skills of new lawyers is indicative of the harm caused by strict adherence to IRAC pedagogy in our teaching of law.[49] Trial and appellate judges

---

they were with rule-based logical briefs). See also Festus Emiri, Mainstreaming an Interdisciplinary Approach to Legal Education: Imperatives for Nigeria's Development [2015] *Proceeding of NALT*, 1.

[43] See generally The Value of IRAC, *The Second Draft* (Legal Writing Institute, Tacoma, Washington, Nov. 1995. (Legal Writing Institute Conference), above n. 14.

[44] Above n. 14 at 1.

[45] For critique of the rule see, Gionfriddo, above n. 16. For flexibility of the rule see, Turner, above n. 7.

[46] Refer to the Nigerian Law School handbook and briefs filed at appellate courts.

[47] Kedia, above n. 13.

[48] For legal academy critique of IRAC, see the 1995 *Second Draft,* devoted to examine IRAC as a model for legal writing. Above n. 14.

[49] For complain of Nigerian judges and lawyers, see. See also the *MacCrate Report*, above n. 38; The *Carnegie Report*, above n. 14; Amy Vorenberg & Margaret S. McCabe, Practice Writing: Responding to the Needs of the Bench and Bar in the First-Year Writing Programs (2009) 2 *Phoenix L. Rev.* 1 (sample of trial judges in several U.S states indicates that they expressed reservations about IRAC as a good organizational structure for organizing writing. In fact, when asked, "Do you find IRAC effective or do

prefer briefs that combine rule explanation with application to client's facts, especially in cases with complexity requiring depth of analysis. The flexible organizational style is most suitable for facts-intensive litigation. An integrated flexible organizational structure encourages centrality of facts and the client's theory of the case, a thing extremely difficult to achieve with the rule-based IRAC paradigm.[50]

IRAC is particularly unhelpful to judges in deciding cases where the legal issues are fairly settled and frequently before the courts. For example, applications for interlocutory injunctions pending final determination of cases and those for stay of execution pending appeal are staple diet in our courts. Movants of such applications would be generally unhelpful to the courts by adopting the rule-based approach in persuading judges to exercise the court's discretion in their clients favour by citing the rule as expounded in say, *Kotoye v CBN*[51] for injunction and *Vaswani Trading Co. v Savalakh*[52] and *Kigo (Nig) Ltd v Holman*[53] for stay of execution and then lacing them with the facts constricted by the syllogism of *IRAC*. Judges know enough of the rules expounded in the cases. What will help them in the exercise of their discretion to grant or refuse an application would be facts construction of applicants' case-theory creating compelling reasons for the orders sought. Yes, the compelling facts-intensive stories which fit a constructed theory of the case. So what is likely to be more useful to them in a brief seeking the material relief may well turn on how the movant matches the rules with the specific narrative of the client to create compelling persuasion for the orders sought. Good brief writing demands an organizational structure that is deep and flexible, combining rule application to the facts specifics of the client to create the client's theory of the case to persuade the court.[54] Rather than stick to a rigid *IRAC* structure, good brief writer goes

---

you prefer organization that combines rule explanation with application to client's facts?' several judges preferred the latter); Graham, above n. 6 at 704; Kedia, above n. 13.

[50] Vorenberg & McCabe survey contains an interesting finding. They provided the judges survey with three students briefs written by their students. Two of the briefs were organized around IRAC, one was not. Most of the judges preferred the brief that was flexible combining rule explanation with client's facts in the same paragraph and section. Vorenberg & McCabe, above n. 49 at 14. See also, Ruminations From the Bench: Brief Writing and Oral Argument in the Fifth Circuit (1995) 70 *Tul. L. Rev.* 187.

[51] [1989] All NLR 76. See especially the judgment of Nnaemeka-Agu, JSC stating that the important issues in the application for interlocutory injunction are (i) that there is a real possibility, not a probability, of success at the trial-that there is a serious question to be tried; (ii) balance of convenience favors the grant (iii) that damages cannot be adequate compensation; (iv) and conduct of the parties.

[52] [1972] All NLR 922, per Coker, JSC.

[53] [1980] NSCC 204, per Kayode Esho, JSC.

[54] For discussion on client's theory of the case and its persuasiveness, see Lucie E. White, Subordination, Rhetorical Survival Skills, and Sunday Shoes: Notes on the Hearing of Mrs. G (1990) 38 *Buffalo L. Rev.* 1 (where the commentators using the story of Mrs. G welfare hearing application reveals that cultural images and long-established legal norms construct the subjectivity and speech of socially subordinate groups, like women, blacks, etc., as inherently inferior to those of dominant groups). See also Derrick

beyond sheer deductive syllogism, combining inductive, problem-solving techniques with it to persuade.

A survey of good briefs filed in courts can give a representative idea of the virility or otherwise of the *IRAC* organizational paradigm. Good brief writers do not think that an organizational structure like *IRAC* is necessary for good brief writing.[55] In one such survey conducted by Kraft of briefs filed in the US Supreme Court, the US Circuit Courts of Appeal, and the Kentucky Supreme Court between 1989 and 2013, he found that while most briefs included elements of conclusion, rule, rule explanation, rule application, and conclusion (*CREAC*), the trend showed a general departure from the strict rule, explanation and application (*R-E-A*) template.[56] In the learned writer's view, most of the briefs rather followed three patterns: (i) they included facts before rule or rule explanation; (ii) they included the rule in a separate section, and started subsequent sections with a discussion of facts, and (iii) they interspersed rule explanation with rule application.

Let us illustrate with two examples of how the flexible style have been used by judges in judicial opinion and lawyers in good brief writing.

1. Judicial Opinion Writing

We have chosen to use the judgment of Peter Gibson J in *Baden v Societe Generale pour Favorise le Developpement du Commerce et d l'Industrie en France SA*,[57] as a good judicial opinion for some reasons. Aside the fact that it is a brilliant writing, it is a fact-intensive, complex case that took 108 hearing days to

---

Bell, *And We Are Not Saved*, 1987 (for critical race theory perspective); Anthony V. Alfieri, The Antinomies of Poverty Law and a Theory of Dialogic Empowerment (1987-88) 16 *N.Y.U. Rev. L & Soc. Change* 659; Patricia J. Williams, *The Alchemy of Race and Rights*, 1991 (literary and legal theory); Kathryn Abrams, Hearing the Call of Stories (1991) 79 *Cal. L. Rev.* 971 (feminist theory); Clark D. Cunningham, The Lawyer as Translator, Representation as Text: Towards an Ethnography of Legal Discourse (1992) 77 *Cornell L. Rev.* 1298 (ethnography discourse); Binny Miller, Give Them Back Their Lives: Recognising Client Narrative in Case Theory (1994) 93 *Mich. L. Rev.* 485 (showing how the practice of lawyering should be reconstructed to embrace a greater role for clients in constructing case theories) [hereinafter referred to as 'Give Them Back']; Edward D. Ohlbaum, Basic Instinct: Case Theory and Courtroom Performance (1993) 66 *Temp. L. Rev.* 1; Binny Miller, Teaching Case Theory (2002) 9 *Clinical L. Rev.* 293.

[56] Kraft, above n. 10.

[57] [1992] 4 All ER 161. This is a case often used by one of the writers of this paper, Festus Emiri, to teach his students writing style in legal method and the concept of *knowing assistance* and *knowing* receipt liability of strangers in trust classes. For similar great style of judicial opinion see the lead judgment of Nnaemeka-Agu in *Kotoye v CBN* [1989] All NLR 76 at 84; *Kigo (Nig) Ltd v Holman Bros. (Nig) Ltd* [1980] NSCC 204, per Kayode Eso, JSC, where His Lordship used dramatic language like "this was the beginning of the drama which eventually culminated in the instant application in this court." Id at 206 lines 28-29; "the next stage in this interesting drama was set on 14th April, 1980." Id at 207 line 6. "Now, it has been necessary to state all these facts antecedent to the present application, before this court, to stay further proceedings before the High Court of Kano, and refer to the activities of learned counsel for the Third Party in the trial court for the reason that the jurisdiction of the court to entertain an application for the stay sought in the instant application is discretionary." Id at 208 lines 1-5.

be concluded. *Baden* was a case about a complex transnational financial scheme was designed to defraud investors. His Lordship's style summarized in the judgment followed a pattern of introducing the facts before rule and rule explanation and thereafter interspersing rule explanation with rule application.

The learned judge started the introduction by narrating the background to the dispute this way:

"A decade or more after the troubles affecting the financial complex known as IOS exited the attention of the financial world, disputes arising from those troubles are still not resolved. In this action the plaintiffs seek to recover a sum a little in excess of $US4m from the defendant (SG), a major French bank which carries on a banking business in, inter alia, the City of London. SG has held that sum in an account designated as a trust account by its customer, Bahamas Commonwealth Bank Ltd (BCB)."

It is from the background that the court went on to describe in detail the complex history and nature of the facts under the subhead/title, history. In the history section, His Lordship catalogues the IOS complex, the dollar funds, the acquisition and reorganization of IOS, change of the investment policies, the transactions that followed, all leading to the Security and Exchange Commission (SEC) proceedings, and SG's involvement and what led to the litigation. It is after this detailed narrative that His Lordship then resorted to the next section, applicable rule.

Noteworthy of mention, the court in laying the background for the dispute using the narrative style above gave life to the dispute by context, stating that the litigation is a fallout from the OIS financial scam. The court did not follow the acontextual style of some judicial opinion writings that would have simply started by just describing the plaintiff's claim, stating for example that "the claim of the plaintiff is for … The plaintiff filed and served his statement of claim …" type of run.

Rather the learned judge used a narrative form of writing, interspersing the facts with law in the rule and rule explanation sections to make the conclusion clear understandable. His Lordship started by first setting out in the introduction a narrative background to the dispute, then proceeding from there to give a background to the claim under the section of history, before stating the before stating the rule and rule explanation and thereafter interspersing rule explanation with rule application is what set the stage to understand the claim of the plaintiff. It is a style very flexible, fact laden and persuasive, not in any way *IRACian*.

2. Good Brief Writing

Good brief writers also employ a similar flexible style.

Let us consider the brief filed by the respondent in response to an appeal seeking to set-aside the judgment granted the respondent by the lower court in *Atlantic Airline v Musa*.[58] The facts of the case had to do with the retention of the respondent by the appellant to provide it professional legal services. At the end of the service in 2010 the respondent delivered a detailed bill for his professional services, under section 16 of the Legal Practitioners Act for the sum of N5m. Unfortunately, the bill was not honored and remained unpaid for four years. It was also not disputed by the appellant. On the strength of it, the respondent applied to the trial court to place the claim under the undefended list from where the respondent sought summary judgment in 2015. On the day the respondent moved for judgment at the trial court, the appellant raised objection to the court's jurisdiction to entertained the suit and also filed an affidavit of intention to defend the suit as provided under the undefended list procedure Order 10 of Gongola State (Civil Procedure) Rules, 2000.

It was the case of the appellant that the judgment obtained by the respondent should be set aside on appeal on the ground that the trial judge erred in law when he entered judgment against the appellant under the undefended list procedure of Order 10 of the Gongola State (Civil Procedure) Rules, 2000, without availing them fair hearing as guaranteed in section 36 of the Constitution of the Federal Republic of Nigeria, by failing to consider its pending applications before entering summary judgment in the respondent's favor.

The respondent reply brief did not follow the IRAC pattern. Rather it simply used a flexible organizational style where facts were interspersed with thesis, rule, rule explanation and legal conclusions that combined elements of logos, pathos and ethos.

For example, in the very beginning of the brief, it drew a taxonomical line between the complaint of the appellant and what is not complained about to enable the court narrow the confines of the appeal. It thereafter states the rule, explains the rule as applied to the legal principle and just intersperse the facts of the case with the applicable principles through inductive reasoning. It began like this:

This brief is in reply to the appellant's brief filed on 15 January 2015 in expatiation of the grounds of appeal filed against the decision of the trial court of the High Court of Gongola State, sitting in Yanbura. The said decision of the court was delivered on 3 January 2015 and is found at pages 40-49 of the records of proceedings.

---

[58] An imaginary case constructed from an appellate brief filed before the Calabar Division of the Court of Appeal.

The respondent who is a senior lawyer was retained by the appellant to provide it with legal services. In 2000, the respondent delivered a detailed bill for his professional services under section 16 of the Legal Practitioners Act, to the appellant for N5m.

After 41 months when the appellant did not contest or dispute any aspect of the said bill, nor paid the bill, after series of demands, the respondent brought an action under the undefended list procedure for his unpaid professional fees. Etc.

It then goes on to state as follows:

"The appellant has urged Your Lordships to resolve the issue as to whether having regard to section 36 of the 1999 Constitution the learned trial judge erred in law when he entered judgment against the appellant without availing them fair hearing.

The appellant has neither contended that Order 10 of the High Court of Gongola State (Civil Procedure) Rules is unconstitutional or offends section 36 of the Constitution.

The appellant has also not complained that the trial judge failed to apply the said Order 10 rule to the facts of case at the trial stage.

The hearing under Order 10 procedure does not cease to be fair where a representation is made by an affected party in accordance with the established procedure for the undefended list. See *CRPIC Ltd v Obongha* (2001) 45 FWLR 353 at 368.

The court can even dispense with any counsel's address before entering judgment in the undefended list procedure of Order 10. *Eneji v Internationals Ltd* (2001) 50 FWLR 765 at 775. See also *Chrisdon Industries Ltd v AIB Ltd* (2002) 128 FWLR 355, where the court held that the provision for showing notice of intention to defend under the undefended list procedure does not require call for argument or hearing an address of counsel. It is the exclusive preserve of the trial court. The movant and defense counsel need not be heard."

It is trite law that an allegation of denial of fair hearing has to be clearly particularized to enable issues to be joined. However, in an apparent effort to justify the claim for breach the appellant has supplied what it would wish the court to take as amounting to breach of fair hearing in his grounds of appeal at pages 100-105 of the record of proceedings as follows: (It then list the facts stated in the pages).

From the records, this was an action commenced under the undefended list procedure. In order to sustain an argument of breach of section 36 of the Constitution, such a breach must of necessity be founded on the undefended list procedure under which this action was commenced.

It is logical to conclude that the appellant complain is limited to the fact that the appellant was not served with hearing notice for the proceedings of 5th

January 2015 and that there were pending applications that were not heard. We submit that in order to sustain an argument for breach of constitutional fair hearing (s.36 of the Constitution) the learned trial judge must have deviated from following the undefended list procedure of Order 10. There is no allegation that the learned trial judge breached any of the stipulations in Order 10 to reach the judgment complained of by the appellant. See *Ekulo Farms Ltd v UBN Plc* (supra).

There is no allegation that the trial court failed to take into account the materials provided by the appellant: the application for objection to the court's jurisdiction and its notice of intention to defend. The appellant has not disputed that where the court finds that the notice does not disclose a defence on merits, the court is at liberty to enter judgment without more. Accordingly, the appellant's argument about pending applications is grossly misplaced and ought to be discounted.

It is also necessary to consider the antecedent of the case in order to show that even though the trial judge needed not consider anything beyond the notice of intention to defend, the judge still out of abundance of caution, considered more than what the law requires. (It then catalogues the facts in a narrative style).

In *Ekulo Farms Ltd v UBN Ltd* [2006] 4 SC 1, the Supreme Court outlined in broad terms the procedure for the undefended list in the following paraphrased words: (states the paraphrased words).

In the circumstance, we urge this court to hold that no breach of fair hearing right has been breached and that the suit was properly decided under the undefended list by the learned trial judge.

What the brief sections above does is an articulation of the facts leading to the appeal, state the relevant question for determination, state the governing rule the court should apply, explains how the rule has been expounded by precedent (by citing the best possible authorities), relate how both the broad and narrow issues meld with the instant facts of the appeal using both inductive and analogical reasons to justify a favourable decision for the respondent. Noteworthy of mention, the rule application section freely interspersed the rule, rule explanation and facts together, drawing inferences and prima facie interim conclusions, before the omnibus conclusion.

The question then is why do good writers use the flexible organisational style, not *IRAC*? Good writers use the flexible style because it is reader-friendly to communicate.[59] Judicial opinion writing and brief writing do not structure their writing using the *IRAC* or *CREAC* paradigm in crafting legal arguments, they merely use elements of the structure. They especially show marked deviation in

---

[59] Kraft, above n. 10.

the "R-A" component of the *IRAC* rule or "R-E-A" component in the *CREAC* rule. The reason for this isn't just a matter of style, or preference. It is deeper. The styles chosen are in part informed by judicial preference to "let the facts do the talking."[60] A brief laced with story is likely to be more persuasive than one that rigidly follows the IRAC template. That explains why most would rather resort to either one or a combination of the three trends emergent in good brief writing: include facts before rule or rule explanation; include the rule in a separate section and start subsequent section with a discussion of facts; and intersperse rule explanation and rule application.

So while beginners in legal writing may need to start with *IRAC,* legal writing teachers should progressively inculcate the flexible style to create potentials for good brief writers.[61]   Generally, good brief writers differ from students' writer in that their writing go beyond the parameters of the formalist analysis using the *IRAC* organisational structure. They rather emphasize facts through storytelling and narrative. It is by teaching our students to write like lawyers that they become great advocates who recognise that law is concerned about real people and the stories that generate controversies located beyond mere form of description of the contending parties as plaintiff and defendant. Students need to be taught that *IRAC* is a mere beginner guide to deductive reasoning, and that the rule is merely a primer and no more. It serves only to raise their thinking ability to think as lawyers. But that is the far it goes. To the extent that lawyering demands acquisition of lawyering skills and values, they will need to master a flexible organisation structure that brings the experience of their client's story to the courtroom.[62] It only when we as teachers instruct our students to master the

---

[60] Susan H. Kosse & David T. ButleRichie, How Judges, Practitioners, and Legal Writing Teachers Access the Writing Skills of New Law Graduates: A Comparative Study (2003) 53 *J. Legal Educ.* 80. See also Symposium, Legal Storytelling (1989) 87 *Mich. L. Rev.* 2073; Symposium, Lawyers as Storytellers & Storytellers as Lawyers: An Interdisciplinary Symposium Exploring the Use of Storytelling in the Practice of Law (1994) 18 *VT. L. Rev.* 565. In fact, judicial writings follow a similar pattern.

[61] Helen A. Anderson, Changing Fashions in Advocacy: 100 Years of Brief-Writing Advise (2010) 11 *J. App. Prac. & Process* 1; Richard A. Posner, Judicial Opinions and Appellate Advocacy in Federal Courts-One Judge's View (2013) 51 *Duq. L. Rev.* 3; Kenneth D. Chestek, The Life of the Law Has Not Been Logic: It Has Been Story (2014) 1 *Savannah L. Rev.* 21.

[62] See George G. Gopen, Keynote Address at the Capital Area Legal Writing Conference, Feb. 26, 2011, in IRAC, REA, Where We Are Now, and Where We Should Be Going in the Teaching of Legal Writing (2011) 17 *J. Legal Writing Inst.* xvii at xviii (there is not and cannot be a single structure that is the right answer to the question of how argumentative thought is best conveyed from the mind of a writer to the mind of the reader). See generally, *The Carnegie Report,* above n. 38; *The Best Practice,* above n. 38. What is more, the word *client* derives from the Latin verb *cluere,* which according to Lucie White mean to "be named, hear oneself named." It was a word that grew from the ancient Roman practice of naming persons under the patronage of patricians as *clientem* because they were known by the name of their patrons. It is in this sense that lawyering is the practice of speaking for the client and therefore ought to be client-centred and client-empowering. See Clark D. Cunningham, above n. 54; Lucie E. White, Goldberg v Kelly on the Paradox of Lawyering for the Poor (1990) 56 *Brook. L. Rev.* 861 at 862 n. 2. Ruth A. Robbins, An Introduction to Applied Storytelling and to this Symposium (2008) 14 *J. Legal Writing Institute* 3. Law and literature is strong current in the legal academy. Robert McPeake, Fitting Stories into

flexible organisational structure of legal writing that we can say we have given them the required arsenal to transform them from amateur students writers to great brief writers, effective advocates for their clients responding to judges expectations. This is a must-do because students must learn that in the real world many legal questions cannot be evaluated under straightjacket formalistic rules and application.

V. Good Writing Entails Persuasion

Judges and lawyers write the way they do using flexible organisational structures because they recognise that good writing must persuade. This way, they merely mimic ancient rhetoricians. Traditional models of legal argumentation based on formal or informal models of logic are increasingly considered to be inadequate for fully describing the persuasiveness of legal argumentation.[63] Ancient rhetoricians unpacked the goal of persuasion as following three paths: the concept of *logos, pathos,* and *ethos.*[64] *Logos* (persuasion accompanied through logical reasoning embodied in the content of the communication) is the process of persuading using substance and logical argument, such as statute law, case-law and policy. *Pathos* (persuasion accomplished through the emotional response of

---

Professional Legal Education-The Missing Ingredient (2007) 41 *L. Teacher Intl' J. Leg. Educ.* 303 (ways of teaching storytelling as a lawyering skill). Generally, three are three strands of the scholarship. The first examines legal issues and representations of lawyers that appear in literary works. The second uses the tools of literary theory to analysis judicial decisions and legislative enactments. The third strand focuses on the transformative power of stories. See Paul Gewirtz, Narrative and Rhetoric in Law, in Peter Brooks & Paul Gewirtz, eds., *Law Stories: Narrative and Rhetoric in Law,* 1996.

[63] Classical rhetoric reputed to have began in the fifth century B.C.E. continued for nearly 1,000 years of the Greco-Roman history. It started with scholars like Socrates, followed by Plato, Aristotle, Cicero and Quintilian. See Aristotle, *The Rhetoric* (trans. W. Rhys Roberts, 1965) available at httpp://www.iastate.edu/honey1/Rhetoric/ (accessed Sep, 2016); Marcus Tullius Cicero, *De Inventione* (trans. H.M. Hubbell, 1949); Marcus Tullius Cicero, *De Oratore* (trans. E.W. Sutton, 1942); Marcus Fabius Quintilian, *Institutio Oratoria* (H.E. Butler, 1954). See Michael Frost, Introduction to Classical Rhetoric: A Lost Heritage (1999) 8 *S. Cal. Interdisc. L.J.* 613 (traces the history of rhetoric and argumentation to Corax of Syracuse). See also, Bernard Jackson, *Law, Fact and Narrative Coherence,* Deborah Charles Pub., 1988; Walter R. Fisher, *Human Communication as Narrative: Towards a Philosophy of Reason, Value, and Action,* U.S.C. 1989; Robert Burns, *A Theory of the Trial,* Princeton Univ. Press, 1999.

[64] Michael R. Smith, *Advanced Legal Writing: Theories* and *Strategies in Persuasive Writing,* Aspen Law & Bus., 2002, 22; Aristotle, *On Rhetoric* (transl. George A. Kennedy, Oxford Univ. Press, 1991); George A. Kennedy, *A New History of Classical Rhetoric,* Princeton Univ. Press, 1998; Stephen Toulmin, *The Use of Argument,* Cambridge Univ. Press, 1958. For detail discussion on a theory of persuasion, see J. Christopher Rideout, Storytelling, Narrative Rationality, and Legal Persuasion (2008) 14 *J. Legal Writing Inst.* 53 (in answer to the question 'what is it about narratives that make them persuasive in the law,' he stated that (1) narratives are innate ways of understanding and structuring human experience; this makes them inherently persuasive; (2) narrative models go beyond models of persuasion based on formal or informal logic, to encompass 'narrative rationality; ' (3) narratives embody several properties that are psychologically persuasive: (a) coherence (a formal property); correspondence (a formal property); (c) fidelity (a substantive property) Id at 55. See also the interesting read, W. Lance Bennett & Martha S. Feldman, *Reconstructing Reality in the Courtroom: Justice and Judgment in American Culture,* Rutgers Univ. Press, 1981 (the social science researchers states that American criminal trial is organized around storytelling).

the audience to the communication) on the other hand is persuasion through emotive argument. *Ethos* (persuasion accomplished through the perceived character or reputation of the speaker) refers to establishing and maintaining credibility in the eyes of the audience by showing intelligence, character and good will.[65] The three paths are often depicted as the "rhetorical triangle:" the three paths leading into one another. *Logos* affects the pathos of the audience and simultaneously affects the perception of the ethos of the author, the pathos of the audience affects how they perceive the ethos of the author and how they receive the logos of the argument.[66]

Aristotle for example, reminded advocates that the rhetorical pathways are fundamentally pragmatic this way: a logical argument will not persuade an audience if the author is perceived as a baboon. Also, a respected author whose reputation is beyond question will not persuade if her argument is riddled with logical fallacies and flaws. Similarly, an ironclad argument delivered in a manner that antagonizes the audience or one in which the audience questions the integrity and credibility of the author will not persuade.[67]

Logos is taught as doctrinal lessons. Students are very familiar with its basic structure: 'think like a lawyer.' That IRAC already teaches them. Traditional legal pedagogy makes it staple legal classroom diet. Pathos and ethos are not usual dietary prescriptions there. The reasons for this are numerous. Logos it is said is what stands out legal argument from other forms of argument. It is what makes law rational and a near science. The knowledge of law and training in logos is what makes law a distinct profession, what makes legal training unique. Yes, it has been suggested that the female embodiment of 'justice' found in law institutions and offices is always blindfolded because we do not want justice to see anything.[68] No one would seriously doubt this stance. Instructively, appellate judges focus more on *logos*. But that is the much it can go. Since lawyering is about persuasion, then attention must necessarily be paid to *pathos* and *ethos*. What is more, to the extent that legal practice focuses on all three aspects of persuasion, legal writing

---

[65] Smith, above n. 64.

[66] Linda Levine & Kurt M. Saunders, Thinking Like a Rhetor (1993) 43 *J. Legal Educ.* 108; Michael Frost, Ethos, Pathos and Legal Audience (1994) 99 *Dick L. Rev.* 85. See also Michael Frost, Justice Scalia's Rhetoric of Dissent: A Greco-Roman Analysis of Scalia's Advocacy in the VMI Case (2002) 91 *KY. L.J.* 167.

[67] Murray, above n. 17; Frost, above n. 66.

[68] Martin Jay, Must Justice Be Blind? The Challenges of Images to the Law, in Costas Douzinas & Lynda Neads, eds., *Law and Image*, Univ. Chicago Press, 1999, 21. See generally, James P. Eyster, Lawyer as Artist: Using Significant Moments and Obtuse Objects to Enhance Advocacy (2008) 14 *J. Legal Writing Inst.* 87 (a discussion of how to apply key techniques of the visual artists-the obtuse objet and significant moments to legal advocacy and their persuasive sting according to art history scholars, aestheticians, psychologists, and psycholinguists). For a discussion on the mental structures (rationality) that raise human cognition, see George Lakoff, *Women, Fire, and Dangerous Things: What Categories Reveal about the Mind*, Univ. Chicago Press, 1987.

teachers must encourage their students to write recursively than sticking to the linear *IRAC* style. Teaching persuasion through the non-rational factors of *pathos* and *ethos* can be achieved by storytelling, while the tension between *logos, pathos* and *ethos* offer teachers opportunity to teach values. There is no question about it: overemphasizing of doctrine at the expense of skills and professional responsibility undermines professionalism and does not train students for the practice of law.[69] To see human conflict through the prism of legal abstraction only cannot help society to challenge the complexity of human conflict.

Facts and narrative reasoning are important components of *pathos.* Accordingly, good writers are encouraged to tell stories in all section of the brief, especially in the argument (*confirmatio*) section of legal documents, the introduction (*exordium*) section, the statement of facts (*narratio*) section, and the conclusion (*peroratio*) section to stress the facts of the case in such a way as to fully engage the emotions of the audience.[70]

Using the respondent brief in *Atlantic Airline v Musa* in Part IV section 2 above, how did the brief writer employ the three elements of persuasion?

The introduction narrates the facts generating the appeal against a judgment in his favour, affording him the opportunity to make an emotional appeal (pathos) for the appeal court to confirm the trial court's judgment. It also uses logos by stating the rule that governed the resolution of the dispute at the lower court, the undefended list procedure of Order 10 of the Gongola High Court Rules. The statement of the case/facts, is a full narrative consisting of logos, pathos and ethos. In it the brief-writer seeks to bring the dispute within the context of the Legal Practitioners Act that provides the legal standard for the demand for professional services (logos). The writer then demonstrates that the bill forwarded to the appellant was not contested or disputes, neither was the bill paid despite repeated demands (pathos). The credibility and reputation of the respondent is bolstered by waiting for upwards of 41 months before commencing an action for recovery (ethos). Next, is the question for determination section. The section supplies the enthymeme relevant to resolve the appeal (logos). Noteworthy however, the section is not couched as a thesis which would have supplied the

---

[69] The first chapter of the *Carnegie Report* (79-81) which identifies and describes the traditional pedagogy of legal education, analogizing it with the concept borrowed from linguistics, describes its four structures: the surface structure, the deep structure, the tacit structure and the shadow structure. The surface structure is that commonly observable in class. The teacher using the Socratic method takes the students through the cases asking a series of questions. The deep structure is the essence of the first. Here the students are encouraged to think like lawyer. The tacit structure is that the student's personal sense of morality is not necessary in resolving legal conflicts. The shadow structure is about clinical training of students to act as lawyers. See above n. 8. The Report states that the weakness of legal education occurs primarily in the tacit and shadow structures. See Mark Yates, The Carnegie Effect: Elevating Practical Training Over Liberal Education in Curricular Reform (2011) 17 *J. Legal Writing Inst.* 233 at 235-236.

[70] Murray, above n. 17.

appeal court a front answer (ethos).[71] In the rule section, the brief-writer provides the legal standard to govern the issue, by supplying the general major premise for the enthymeme [or what some may prefer to call the deductive syllogism] (logos). In this section also the writer demonstrates his skills in researching the law that the complain of the appellant is not about how the undefended list procedure plays out in litigation, thereby bring to fore his grounding as respected researcher who has distilled the substance of the appeal (ethos). The section on rule explanation combines all the three forms of persuasion. In explaining how the undefended list procedure has been interpreted and applied based on inductive reasoning, the writer applies logos. By further demonstrating how the courts have analyzed and synthesized in factual situations over time the rule on undefended list procedure, he induces the reader emotionally to apply the rules in the instant case in the respondent's favour. The brilliant synthesizing of the cases for the judges so that they have no need to do the research themselves is credibility plus for the writer (ethos). The rule application/facts section is in fact employs several levels of logos, pathos and ethos, as the brief-writer intersperse rule, rule explanation, stories and conclusion into one mold and square. The minor premise for the enthymeme on the issue of alleged breach is analyzed (logos). He uses the narrative reasoning to make the necessary emotive appeal (pathos), while the proper intersperse of the facts with the rules of precedent establishes the writers 'reputation as a good brief-writer in the eyes of the judges (ethos). The section on conclusion is it. It reaches a conclusion on the enthymeme (logos) and indicates to the reader that the discussion has come to an end, the enthymeme properly applied (ethos).

Any lawyer reading the brief will readily see that even though the brief does not follow the *IRAC* structure, it is a good brief. All its content follows an agreed-upon analytical elements intelligent by lawyers and judges modest count of a good brief. It articulates the rule, explains it and any ambiguities thereto, stating how the rule should apply in the instant case. Noteworthy of mention, it uses the intersperse style of argumentation. Facts and the rules are argued together in all material sections from introduction to conclusion, thereby adopting the three pathways of persuasion, logos, pathos and ethos, without necessarily following a rigid rule-based *IRAC* formula that keeps the components tightly separated from one another. The brief writer constructs her own schemata for communicating legal analysis in a manner within the bracket of grammar understandable to the legal community and readers.

---

[71] Framing question for determination in the form of thesis is not a common practice with Nigerian lawyers, but it enjoys the advantage of supplying an interim conclusion, which is pleasing to impatient readers. See Murray, above n. 17.

This is the kind of brief-writing style that our students need to learn about. That legal writing requires a variety of ways to communicate the facts of any given case, and that style can differ depending on the type of analysis required (whether it is a facts-intensive case or rule-intensive litigation). For example, if an analysis requires discussion on policy, such as is usually the case in regulatory practice, rule explanation may be heavier with lighter facts/scientific articulation. If on the other hand, it is a matter having to do with say, custody or matters of asylum or matrimonial proceedings, which require intensive-facts litigation, stories will be heavier than rule explanation.[72]

Recognizing that legal reasoning often rest on probabilities is what should encourage legal writing teachers to model analysis in ways that incorporates logos, pathos and ethos in writing assignments, a project greatly helped by the indeterminacy thesis of facts and language.[73]

VI. Comparing the Persuasive Power of *IRAC* with the Flexible (Non-*IRAC*) Styles of Writing

All of this talk will be unhelpful if we fail to compare the persuasiveness of *IRAC* and non-*IRAC* structure of legal writing, using writing analogy drawn from non-flexible and flexible, contextual styles. First let us illustrate the point from a variety of employment perspective requiring legal writing. Legal employment was traditional thought to fall within two categories: litigation and transactional lawyering. With the growth of regulation in the modern state, we may now add regulatory practice, as a new area of legal practice.[74] In regulatory practice, lawyers spend time advising clients about the nature and scope of their obligations under various regulatory regimes, ranging from employment, banking, telecommunication, food and drug, health care, immigration, tax, transportation and a host many others; while representing their clients before government regulators, whether in drafting comments in response to notices of proposed rulemaking or in agency-level enforcement proceedings. On the government side, regulatory lawyers focus on writing legislation, developing regulations, drafting guidance documents, and pursuing enforcement actions. We have therefore chosen to discuss the persuasive viability of the *IRAC* and non-*IRAC*

---

[72] For illustrative brief writing of fact-intensive cases, see for example, Miller, above n. 54; White, above n. 54; Stacy Caplow, Putting the "I" in Wr*t*ng: Drafting an A/Effective Personal Statement to Tell a Winning Refuge Story (2008) 14 *J. Legal Writing Inst.* 249 (the use of pathos in asylum law).

[73] For example, see Michael D. Murray, above n. 64. See also, Festus Emiri & Ayuba Giwa, Metaphoric Thinking About Law as Language and Lawyering as Translation: Reflection on Legal Clinic [2008] *Enugu State University of Technology Journal of Public Law* 15.

[74] Kristin E. Hickman, Designing a Broader Regulatory Practice Curriculum, *RegBlog*, Penn Programme on Regulation, Aug. 15, 2016.

organizational structure in legal writing within the three categories: transactional lawyering, regulatory practice and litigation practice.

1. Transactional Documents

Let us first consider transactional legal writing. How can lawyers be more persuasive in drafting transactional documents? Does the linear, stock-position writing or the flexible, narrative technique more properly persuade and communicate?[75] What analogical lessons can be learnt from this comparism, that can be transposed to the linear IRAC and flexible non-IRAC techniques of writing? It is generally reasoned that the inflexible, copied from precedent style of writing or drafting is what matters in transactional documents. Contextual, flexible, story like style should have no place in drafting transactional document. Such reasoning is rooted in the thinking that documents are essentially expository texts, designed to inform rather than relay a story. For example, in a simple conveyance, all the document need tell (so it is erroneously thought) to state that the seller desires to sell at a given price and the buyer is interested in the purchase. The usual conveyancing clause relating to property description, covenants and the like are added to complete documentation.

Storytelling teachers however know better. We say that the fact that documents are essentially expository should not ordinarily abyss the narrative style in their drafting. It is flawed reasoning to think that stories enjoy a lesser place of prominence in transactional lawyering.[76] The reason isn't farfetched. Think for once. Every transaction is in truth a story. It is the stories that give life to transactions. It is it that metamorphoses to become the basis of agreements and the ultimate clauses of documents executed by the parties. Think for once, is a conveyance not a story of negotiation, title investigation, and the purchase agreement? If it is, then it is plausible to imagine that the ability of lawyers to visualise and conceptualise transactions as stories benefits the negotiation, drafting, implementation, interpretation, and the ultimate enforceability of the transaction document.[77]

Let us consider how good lawyering requires contextualising transactional documents in areas where there is stock-story perception.[78] The existence of

---

[75] Susan M. Chesler & Karen J. Sneddon, Once Upon a Transaction: Narrative Techniques and Drafting (2016) 68 *Oklahoma L. Rev.* 263

[76] Chesler & Sneddon, above n. 75 (The learned writers drawing analogical on narrative techniques highlight the use of stock stories, plot and narrative movement, character, point of view, narrative setting, themes, and motifs across a spectrum of transactional documents).

[77] Chesler & Sneddon, above n. 75 at 268 ("narrative techniques further the attorney-client relationship by promoting a closer examination of individual client goals and designing documents to further those goals").

[78] Stock stories are conventional story type stripped of essential details but they carry cognitive models easily inferred by those who hear or perceive them. For example, it is easy to stereotype a man on

adverse stock story should discourage linear drafting style without effort to customize the document to reflect the client's specific goals. One such areas highlighted by Chesler and Sneddon, is premarital (prenuptial) agreement. Medieval history tells us that these were agreements specifically designed for protection of women at a time when they enjoyed no property rights. They were essentially conceived to detail financial and non-financial responsibilities in the economic alliances between families created by marriage. Courts were however reluctant in enforcing them because they were thought of as encouraging divorces. That is the stock story behind premarital agreements.[79] It is also the thinking that since most premarital agreements were widely used by the rich, then such agreements is limited to high-net-worth individuals or families. That is the stock character of ante nuptial agreements.

Faced with this stock position, how would students stewed in the *IRAC* linear writing style draft a premarital agreement for a client? The natural drafting technique after receiving client's instruction would be to take a precedent book, copy and paste with a few modifications. That being the case, they would have done nothing to thinker the stock story surrounding the type of agreement. In the event of litigation arising from the document, the interpreting authority is deprived the narrative benefits the client's specific needs so its implementation, interpretation, and the ultimate enforceability of the transaction document may just well follow the usual run of reluctance by the court to enforce.

All of that can change by simply using a recursive, storytelling writing technique that tells a story. Employing, say the narrative style, enables the drafter to take deliberate steps to thinker and reframe the document in a way that can supplant stock position. After all, what is wrong to clarify financial aspects of marriage that will eventually end in death or divorce? The learned writers give a few examples of how the document can be contextualized to displace stock story misunderstandings. One simple way suggested is to modify the standard acontextual premarital recital. The standard draft would look like this:

---

dreadlocks wearing jean as a Rastafarian. Such automatic identification may prevent audience engagement with contrary narrative experience. For reading on stock story and cognition see, Vicki Schultz, Telling Stories About Women and Work: Judicial Interpretation of Sex Segregation in the Workplace in Title VII Cases Raising the Lack of Interest Argument (1990) 103 *Harv. L. Rev.* 1749; Mary Chiarella, Silence in Court: The Devaluation of the Stories of Nurses in the Narratives of Health Law (2000) 7 *Nursing Inquiry* 191 (the stock story of nurses as caregivers to patients, handmaiden of doctors or ministering angels, undermines the status of nurses which translated to a framework that devalues their professional opinion); Stephen Paskey, The Law Is Made of Stories (2014) 11 *Legal Comm. & Rhetoric: JALWD* 51 at 69.

[79] For a history and jurisprudence of premarital agreements, see Baker, History of English Law, *Snell's Equity*; Judith Younger, Perspectives on Ante-nuptial Agreements (1988) 40 *Rutgers L. Rev.* 1059; Brian Bix, Bargaining in the Shadow of Love: The Enforcement of Premarital Agreements and How We Think About Marriage (1998) 40 *WM & Mary L. Rev.* 145; J. Thomas Oldman, With All My Worldly Goods I Thee Endow, or Maybe Not: A Reevaluation of the Uniform Premarital Agreement Act After Three Decades (2001) 19 *Duke J. Gender L. & Pol'y* 83.

A. Marriage is intended soon between the parties.

B. Each party desires, before entering into the marriage, to know just what the rights of property are to be in each other's estate.

No question about it. The recital is accurate. But it misses context.[80] So it falls within the mould of stock story surrounding premarital agreements. To avoid the stock-position label, the recital could well be reframed this way:

A. Each party acknowledges and stipulates the purpose of this Agreement is not to promote or procure a divorce or dissolution of marriage, but to provide for marital tranquillity by agreeing on the property and support rights of each other at the commencement of marriage.

B. The parties have determined that the marriage between then shall have a better chance of success if the rights and claims that accrue to each of them as a result of their marriage are determined and finalized by this Agreement.

This later writing technique says it all. It contextualizes the party's intention, supplants the stock position, eliminates ambiguity, reframes the narrative by highlighting the party's specific goals. Deliberate use of this narrative non-IRAC paradigm as in the example above, puts the clients on the centre burner and leverages their presence to further their intention.[81]

2. Regulatory legal writing.

It can no longer be seriously doubted that regulation is now part of modern society. Virtually no part of society or our lives is untouched by regulation. Government is gradually turning modern societies to regulatory states. There is virtually no part of our lives unregulated by the state. The state regulates education, food, movement, businesses etc. It regulates who can vote, how to vote, what we eat, listen to or hear from the radio or television, and many others. It is not uncommon to hear individuals, groups and businesses that rail under legislation and regulations which threaten their existence and concerns question the ambits of the powers of the state. It is therefore important to legally analysis the range of activities covered in the modern state by growing legislation and regulation, especially in the context of whether the regulatory state is effectively mitigating the economic and non-economic problems regulation addresses. Yes,

---

[80] Chesler & Sneddon, above n. 75 at 273.

[81] On furthering other narrative techniques in transactional drafting, see Chesler & Sneddon, above n. 75. See also Frank L McGuane, Jr. & Kathleen A. Hogan, Drafting the Agreement Not to Encourage Dissolution, in *Colorado Prac., Family Law & Practice*, chapter 39.7, Drafting the Agreement-Not to Encourage Dissolution, 2nd ed. 2012, cited in Chesler & Sneddon, Id at 273 n. 45 (narrative in ante nuptial agreement); Joseph M. Williams & Gregory G. Colomb, Telling Clear Stories: A Principle of Revision that Demands a Good Character (1996) 5 *Persp. Teaching Legal Res. & Writing* 14 (on descriptive information about the parties in the background or recital section of agreements to provide three dimensional reference to the parties, such as on which includes (i) the human character of the parties, say (ii) seller and (iii) buyer rather than the two-dimensional reference of only seller and buyer).

from communication fees, grazing, food safety, financial institutions to welfare and education, government reels out one form of regulation or the other.[82] The key to regulatory law is rooted in the philosophy that legal rules are nothing but responses to market failure.[83]

How can narratives be interspersed with regulation to persuade. Let us imagine that the government of Layanda, a pastoral and agrarian country seeks to acquire land from farmers to be used as ranches for pastoral purposes because of constant clashes between nomadic herdsmen and farmers over grazing land. Assuming a lawyer is hired to oppose the legislative proposal before Parliament, how can she structure persuasive writing in this regard? An integrated technique using *logos, pathos* and *ethos* stands the chance more of persuading than a non-narrative rule-based approach.

She may need to draft the letter using the section technique: beginning with the narrative section, using *pathos*. This section would ordinarily employ the storytelling technique- a narrative plot telling how farmer come unto their land, how land is reified and connected with ancestralship, why farming is an integral part of the lives of her clients, transcending property-personhood dichotomy, how her clients stable agrarian living, culture, tradition and existence is troubled by herdsmen, what efforts have been put in place to peacefully resolve the troubles, how it has failed to resolve the trouble, and why their ancestral rights (as protagonists) should be protected in the face of two invading antagonists, the herdsmen, with implicit support of the state; why it should be of concern in a modern democratic state; and the moral justification for preventing taking.[84]

It is after a narrative of this sort that the lawyer can then resort to *logos*, sometimes mixing it with *pathos* and *ethos* to create effect, in the section on rules, rules explanation, interpretation of law, policy and application. The section on

---

[82] For literature on regulatory law, see Sidney A. Shapiro & Joseph P. Tomain, *Regulatory Law and Policy*, 1993; Stephen Breyer, *Regulation and Its Reform*, 1984; Samuel Peltzman, Towards a More General Theory of Regulation (1976) 19 *J. L. & Econ.* 211; Sidney A. Shapiro, Keeping the Baby and Throwing Out the Bathwater: Justice Breyer's Critique of Regulation (1995) 8 *Admin. L.J. Am. Univ.* 721; John Manning & Matthew, Legislation and Regulation; Lisa, Edward Rubin & Kevin Stack, *The Regulatory State*; Geoffrey P. Miller, *The Law of Governance, Risk Management and Compliance* (focus on risk definition, assessment, and management, which requires the identification of risk and ex ante preventive action); See also Penn Programme on Regulation at the University of Pennsylvania, *RegBlog*, especially *RegBlog* five-part series, Innovations in Teaching Regulatory Law, Aug. 15, 2016. Generally, after the financial thunderstorms between 2007 and 2009 in the U.S. compliance and regulatory programmes sprouted like mushrooms in both the U.S and around the world.

[83] Joseph P. Tomain & Sidney A. Shapiro, Analysing Government Regulation (1997) 49 *Admin. L. Rev.* 376 at 402 ("The presence of ... market failure serves as a justification for the government to enter and fix a market in order to achieve better allocative efficiency. . .. regulation is unnecessary in the absence of efficiency defects.")

[84] This type of dramatic introduction aligns with literary theory and can be persuasive to the reader. For illustration of its usefulness of pathos in persuasion, see Elyse Pepper, The Case for "Thinking Like a Filmmaker:" Using Lars von Trier's Dogville as a Model for Writing a Statement of Facts (2008) 14 *J. Legal Writing Inst.* 171; Stacy Caplow, above n. 72 (the use of pathos in asylum law).

rules could begin by asking the rhetoric question of 'why government regulate activities?' from there the argument could build up to rule explanation. The state regulates for two main reasons: (i) for economic or (ii) non-economic (social) reasons. But in all cases to correct market failure.[85] The reason for this is because legal economists have long believed that the invisible hand of the market creates allocative efficiency and distributive gains.[86] Under an economic justification, an absence of market failure makes it unnecessary for government to regulate, such as change the assignment of rights and obligations, which the bill proposes.[87] However, since markets can sometimes be defective (which is referred to as 'market failure') their will be justification for government to regulate market to create the necessary allocative efficiency. For social justification, the analysis starts from the premise that government is necessitated by a people who set up a political structure on certain core values (generally referred to in economics are 'market inalienable') on how they wish to be organised.[88] If markets therefore

---

[85] For literature analysis of the economic justification for regulation see, Sidney A. Shapiro & Joseph O. Tomain, *Regulatory Law and Policy: Cases and Materials,* LexisNexis, 1993; Stephen G. Breyer & Richard B. Stewart, *Administrative Law and Regulatory Policy: Problems Text and Cases,* 3rd ed., Aspen Pub., 1992, 5-11, (7th ed. 2015); Richard Posner, *Economic Analysis of Law,* 4th ed., 1992, 367-368; Joseph P. Tomain & Sidney A. Shapiro, Analysing Government Regulation (1997) *Admin. L. Rev.* 377. It must be noted however that not every market failure invites an ex ante regulatory solution. A great deal of market failures are addressed directly by courts through common-law or statutory remedies that award damages ex post to injured persons. Thus, regulation would be necessary if a market fails, and courts are unable to address the problem with the remedial ambits of law. See also George J. Stigler, The Theory of Economic (1971) 2 *Bell J. Econ. & Mgmt. Sci.* 3; Richard A. Posner, Theories of Economic Regulation (1974) 5 *Bell J. Econ. & Mgmt. Sci.* 335; Samuel Peltzman, Towards a More General Theory of Regulation (1976) 19 *J. Law & Econ.* 211; Benjamin H. Barton, Why Do We Regulate Lawyers? An Economic Analysis of the Justification for Entry and Conduct Regulation (2001) 33 *Ariz. St. L.J.* 429.

[86] Adam Smith, *Wealth of the Nation.* Global demand for deregulation is grounded on the assumption that free market is better than government regulation. See Herbert Hovenkamp, *Enterprise and American Law: 1836-1937,* Cambridge, Massachusetts: Harvard Univ. Press, 1991; Cass R. Sunstein, *After the Rights Revolution, Preconceiving the Regulatory State,* 1990. See also for example Elizabeth Landes and Richard Posner, The Economics of Baby Shortage, (1987) 7 *J. Leg. St.* 323 (advocates an adoption market for babies). But cf. Frankel & Miller, The Inapplicability of Market Theory to Adoption (1986) 67 *Boston Univ. L. Rev.* 99; Prichard, A Market for Babies? (1984) 34 *Univ. Toronto L.J.* 341.

[87] Ronald Coase, The Problem of Social Cost (1960) 3 *J. Law & Econ.* 1; see reprinted in Ronald Coase, *The Firm, the Market, and the Law,* Chicago Univ. Press, 1988. The paper is reputed to be the most cited law paper in the world. See Fred R. Shapiro, The Most Cited Law Review Article Revisited (1996) 71 *Chi.-Kent L. Rev.* 751. See also, W.N. Landes & Richard Posner, The Influence of Economics on Law: A Quantitative Study (1993) 36 *J. of Law & Econs. 385,* (on recent study which suggest that the major American law journals cite articles using the economic approach more than articles using other approach in legal scholarship).

[88] Market inalienable follows commodification argument that certain kind of activities are of intrinsic value that a market valuation of them is inappropriate in that it distorts significantly their tangibility. Inappropriateness of market principles to such values has often rested on lines of property-personhood dichotomy and incommensurability hypothesis. See *Hegel's Philosophy of Rights,* London: Oxford Univ. Press, translated by T.M. Knox, 1952, s.44) cited in Neil Neil Duxbury, Do Markets Degrade? (1996) 59 *MLR* 331. For further reading on incommensurability in philosophical literature see, Joseph Raz, Mixing Values, *Proceedings of the Aristotelian Society* 83; J. Griffin, Mixing Values, (1991) 65 *Proceedings of the Aristotelian Society* 65; J. Griffin, Are There Incommensurable Values? (1977) 7 *Philosophy & Public Affairs* 39; Joseph Raz, *The Morality of Freedom,* Oxford: Clarendon Press, 1986, 339-340; Margaret

operate in such manner that discounts the values, the government will be justified in intervening to correct the defects by conforming market operation to those values. In effect, law can be used to also constrain markets. From this paradigm, regulation is unnecessary in the absence of efficiency defects.[89]

Honourable Parliamentarians, the difference between economic and social justification for regulation can be liken to that between *efficiency* and *equity.* While both can be strong currents in any political system, trumping one another, both cannot be ignored in regulatory.[90]

Economic regulation addresses three types of market failures- (i) natural monopoly; (ii) excessive competition; (iii) and economic rents. Regulatory prescription for correction are either by price control or entry and exit controls.

On the other hand, non-economic reasons for regulation addresses four market failures: negative externalities, asymmetric information, scarcity and public goods. Government response to this market failure is with the tools of regulatory or allocative controls.

Why is a discussion on the justificatory bases for regulation and the tools of regulation necessary? Simply this. To prevent what Justice Breyer has termed regulatory mismatches.[91]

The next section could then be termed "the bill and justificatory analysis."

In this section, the writer situates the analysis in the context of the bill, by analysing why and how it possibly sits outside of or in the regulatory square in section 2 above. An intersperse discussion employing the triangular persuasion techniques will come to fuller play here.

For example, the writer could employ the Coase theorem regulating basic assignment of rights in the context of incompatible-users right, analogically extending it to the herdsmen-farmers incompatible land use, to show that forced

---

Radin, *Reinterpreting Property,* Chicago: Univ. of Chicago Press, 1993; Brian Bix, *Law, Language and Legal Determinacy,* Oxford: Clarendon Press, 1993, 96; Cass Sunstein, Incommensurability and Valuation in Law (1994) 92 *Michigan L. Rev.* 779, Anderson, *Value in Ethics and Economics,* Cambridge, Mass: Harvard Univ. Press, 150. But cf. Schnably, Property and Pragmatism: A Critique of Radin's Theory of Property and Personhood (1993) 45 *Stanford L. Rev.* 347. Neil Duxbury, Law, Markets and Valuation (1995) 61 *Brooklyn L. Rev.* 657; Guido Calabresi & Douglas Melamed, Property Rules, Liability Rules and Inalienability: One View of the Cathedral (1972) 85 *Harv. Law Rev.* 1089; Festus Emiri, A Market Approach to Vocational Legal Education in Nigeria in *Trajectory of Nigerian Law: Underneath is Festschrift of Dean Smith* (ed. Ibidapo-Obe, Lagos: Lagos Univ. Press, 2015, 144.

[89] Tomain & Shapiro, above n. 78.

[90] Arthur A. Leff, Economic Analysis of Law: Some Realism about Nominalism (1974) 60 *Virginia L. Rev.* 451 (a critique of pure economic analysis to legal and social questions in reaction to the first publication of Richard A. Posner's, *Economic Analysis of Law* book).

[91] Stephen Breyer, *Regulation and its Reform,* Cambridge, MA: Harvard Univ. Press, 1982, 191-368; Stephen Breyer, Analyzing Regulatory Failure: Mismatches, Less Restrictive Alternatives and Reform (1979) 92 *Harv. L. Rev.* 549 at 586-604.

taking in the form of compulsory acquisition power vested in the proposed commission does not align with economic logic. [92]

In this section, the writer would be required to use the form of narrative that brings to fore, character development like a fiction writer, so that the reader can quickly spot the protagonist worthy of sympathy against the antagonist. The persuasive, skilled writer is here required to provide proof of each character in the trouble by piling objective detail, arranged in such a way to evoke emotional response by the reader. Again, argument using both logos, pathos and ethos. The persuasive writer can then launch more missiles against the bill by drawing on the specific narrative of her client, regulatory justification, arguments showing why the bill does not come within the framework justification for economic or non-economic reasons and conclude.

No question about it. An argument that employs the three dimensions of rhetoric would be more convincing to Parliament than the linear inflexible writing style.

3. Litigation (brief) writing

We shall unashamedly use the scenario of Chestek to navigate the richness of flexible organizational structure over the usual non-flexible style. We have chosen to draw on the scenario used by the learned writer for many reasons.[93] (List the reasons)

---

[92] Coase theorem is the most celebrated application of the concept of opportunity cost. See Ronald H. Coase, The Problem of Social Cost, (1960) 3 *Law & Economics* 1, see reprint in Coase, *The Firm, the Market, and the Law,* Chicago Univ. Press, 1988. See also Ronald Coase, The Nature of the Firm (1937) 4 *Economica* 386. The theorem posits that under conditions of rational cooperation, full information and zero transactional costs, parties will negotiate around inefficiencies to allocate rights in order to establish optimal level of resource deployment. See also George Stigler, Economics: The Imperial Science? (1984) 86 *Scand. J. Econ* 301 at 304. Economists also think so of law. Efficiency in a legal situation arises if a right is given to a party willing to pay more for it. This explains why if the Coasean market is unavailable courts are urged to imagine what the parties would have agreed to in a hypothetical Coasean market. Since the right to a resource will have been secured by the party willing to pay most for it, court are expected to mimic by auctioning entitlements to those who value them most - judged by each litigant's willingness to pay. See Jules Coleman, Economics and the Law: A Critical Review of the Foundations of the Economic Approach to Law (1984) 94 *Ethics* 649, Richard Posner, *Economic Analysis of Law,*8th ed., 2011. But cf. David Campbell, 'Ayer versus Coase; An Attempt to Recover the Issue of Equality in Law and Economics,' (1994) 21 *J. Law &* Society 434, for critique of law and economics pure materialistic theory of rights. But economists defend its position on the grounds that the term 'efficiency' when used to denote allocation of resources in which value is maximised does not extend to ethical criterion as basis for social decision-making. See Richard Posner, p. 16. But cf. Richard Posner, *The Problem of Jurisprudence,* Harvard Univ. Press, 1990, 375 (where learned writer doubted efficiency as an overreaching normative basis for law) and Guido Calabresi, *The Costs of Accidents: A Legal and Economic Analysis,* New Haven: Yale Univ. Press, 1970, 17-18 (argues that while efficiency should not be disregarded the legal system should draw a balance between consequentialist and principle-based ethics).

[93] Kenneth D. Chestek, The Plot Thickens: The Appellate Brief as Story (2008) 14 *J. Legal Writing Inst.* 127. For other great stories on how lawyers have written persuasive briefs, see

The essence of the appellate brief is a story of adoption by a homosexual parent resisted by the state.[94] It is the story of Margaret Rubin, who is devastated by the loss of her homosexual partner, Francie Kohler, and the attempt of the legal system to take away her son from her, on the grounds that the marriage is not recognized by the *lex fori,* Old York, the residence of the parties. The gist of the matter is that both couple married of ten years and had a son, Johnnie, through *in vitro* fertilization (IVF). The marriage was entered into in Vermont, a state that permits the union of gay and lesbian couples. So what Margaret and Francie did was to leave Old York, a state that does not approve of lesbian marriage to marry in Vermont, a state that recognizes lesbian marriages. In fact, the Old York Supreme Court refuses to recognize the validity of Vermont gay marriages.

On the death of Francie, Margaret wanted to adopt Johnnie and continue to raise him. But Margaret's mother who has always been opposed to the lesbian marriage resisted the adoption. She asked the Old York State to declare Johnnie a dependent child and place him in a foster home because under the law Margaret has no legal claim to guardianship. The law does not recognize lesbian marriages. What is more, the state adoption prohibits homosexuals from adoption. That is the stage plotted in the story.

Faced with this fact-intensive situation what style of writing would be more persuasive to convince a court to permit Margaret to adopt Johnnie, a flexible or non-flexible analysis? What would be the shape of the IRAC argument here for Margaret? You can imagine it going this way: a review of the constitutionality of the Old York State adoption law. It will be dry and simply abstract with little or no power to convince. The technique will leave little room to dramatize the humanness of Margaret.

It can read this way:

1. *Section on Introduction*

This is an application by Margaret Rubin to adopt Johnnie, her son, against the wish of Francie Kohler's mother asking that Johnnie be declared a dependent child, placing him in a foster home. Margaret married Francie in 2000, ten year ago in Vermont, a state that permits gay and lesbian marriages. In the couple desire to mature and raise a child, they decided to go through IVF, which help give birth to Johnnie in 2003.

The couple and their son lived happily thereafter in Old York until Francie was killed in a car-pedestrian accident, necessitating the present application by Margaret to adopt Johnnie with a view of continuing his care under her superintendence. It is this application that Francie's mother is opposed to.

---

[94] This story is fictional, product of a modified moot court problem from Indianapolis School of Law, Indiana University in 2004. See Chestek, above n. 93 at 128 n. 1.

2. *Section on Issue(s) for Determination*

The main issue that arises for determination in this case is whether it is constitutional for the Old York statute to deny Margaret adoption rights over Johnnie, her child or put otherwise, whether Margaret should be entitled to succeed in her application for adoption under the adoption statute of Old York State.

3. *Section on Rule*

Section 19-67-2 provides that the following persons are eligible to adopt: (1) a husband and wife together, or (2) an adult who is not married. Subsection (B) however states that "homosexuals are not eligible to adopt under the statute.

Noteworthy of mention, subsection (B) was not in the original legislation. It was only added after a highly publicized incident of a prominent musician was convicted for sexually abusing an adopted child. See *State v Smith* (1985) 489 O.Y. 142.

This said prohibition violates the constitution of the United States, especially the protected rights to privacy; right to family integrity; due process right and it discriminates homosexual rights to equal treatment.

(The remaining part of the section would then go on to relate how it does in specifics of say the Fourteenth Amendment, Due Process Clause (Amend. XIV, cl.3), Equal Protection Clause (Amend XIV, cl. 4) and the like)

It will end by asking the court to declare the Old York statute unconstitutional, especially when it is not narrowly tailored to serve a "compelling state interest."

4. *Section on Application of Rules*

This section would ordinarily synthesize the facts of the case with the rules asking the court to scrutinize the state legislation in the context of the constitution and the peculiar facts of Margaret.

5. *Section on Conclusion*

This section will pray the court to overturn the state legislation and declare Margaret eligible for adoption of Johnnie.

That is how an *IRAC* brief is likely to be structured. If in the brief-writer's opinion the brief involves multiple issues and sub-issues than the one issue plotted in this chapter, then the writer will simply do a brief with multiple syllogisms. The writer may have to repeat the IRAC structure in multiple sections and sub-section, which ordinarily would involve rule, application and conclusion being repeated. To say the least, that can make the brief burdensome and a monotonous read.[95] Whether the single issue or multiple issues brief *IRAC* style is used, the structure above certainly feels linear, mechanical and abstract. A heavy reliance on *logos*, with little of *pathos* and *ethos*.[96]

The *IRAC* brief plotted above has noticeable features: (i) It is rule-based. The U.S. Constitution is analyzed and applied to the state legislation as possible topics for court scrutiny to determine if it is rational in the context of legitimate state interest; (ii) It is deeply rooted in rules, with little space for human narrative. The issue for determination is what sets the stage for the proper level of scrutiny. Invariably, the "R" becomes confined to a pure question of law, previous decisions of court measuring the application of the constitution to matters of rights; and (iii) Operating under the *logos* bracket of *IRAC* leaves little room to personalize the story of Margaret. A brief written in that style will hardly persuade. Such a mechanical attack on the statute will hardly persuade a court usually more interested in preserving the status of legislation.

A non-*IRAC* structure that plays the human drama of the case is more likely to help overcome the statutory barriers. Consciously thinking about the case as one requiring human elements of character, conflict, theme, and point of view can add the missing link. The learned writer suggests that employing the style of fictional writing can do the magic.[97] The transformational appellant brief written to the Supreme Court of Old York State is compelling that we have chosen to highlight some material sections of the brief to illustrated the persuasiveness of narrative structured briefs in especially facts-intensive legal writing. Its flow using narrative style would follow an organizational structure like this:

1. Section on Argument

---

[95] See Chestek, above n 93. But cf. Tracy Turner, Flexible IRAC: A Best Practice Guide (2015) 20 *J. Legal Writing Inst.* 233 (where the learned writer seeks to free IRAC from the its shackles by creating a best practice guide to it. The article argues that IRAC core syllogistic reasoning is still the template for good writing. See for example, outside the one-sequence IRAC, the writer makes useful suggestions on how to apply (i) "alternating IRAC" (IRARARAC)-places each application paragraph right after the corresponding rule paragraph so that a principle of law is applied as soon as it is introduced; (ii) "IRAC by paragraph" (IRACIRAIRAC)-an IRAC structure which bring each R and A together into a paragraph and add a topic sentence to unite them; (iii) "IRAC sentence"-an assertion about the legal impact of a fact followed by a parenthetical citation that proves the asserted impact; (iv) "narrative add-ons: mixing facts into the I of IRAC"-adding a narrative element to IRAC by using the facts of the case to introduce and set the stage for each RA sequence to engage and persuade the reader. See also, Laura P. Graham, Why-RAC? Revisiting the Traditional Paradigm for Writing About Legal Analysis (2015) 63 *Kansas L. Rev.* 681 at 693 (where the writer suggests a fresh view of IRAC that recognizes its value as a basic analytical framework but loosens its grip on students as legal writers).

[96] Chestek, above n. 93 at 163.

[97] Fiction writer and film producers often plot stories using the structure of setting, conflict, character, point of view/voice, theme, plot, introduction/exposition, complicated incidents/rising action, climax, resolution/falling action, denouement and conclusion. See Anthony G. Amsterdam & Jerome S. Bruner, *Minding the Law*, Harv. Univ. Press, 2000, 20; Chestek, above n. 87; Elyse Pepper, The Case for Thinking Like a Filmmaker: Using Lars von Trier's Dogville as a Model for Writing a Statement of Facts (2008) 14 *J. Legal Writing Inst.* 171; James P. Eyster, Lawyer as Artist: Using Significant Moments and Obtuse Objects to Enhance Advocacy (2008) 14 *J. Legal Writing Inst.* 87

Exposition (foundational law regarding standard of review, road map, legal conflict revealed)

A. Rising Action

i) First sub-plot (due process claim)-legal setting explained

Right to privacy and family integrity

    ii)   Second sub-plot (equal protection claim)-legal setting explained

             Suspect classification and quasi-suspect classification

{CLIMAX (the factual and legal settings are complete, the conflict is apparent, the protagonists are at maximum peril)}

B. Falling action

i) Safe escape from peril tested (strict/intermediate scrutiny)

ii) Risky escape from peril tested (rational basis review)

C. Conclusion (denouement)

How does it all play out in the narrative constructed? Let us do an abstract of a few personalization highlighted by the learned writer. The facts section is very revealing. It goes like this:

"Margaret and Francie only wanted a child.

Having committed themselves to each other emotionally and legally, they decided, as do many committed couples, that they wanted to raise a family. But the state of Old York told them that they were unfit parents, simply because they loved each other. Without knowing anything about the depth and sincerity of Margaret and Francie commitment to each other, and without any individualized investigation into their fitness as parents, the state categorically declared that they, along with all other gay and lesbian citizens, were unfit to adopt and raise children."

It then goes on to narrate how the couple devoted to their dream travelled to Vermont to legalize their relationship; how they attempted without success to seek agencies approval to adopt; how they then resorted to IVF which eventually produced Johnnie; what adjustment they made in their personal lives to create a happy family life and conducive environment for raising their child; how Francie got killed in an accident; the bond between Margaret and Johnnie; etc.

This narrative plot brings to fore the human elements of character (the story of a loving family, the kind law should promote, the hurdle erected by the state which prevents them to marry and raise a family, how they as protagonist scaled the pillars of hurdle erected by the state as antagonist, by the couple resort to travel to Vermont for their marriage and modern reproductive technology to raise a family). This is no doubt a great introduction preluding the beginning of the "rising action" of the story plot.

The rising action is the sudden intestate death of Francie, the couple not having planed and arranged their affairs. This absence is what introduces another antagonist to the scene, the mother of Francie, who now seeks a custodial regime over Johnnie. The rising action is part of the facts section which provides the setting for a discussion of the legal section, the relevant rules that govern the resolution of the facts situation.

Since the statute prohibits lesbian adoption, the strategy most likely to persuade will be to create at least a plausible reason to preserve the stable family life for Margaret and Johnnie, by showing the irrationality of disrupting a stable, loving home, and putting Johnnie in a state facility most probably devoid of love and attention. Here the writer gives a history of the unreasonableness of the prohibition, showing that it is adopted out of animus towards homosexuals without individualization perspective and consideration of the "best interest" of the child analysis and further that it is not one within the protected state legitimate interest.

No question about it. This narrative non-*IRAC* organization structure is more persuasive and compelling for being client-centered. The article happily tells that the brief written in the narrative form was successful as the Supreme Court of Old York held in favor of Margaret. The lesson from the narrative brief is that thinking about lawyering as storytelling gives us the opportunity to look behind and between black letter rules, which possibly reveals facts, language, structure and ideas that go beyond abstract stipulations of statute and opinion of courts.[98] Narrative style briefs help lawyers to wrestle with the law, to have it fit into their client's lived realities and experience, rather than funneling their realities into what they think law requires. This is a hallmark of good legal writing.[99]

VII. How to Teaching Robust Legal Writing Skills

The rest of this chapter will be devoted to what teachers can do to free their students from the shackles of *IRAC*. The paradigm no doubt can be a helpful tool for beginners of legal writing, who are faced with how to synthesis human complexities into logical form of reasoning. The basic quarrel with it is its inflexibility in capturing and evaluating legal questions by sheer rule-based formula.

How have some teachers been able to recreate flexible writing styles? Some commentators however thinks that *IRAC* should not be sacrificed for client's centeredness, urging that both are not necessarily adverse concepts.[100] Turner for

---

[98] Carolyn Grose, Storytelling Across the Curriculum: From Margin to Center, from Clinic to Classroom (2010) 7 *J. Ass'n Legal Writing Directors* 37. On the need to develop case theory with the client at the centre, see cite from simulation paper.

[99] Carolyn Grose, Of Victims, Villains and Fairy Godmothers: Regnant Tales of Predatory Lending (2010) 2 *Northeastern Univ. L.J.* 97.

[100] Tracy Turner, above n. 95 (demonstrates who IRAC can be adapted to integrate narrative details often discouraged by rigid adherence to IRAC).

example, argues that teachers can re-create flexible I*RAC* to capture complex analysis without discarding *IRAC.* Her argument is that the paradigm is useful in legal writing if teachers can identify its variants under a common vocabulary that can be tailor-specific to the facts in controversy. So rather than abandon IRAC, she argues for its more sophisticated adaptations.[101] Let us examine her thesis in the context of a multidisciplinary approach.

In a bid to save *IRAC* the learned articulates four adaptation of the rule that should align it with fact centred lawyering: (i) one sequence *IRAC* (IRRRAAAC); (ii) alternating *IRAC* (IRACARAC); (iii) IRAC by paragraph (IRA-IRA-IRA-C); and (iv) the IRAC sentence.[102] Even at this, she recognizes that the four flexible adaptation of *IRAC* will be limited in injecting narrative elements within them. To cure the suppose deficiency, she suggests what can be called *narrative add-ons* in mixing facts with the "I" of *IRAC.* The technique requires that the narrative element to *IRAC* should use the facts of the case to introduce and set the stage for each "RA" sequence.[103] The addition of narratives makes brief more persuasive.[104] Narrative introduction to the "R-A" sequence fits naturally more in the *IRAC* by paragraph structure (iii); than the other *IRAC* structures (i), (ii) and (iv).[105] These notwithstanding, the thesis paragraph in all the four flexible *IRAC* can be used to weld facts to the law to escape the monotony of a universal, rigid *IRAC* structure. She therefore encourages an incremental approach to organizational writing techniques starting with *IRAC* and then moving on as the students mature to the variety of *IRAC* models that incorporates narrative elements in a creative, self-reliant way.[106] That is itself a useful suggestion, but the flexible Chestek brief in "The Plot Thickens" referred to in Part VII section 3 above hardly follows any of the Turner's suggested style.[107]

---

[101] Turner, above n. 95. See also Tracy Turner, Finding Consensus in Legal Writing Discourse Regarding Organizational Structure: A Review and Analysis of the Use of IRAC and Its Progenies (2012) 9 *Legal Comm. & Rhetoric: JALWD* 351 (listing forty articles that discuss the benefit of IRAC, stating that the various acronyms formulated as alternatives to IRAC show no marked departure from the core concept of IRAC).

[102] Turner, above n. 95 at 237.

[103] Id at 258.

[104] Kenneth D. Chestek, Judging by the Numbers: An Empirical Study of the Power of Story (2010) 7 *J. ALWD* 8 ("a brief that relies purely on a logos-based argument will be lifeless, just as a single strand of the DNA molecule is incomplete. Winding in a solid story-based argument will bring the brief to life.)" Id at 18. See also Linda Edwards, Convergence of Analogical of Analogical and Dialectic Imagination in Legal Discourse (1996) 20 *Legal Stud. F.* 13.

[105] Turner, above n. 95 at 262 and 264.

[106] Turner, above n. 95 at 273 ("The faculty advisor of our moot court team has told me that the IRAC modifications are helpful to transitioning students from first-year course to moot court brief writing: rigidly IRAC-ed briefs do not tend to win competitions.)"

[107] Chestek, above n 93. See also the judicial opinion in Baden, *Kotoye v CBN* [1989] All NLR 76; *Kigo v Holman* [1980] NSCC 204, per Kayode Esho, JSC.

Maybe we should let our readers see how we teach narrative elements using non-*IRAC* structure in our legal methods and writing class. We often use the *Speluncean Explorers* as our teaching case. It is an imaginative case written by Fuller in 1949.[108] Largely taking the form of a fictional judgment, it presents the case involving five explorers who were caved in following a landslide in a cave. They learn via radio communication that without food they would likely to starve to death before rescue. On this basis, they decide through throwing of a dice who should be killed and eaten for nourishment until rescue come their way. After the four survivors are rescued, they are charged and found guilty of the murder of the fifth explorer.

The appeal court offers five judicial responses to the facts whether they should be found guilty of breaching the law. Two judges affirm the conviction, two other overturn the conviction. The fifth judge is unable to reach a conclusion, so recuses himself. Since the court's decision is a tie, the original conviction stands.

We have used the *Speluncean* case over the years to teach our students how to analyse legal problems without necessarily following an *IRAC* style so that they can reason on basis gravitational organization scheme congruent with great brief writers' style and techniques. Immediately after mentioning the *IRAC* style, without emphasis that it is paradigmatic, we assign our students the *Speluncean* case to read and write their brief either in support of an affirmation of the four explorers conviction or in acquittal. We only forward to them the judgment of Truepenny, CJ, which states the facts of the case, the law applicable law and His Lordship's judgment that the facts are suitable for executive clemency to mitigate the rigors of law.

After assigning the students to read the case, we ask that they also read the Criminal Code provision on unlawful homicide of murder.[109] Their writing assignment on murder takes this form:

1. Read the facts in the Speluncean's case.
2. Read the law on murder in Nigeria, especially section 316 that define the ingredients of the offence.
3. As you read the case, make note of facts which suggest that the four explorers can prima facie be tried for murder of Whetmore.
4. Identify and note what broad issues for determination you think the court ought to resolve.

---

[108] it is based on an article by legal philosopher Lon L. Fuller, first published in the *Boner City* in 1949. The five possible solutions were delivered by judges sitting on the fictional "Supreme Court of Newgarth" in the year 4300. See Lon L. Fuller, The Case of the Speluncean Explorers (1949) 62 *Harv. L. Rev.*

[109] Criminal Code Act, s. 316 (definition of murder), Cap LFN 2004.

5. Read the case and law again, this time noting what you consider to be the narrow issues that flow from the broad issues that need to be resolved by the court.

6. As you read the case again, identify what policy matters can impact on the construction of the narrow questions for determination.

7. Using legal imagination, common sense and your experience about cave exploration, if any, reconstruct what narrow questions and facts you consider more significant in resolving the broad question you identify in step 4.

8. What facts will you use in resolving the narrow questions and how do you think this merges with the applicable rule.

9. Based on your reformulated narrow issue and step 7, write a brief of argument to the court how the issue you identify should be resolved.

Most of our students after following steps 1 and 2 come up to think that a prima facie indictment can be raised for a murder trial of the four explorers. From there they generally frame the broad issue for determination to be "whether or not the killing of Whetmore by the four defendants amount to murder under section 316 of the Criminal Code Act?" [Refer to this as "I" of the IRAC]

However, after rereading the case (step 5) they formulate some narrow issues which they suggest are helpful in defining and explaining the broad issue. [Refer to as rule explanation] Some at this point narrow the issues to questions such as "are the facts of this case not sufficiently peculiar to warrant the law permitting a discretion with respect to the penalty?" do not the extreme condition the defendants found themselves not qualify as self-defence; should the law on murder, a positive legislation trump the law of nature; what is the effect of law of contract entered into by all the explorers on the law of murder; does the extra-territorial place where the killing took place within the contemplation of the law on murder? Following steps 7 and 8 enables our students to identify more narrow issues such as the absurdity in sentencing the defendants to death remembering that saving them cost the state ten heroic workmen; etc.

By the time our students arrive at step 9 their brief is robust. The briefs are returned to them and the four other judgments delivered by Foster, Tatting, Keen and Handy, JJ of the Supreme Court of Newgarth are handed over to them to study.

The next writing class is used to draw out lesson on legal analysis and reasoning. They find that by noting and drawing the broad issues for determination in step 4 they have articulated the "I" of *IRAC*, step 5 helps them intersperse narrative construct with possible narrow issues. They at this stage are deepening reasoning in a way that issues connect with rule explanation and the facts of the case (something close to the *narrative add-ons* in the "R-A" sequence of the Tracy's flexible *IRAC* by paragraph structure. Steps 7 and 8 relate to more narratives and the conclusion (analogue to "A-C" of *IRAC*). As we review the judgments delivered by the other four judges, which they compare to their written briefs, they see that their briefs and the judicial opinion they have read in the case do not necessarily follow *IRAC*, but they all share what can be termed "gravitational or intellectual elements" of rules of law, explanation of the rules, and application of the rules to facts. We only mention to them about *IRAC* so that they know it is a style of analysis stepped in syllogism generally useful as primer in analysing simply disputes. This way they are not trained to be "knowledge-builders or legal creators" (who project client-cantered lawyering and client's theory of the case), rather than "knowledge-tellers or legal technicians" (who must funnel their client's reality to rules).[110]

What the examples above drives home is the point that *IRAC* can be useful in organizing thought process, especially for beginners and those slow in creative writing, but it is incapable of accounting for all the nuances of legal analysis and writing which reflects the complexities of human disagreements. That being so, writing teachers should help their students develop the flexible style of writing with gravitational fidelity for clear understandable. Since law and facts remain indeterminate, writing styles must recognize the importance of the three pillars of classical rhetoric-*logos, ethos,* and *pathos,* as a slavish adherence to *IRAC* and similar formulations sucks the life out of human conflicts.[111]

Graham also has suggested how teachers can help their students learn the flexible writing style without necessarily clinging to *IRAC.* His example is interesting. He states that he does it by deliberately incorporation of pre-writing into his writing class.[112] The learned scholar says he rarely mentions *IRAC* when teaching pre-writing strategies, although the teaching techniques used does cover the four components of *IRAC.[113]* His strategy has been useful in preparing his students to recognize the flexible nature of legal writing which incorporates

---

[110] See Paula Lustbader, Construction Sites, Building Types, and Bridging Gaps: A Cognitive Theory of the Learning Progression of Law Students (1997) 33 *Willamette L. Rev.* 314; Graham, above n at 708.

[111] Laura P. Graham, above n. 6 at 693. See also Chestek, above n. 93 (emphasizing the storytelling dimension in writing as critique of the IRAC paradigmatic structure, the commentator stated: " 'I' refers to the legal issue under consideration. No people in there. The same goes for 'R,' the rule. . . . 'A' has a bit of promise, if you take 'A' to mean application, but even then, people are just objects upon which the rule operates. And if you take 'A' to mean analysis, that is just more processing of the legal rule. The 'C,' or conclusion, is then just the legal conclusion that follows logically from the previous pieces. Law, law, law. Where did the people go in this process? Law, and the legal system, should be about people. It decides disputes between people and provides people with neutral rules conduct in civilized society. It is a tool to enrich and order peoples' lives. So why do legal briefs focus so much o the abstract law and overlook the people?" id at 129-130; Bret Rappaport, Tapping the Human Adaptive Origins of Storytelling by Requiring Legal Writing Students to Read a Novel in Order to Appreciate How Character, Setting, Plot, Theme, and Tone (CSPTT) Are as Important as IRAC (2008) 25 *T.M. Cooley L. Rev.* 267

[112] See Graham, above 6 at 706.

[113] Id at 707.

lawyers "agreed-upon analytical elements," such as rule articulation, citation and explanation of best possible authority for the rule, possible ambiguities of the rule and how the rule has been applied in the past, and how the rule should be analogically applied to the present case, how the facts persuade a conclusion in favor of the client etc. without mentioning the *IRAC* formula. The theory of agreed-upon analytical elements or what is termed "intellectual location" works like the underlying grammar for legal discourse and writing. We expect a well written memorandum or brief to feature and give attention to those common nuances. And that is what good brief writers do.

We would like to conclude this section with the admonition of Chestek on writing technique: "I do not contend that *IRAC* and its brethren are inherently bad. *IRAC* clearly has a place in legal writing; it is a very useful tool for explaining and examining logical pieces of the legal puzzle that every case presents. But its utility is limited to small scale organization and legal reasoning; when used to create the superstructure of a brief, it can lead to formulaic writing devoid of personal stories that form the conflict being presented in court. In short, *IRAC* is a building block-merely one type of material that a writer can use to construct a solid brief. My premise here is that what the writer builds with these blocks, the client's story, should be organized as a narrative."[114]

VIII. Conclusion

It cannot be seriously doubted that *IRAC* provides an intellectual framework of synthesizing legal reasoning by making law's complexity more manageable and that it allows lawyers to communicate with each other on common grounds in analyzing social realities in a principled, rational manner. It can be termed the grammar structure of legal discourse. But that is the much it does. It is however harmful to treat it as the only way to good legal writing. Recognizing this fact should motivate teachers to help their students outgrow the amateur, basic analytical skills underlined in *IRAC* and its other cousins to more flexible writing techniques for analyzing complex, sophisticated social realities and experiences in the social world. They must heed the warning: there is not and cannot be a single structure on how legal argumentative thought is best communicated. *IRAC* can be useful, but it is just one building block in the architectural edifice of legal analysis, and legal writing teachers should not overemphasize it to the detriments of the kaleidoscope and mosaic nature of legal analysis and reasoning. The Greek mythology of the *Procrustean bed* is enough caution for those who want to train great brief-writers.[115]

---

[114] Chestek, above n 93 at 132.

[115] The Procrustean bed symbolizes a standard that is enforced uniformly without regard to individuality. It derives from the Greek mythical giant Procrustes or the mode of torture practiced by him. According to

A final word! Good writing uses reflective techniques and approach the writing process recursively by adopting specific rhetorical strategies for deep legal analysis.[116] IRAC is only a useful tool at the preliminary stage of the legal development of our students. And even at that, a rigid insistence on it as the organizational tool for writing can be dangerous. As teachers our goal should be to help them move quickly to complex analysis by drawing on other methods of organizing writing that better promotes our students' cognitive growth as useful members of the legal discourse community.[117] The writer's focus must be reader-centered with communicative purpose as objective. The non-*IRAC* narrative style is what best suits this objective in legal writing and it should by encouraged by legal writing teachers to broaden the imagination of would-be-lawyers to the social realities and sometimes conflict and complex commitments negotiated through the prism of law and the legal system.

IRAC was conceived primarily as an analytical tool, it must not be converted into a writing formula!

George Gopen, Procrustean lived off the road from Athens to Eleusis. Each evening he offered hospitality to travellers on the road. While the food and wine he offered his guest were fine, the sleeping arrangement was not. The guest was required to fit perfectly to the iron bed he constructed. If the guest was taller than the bed, he would cut off the guest feet and legs to fit into the bed. The obvious effect is that the guest will die. See George G. Gopen, Keynote Address at the Capital Area Legal Writing Conference, Feb. 26, 2011, in IRAC, REA, Where We Are Now, and Where We Should Be Going in the Teaching of Legal Writing (2011) 17 *J. Legal Writing Inst.* xix

[116] Paula Lustbader, Construction Sites, Building Types, and Bridging Gaps: A Cognitive Theory of the Learning Progression of Law Students (1997) 33 *Willamette L. Rev.* 317 (identifies four stages in the legal development of law students-the technician, drafter, designer and creator stages).

[117] Graham, above n. 6 at 704.

Chapter 11

Narrative Pedagogy

Introduction

This chapter asserts that legal storytelling is a powerful tool for transmitting lawyering skills to students via simulation. Working through the basic theories of storytelling and skills of case-theory, it reveals how law should give the client her voice, and why such a bent aligns with the etymological understanding of lawyering. The chapter illustrates how this can be usefully employed in litigation and transactional practice of lawyering. It concludes by urging an incorporation of a storytelling and legal construction of facts approach to law in law faculty curriculum and scholarship.

The narrative pedagogy in teaching law is both novel and innovative. It is a form of scholarship that integrates an understanding of the human condition with the experience of law. That being so, as a pedagogy it is based on an understanding of the human learning process and a desire that students understand the human dimension of law. It essentially is an antidote to students' reliance on restrictive positivism. It demonstrates how human experience is the springboard for legal doctrines and their development. It also shows how rules are in reality value-laden, rather than value-neutral.[1] At a level of generality, the narrative pedagogy is a useful tool intended to ease information into students' long-term memory.

Stories get at the human element of conflicts that become lawsuits. They are just what make law sensible. Stories convey meaning to every practice, teaching and acting of law.[2] For instance, think for once. How would it be to read a law

---

[1] Beryl Blaustone, Teaching Evidence: Storytelling in the Classroom (1992) 41 *Amer. U.L. Rev.* 453 (discussion on how the author uses John Henry Wigmore's personal life to create short stories that review the major premises and structures of the rules of evidence law. The effect makes the scholar real in the minds of students, as well as make the reasoning process directly inferable from the facts of the stories). Wigmore was considered the greatest Anglo-American scholar on evidence law. See John H. Wigmore, *Evidence in Trials at Common Law*, 1979 (J.H. Chadbourn, rev. 1979). See also on how stories recreate humanism in learning law, Angela P. Harris & Marjorie M. Schultz, A(nother) Critique of Pure Reason": Toward Civic Virtue in Legal Education (1993) 45. *Stan. L. Rev.* 1773.

[2] For example, in clinical teaching, storytelling has been used as a tool to help students hear and incorporate the voices of "outsiders" as they engage in and practice various lawyering skills, and to challenge them to think creatively and compassionately about their case strategy and practice. Lucie White's "Sunday Shoes" and Binny Miller's "Give Them Back Their Lives" articles are two good examples of narrative theory and

report without mention of the stories (facts) leading to the dispute resolved by the court. Readers would not be far from imagining that judges have become some prophets of law telling strange abstract law or at best imagine that judges are engaged in some form of philosophy. How would it be for example, to just tell first year students in contract law the holding in *Carlie* v. *Carbolic Smoke Ball Co*[3] without narrating the story leading up to the *ratio* that an offer can be made to the whole world? Hard to imagine. Admittedly, stories are what make law sensible to us. But the some in the legal community scoff at stories. They are rather very quick to associate law with reason and logic. In fact, most scorn at stories for bringing emotion or experience into what they consider the pure laws' empire. But this is simply superficial thinking, which by modest count it is deflationary. It cannot be seriously doubted that experience has a place in the construction of knowledge. Stories as communicated experience creates, reinforces or changes existing knowledge and belief. The heightening importance of stories find justification in the redirection of legal education from liberal studies to professionalism[4] and judicial calls for "let the facts do the talking."[5]

---

storytelling practice that many clinical teachers use either explicitly or behind the scenes in their supervision of clinical students or their seminar teaching. See Lucie White, Subordination, Rhetorical Survival Skills and Sunday Shoes: Notes on the Hiring of Ms. G. (1990) 38 *Buff. L. Rev.* 1 (a story about the writer as a young legal aid lawyer representing a client in a welfare overpayment case. The piece explores the complexity of the lawyer-client relationship and introduces the important "critical lawyering theory" idea that the client is the expert about her own life and that the lawyer must collaborate with her to construct and tell a story that adequately and authentically represents her); Binny Miller, Give Them Back Their Lives: Client Narrative and Case Theory (1994) 93 *Mich. L. Rev.* 485 (in this article the writer describes the multi-layered process of constructing case theories and the need for awareness of the ways in which the lawyer and client bring different pieces of themselves to the process of constructing those stories). See also, Martha C. Nussbaum, Cultivating Humanity in Legal Education (2003) 70 *U. Chi. L. Rev.* 265I believe narrative theory and storytelling can be used even more fundamentally in the law school curriculum, cutting across types of courses and types of lawyering.

3 [1854] AC 23.

4 For discussion on tilt towards professionalism in legal education, see William M. Sullivan, et al. eds. *Carnegie Fund for the Advancement of Teaching, Educating Lawyers: Preparation for the Profession of Law,* 2007 (hereinafter called the *Carnegie Report*) (Report of Carnegie Foundation for the Advancement of Teaching, Preparation for the Professions Program (PPP) 2007, Legal Education Report based on a survey of more than two hundred law faculties (schools) in the US and Canada in 1999). See also, H.R. Cort & J.L. Sammons, The Search for Good Lawyering: A Concept and Model for Lawyering Competencies (1980) 29 *Cleveland State L. Rev.* 397; Mark Yates, The Carnegie Effect: Elevating Practical Training Over Liberal Education in Curriculum Reform (2001) 17 *J. Legal Writing Inst.* 233; James R. Maxeiner, Educating Lawyers Now and Then: Two Carnegie Critiques of the Common Law and Case Method (2007) 35 *International J. Leg. Info.* 1; John B. Garvey & Anne F. Zinkin, Making Law Students Client-Ready: A New Model in Legal Education (2009) 1 *Duke Forum Law & Soc. Change* 101; Karen Tokarz, et al, Legal Education at a Crossroad: Innovation, Integration, and Pluralism Required (2014) 43 *Washington Univ. J Law & Policy* 11. Emphasizing the importance of preparing students for professional practice, Robert MacCrate in forward to *Best Practices* stated: "The central message in both Best Practices and in the contemporaneous Carnegie Report is that law schools should broaden the range of lessons they teach, reducing doctrinal education that uses the Socratic dialogue and case method: integrate the teaching of knowledge, skills and values, and not treat them as separate subjects in separate courses: and give greater attention to instruction in professionalism." See also Roy Stuckey et. al., *Best Practices for Legal Education: A Vision and a Roadmap,* 2007 (hereinafter called *Best Practices*) and generally,

The emergence of realist scholarship, legal writing curriculum, legal clinics and calls to tilt legal education towards professionalism have all combined to heightening the place of stories in legal education and lawyering. Most legal writers and clinicians in fact suggest that stories constitute the backbone of the very important theory of the client's case, which is the essence of client-centred lawyering.[6]

This chapter sets out to discuss how law teachers can use simulation stories to deepen students' learning in the three dimensions of professional education, namely thinking, performing, and behaving. In the introductory Part, we briefly show why storytelling should be encouraged in professional legal education. The next Part reveals the exponential power of stories and why it must not be ignored by the legal academy. Part III, shows the place of stories in the storytelling pedagogy. Part IV, analysis how simulation as a teaching pedagogy helps to illuminate and synthesize knowledge of abstract legal doctrines taught by traditional pedagogy. Part V, is a demonstration of how teachers have used stories in simulation classes to stimulate learning in the three dimensions of legal education, especially in expanding the meaning of "what happened." In this part, we offer an example of how we have used simulation in large classes to teach using the Yoyo hypo example. In Part VI, we connect stories and simulation with the emerging concept of client-centred lawyering, using the Elmer Davis case to draw necessary entailment. Ethical issues that can be triggered by client-centred lawyering are discussed in Part VII. The penultimate Part VIII, encourages the introduction of simulation and stories across curriculum for its beneficial reasons. Part IX, concludes that to the extent that simulation teaches our students to be problem solvers, giving them the opportunity to reflect on what they have learnt and how they learned it, it enforces lawyering skills that is enduring, which should be encouraged by the legal academy.

Association of American Law School, Conference on the Future of Law School Curriculum: Brochure (Seattle, 2011). But cf. Kristen Holmquist, Challenging Carnegie (2012) 61 *J. Legal Educ.* 353

[5] Jim Regnier, Appellate Briefing: A Judicial Perspective (2003) 11 *Persp.: Teaching Legal Res. & Writing* 72 at 73.

[6] The word *client* derives from the Latin verb *cluere*, which according to Lucie White mean to "be named, hear oneself named." It was a word that grew from the ancient Roman practice of naming persons under the patronage of patricians as *clientem* because they were known by the name of their patrons. It is in this sense that lawyering is the practice of speaking for the client and therefore ought to be client-centred and client-empowering. For discussion and application of client-centred lawyering, see Lucie E. White, *Goldberg v Kelly* on the Paradox of Lawyering for the Poor (1990) 56 *Brook. L. Rev.* Clark D. Cunningham, Lawyer as Translator Representation as Text: Towards an Ethnography of Legal Discourse (1992) 77 *Cornell L. Rev.* 1298; Ruth A. Robbins, An Introduction to Applied Storytelling and to this Symposium (2008) 14 *J. Legal Writing Institute* 3.

Emergence of Stories in Legal Scholarship

Since the publication of the book, *The Legal Imagination*,[7] many legal writing and skill teachers have been prompted to explore the common attributes and function of legal acts and literary works.[8] Storytelling has found its way into the teaching of law modular subject curriculum in many jurisdictions.[9] Increasingly, law teachers

---

[7] James B. White, *The Legal Imagination,* Chicago: Univ. Chicago Press, 1973 (abridged edition, 1985). Law and literature is now a strong current in the legal academy. See Robert McPeake, Fitting Stories into Professional Legal Education-The Missing Ingredient (2007) 41 *L. Teacher Intl'J. Leg. Educ.* 303 (ways of teaching storytelling as a lawyering skill). According to Gewirtz, three are three main strands of law and literature scholarship. The first examines legal issues and representations of lawyers that appear in literary works. The second uses the tools of literary theory to analysis judicial decisions and legislative enactments. The third strand, focuses on the transformative power of stories. See Paul Gewirtz, Narrative and Rhetoric in Law, in Peter Brooks & Paul Gewirtz, eds., *Law Stories: Narrative and Rhetoric in Law,* 1996. The place of stories in law is far in history. Prior to Wigmore's impressive compilation in 1912 of legal novels, literary critics had noted the prominent role played by lawyers and courtroom scenes in plays and novel. See J. Wigmore, A List of One Hundred Legal Novels (1922) 17 *Illinois L. Rev.* 26; William Andrews, *The Lawyer in History, Literature and Humour,* 1896, both cited in Paul J. Heald, *Guide to Law and Literature for Teachers, Students, and Researchers,* North Carolina, Durham: Carolina Academic Press, 1998, 7.

[8] Ronald Dworkin, How Law is Like Literature, in A Matter of Principle, Cambridge: Harvard Univ. Press, 1985; Robin West, Narrative, Authority & Law, Ann Arbor: Univ. Michigan Press, 1993; Wai Che Dimock, Residues of Justice: Literature, Law, and Philosophy, Berkeley: Univ. California Press, 1996; Lenora Ledwon, ed., Law and Literature: Text and Theory, New York: Garland, 1996; Heald, above n.5 at 9. See also, David R. Papke, Law and Literature: A Commentary and Bibliography of Secondary Works (1980) 73 Law Lib. J. 41; David Luban, Paternalism and the Legal Profession (1981) Wisconsin L. Rev. 454; James B. White, Law as Language: Reading Law and Reading Literature (1982) 60 Texas L. Rev. 415 (connects law with literature); Symposium, Legal Storytelling (1989) 87 Mich. L. Rev. 2073-2494; Kim Lane Scheppele, Forward: Telling Stories (1989) 87 Michigan L.Rev.2073 (discussing "point of viewlessness"); James Elkins, A Bibliography of Narrative (1990) 40 J. Legal Educ. 203; Daniel Farber & Suzanna Sherry, Telling Stories out of School: An Essay on Legal Narratives (1993) 45 Stan. L. Rev. 807; Elizabeth V. Gemmette, Law and Literature: Joining the Class Action (1995) 29 Val. L. Rev. 665 (a survey revealing that the course is taught in 84 law schools in the U.S.); Carolyn Grose, Storytelling Across the Curriculum: From Margin to Center, From Clinic to the Classroom (2000) 7 J. Ass. Legal Writing Directors 37; Symposium: Law, Knowledge, and the Academy (2002) 115 Harv. L. Rev. 1278; Festus Emiri, A Plea for Legal Narrative in Legal Education, (2004) 1 Delta State University Public Law Series 1; Festus Emiri, Legal Storytelling and Perception (2004) 1 Annuals of Nigerian Law 203; Shulamit Almog, Windows and Windows: Reflections on Law and Literature in the Digital Age (2007) 57 Univ. Toronto L.J. 755 (where the learned writer uses Shakespeare's Measure for Measure to teach poetic justice in law and literature); Festus Emiri & Ayuba Giwa, Metaphoric Thinking About Law as Language and Lawyering as Translation: Reflection on Legal Clinic [2008] Enugu State University of Technology Journal of Public Law 15. But cf. Richard A. Posner, Law and Literature: A Misunderstood Relation, Cambridge: Harvard Univ. Press, 1988; Richard Posner, Law and Literature: A Relation Reargued (1986) 72 Virginia L. Rev. 1351 (where the writer argues that the use of literature in the interpretation of legal texts by method of literary criticism and its use to improve judicial opinions are overstated).

[9] For advocates of incorporating literature to law curriculum in the United States, see David Ray Papke, *Narratives and the Legal Discourse,* Deborah Charles Pub., 1991. See also, James Elkins, Writing Our Lives: Making Introspective Writing a Part of Legal Education (1993) 29 *Willamette L. Rev.* 45. Stories can be created using different styles of writing, such as dialogue, narratives or parables. See Drucilla Cornell, Two Lectures on the Normative Dimensions of Community in the Law: In Defence of Dialogic Reciprocity (1987) 54 *Tennessee. L. Rev.* 335 (example of dialogue), Robert Williams, Taking Rights Aggressively: The Perils and Promise of Critical Legal Theory for People of Colour (1987) 5 *Law & Inequality* 103 (parable using King David and Bathseba); Jeremy Paul, A Bedtime Story (1988) 74 *Virginia. L. Rev.* 915 (combines dialogue and parables). Generally, on creating a felt connection to trigger empathy see Toni M. Massaro, Empathy, Legal Storytelling, and the Rule of Law: New Words, Old

are beginning to recognize the power of stories in grounding legal understanding using stories to connect law with human experience.[10] It provides a way of understanding the plurality of social life negotiated by law, especially in giving insight to how law functions to include or exclude.[11] One reason for this has been the close association storytelling shares with the construction of legal meaning 'from the ground up', a form of scholarship subscribed to by 'outsider jurist.' Stories re-present experience, a vital ingredient in the construction of knowledge. It carries great power because of its ability to convey truths in that it can introduce imagination and new viewpoints thought established. It is therefore not surprising that its place in the legal process is emerging strong. It often provides the most unconventional missile to challenge established ways of thinking and received wisdom because it is 'counter-hegemonic'.[12] It is suggested that stories derive their potency from ability to convey truth in non-coercive ways that enable the hearer to challenge received wisdom. One example familair to many will do. It is the story of the encounter between Prophet Nathan and King David. [13] To lay bear the King's sin of adultery, covetinousness and murder, the prophet told a story that made it easy for the king to reach proper logical conclusion in a non-coercive manner. Certainly, that was a better way to make the king remoseful than

---

Wounds ((1989) 87 *Michigan L. Rev.* 2099. On use and power of stories or narratives in law, see, James Boyd White, *Legal Imagination*, Boston: Little, Brown, 1973 ("Think of or read a law case, imagine the characters freed from the page and live in a storyland, and ask what their story would be like. You are familiar for example, with the ubiquitous personage of the law of torts, the Reasonable Man, and could write a story about him, I suppose: A Day in the Life of the Reasonable Man. ... If you cannot imagine that a novel built around characters defined in this way would have any interest for you, how can legal talk about such characters, the same events, have any interest?")

[10] For illustrative examples see, Cunningham, above n.4; Lucie E. White, Subordination, Rhetorical Survival Skills, and Sunday Shoes: Notes on the Hearing of Mrs. G (1990) 38 *Buffalo L. Rev.* 1 (where the commentators using the story of Mrs. G welfare hearing application reveals that cultural images and long-established legal norms construct the subjectivity and speech of socially subordinate groups, like women, blacks etc., as inherently inferior to those of dominant groups). See also Binny Miller, Give Them Back Their Lives: Recognising Client Narrative in Case Theory (1994) 93 *Mich. L. Rev.* 485 (showing how the practice of lawyering should be reconstructed to embrace a greater role for clients in constructing case theories).

[11] On the immense value of legal storytelling, see for general reading J.B. White, *Legal Imagination* (1973); Lopez, Lay Lawyering (1984) 34 *UCLA LR* 1; Symposium (1988-1999) 87 *Mich. L. Rev.* 2073; Symposium (1988) 39 *Mercer LR* 739. See also West, Jurisprudence as Narrative: An Aesthetic Analysis of Modern Legal Theory (1985) 60 *NYU L.R.* 145; Gerald Torres, Translation and Stories (2002) 115 *Harv. LR* 1362; O.F. Emiri, A Plea for Legal Narrative in Legal Education, (2004) 1 *Delta State University Public Law Series*1, Festus Emiri, above n. 6; Festus Emiri & Ayuba Giwa, above n. 6. But some commentators have castigated much of emerging scholarship that seeks the contextualization of law in the context of concrete experience that does not conform to 'stock' positions in law. For example, see Posner's recent attack on "outsider jurisprudence in the form of law and literature in Richard A. Posner, *Law and Literature: A Misunderstood Relation,* Cambridge: Harvard University Press, 1988. But cf. review and counter argument to his work by James B. White, What Can A Lawyer Learn From Literature? (1989) 102 *Harv. L. R.* 2015.

[12] Scheppele, above n. 6.

[13] Holy Bible, 2 Samuel 12: 1-13.

an abstract appeal to the blackletters of the Mosiac Law that condemned the king's excesses.

Lawyering as storytelling is now in vogue. For example, in 2007 over eighty professors, judges, practitioners, and students attended the Applied Legal Storytelling conference entitled *Once upon a Legal Time: Developing the Skills of Storytelling in Law* in London to brainstorm on the place of storytelling in teaching pedagogy and in practice.[14] There has since then being growing call for storytelling to be taught as skill in faculties of law, recognizing that interplay of law, language and experience can enrich legal consciousness in creating indeterminacy hypothesises about facts and law.[15]

What is more, the legal academy and legal practitioners are beginning to recognise that at a theoretical and substantive level, law is increasingly becoming more about facts than abstract doctrines.[16] The example of the Roman jurist Ulpian (160-228 AD) from the delict of theft (tort in Roman law) is one such pointer of the connection between facts and law.[17] The jurist ask the question who will have an action for the theft of a letter sent but intercepted before it arrives to the addressee? He said in order to answer the question one must first ask who does the letter belong to: sender or addressee. If it was given to the agent or slave of the addressee, then the addressee can be treated as owner, especially if he has an interest in becoming the owner. If on the other hand, the sender sent it on the understanding that it would be returned to him, then he retained ownership. Returning to the question of whom a right of action rested, he stated that it would revolve on who had an interest in the letter not being stolen. So can the messenger bring an action? Yes, if he had undertaken to safely deliver, in which case his situation becomes analogous to an innkeeper. The learned writer Samuel, has used Ulpian's discourse to illustrate how the law of obligations interrelates with reasoning,[18] but for our storytelling purpose, the Ulpian discourse is material in

---

[14] Conference held at the City Law School in London, United Kingdom, from July 18-20, 2007, sponsored by the Gray's Inn of Court/City Law School and Legal Writing Institute. This 2007 conference was a way for academics and practitioners to continue the dialogue that began at the 2005 Power of Stories conference held at the University of Gloucester, a conference reputed to be the first of an open call for conversation about story and narrative. See Ruth A. Robbins, An Introduction to Applied Storytelling and to this Symposium (2008) 14 *J. Legal Writing Institute* 3 at 5. The conference states the following as reason for the applied legal storytelling conference: 'the organisers wished to create a sustainable dialogue about the application of storytelling elements to the practice and pedagogy of law. . . .. We are committed to spotlighting the concept of story in a way that will directly and tangibly benefit law students (i.e. future lawyers) and legal practitioners (i.e. former law students).

[15] See Brian Bix, *Law, Language, and* Legal *Determinacy,* Oxford: Clarendon Press, 1993. For how stories create facts fault-lines in perception, see Festus Emiri, Legal Storytelling and Perception (2004) 1 *Annual of Nigeria Law* 131.

[16] Festus Emiri & Felicia Eimunjeze, Legal Reasoning, Epistemology and Comparative Law: Some Reflection on the Law of Obligations (2012) *U. Ibadan L.J.*

[17] Digest of Justinian/Dalloz, D. 47.2.14.17.

[18] Geoffrey Samuel at 6; Geoffrey Samuel, *The Foundations of Legal Reasoning*, Maklu, 1994, 193-196.

'letting the facts do the talking.' The facts about the status of the messenger, his undertaking, the interest of the sender and the addressee become focal questions for how to design the remedy for the delict. Law is therefore much about the construction of facts as it is about the application of abstract doctrines.[19]

Not surprising, in the adjudication process the important role of the fact-finder's role ultimately rest on facts and inference drawn from them, than on the law. Facts travel the gamut of law, through investigation, mediation, negotiation, advice, sentencing, and trial.[20] That being so, storytelling is a required skill for all lawyers, no matter the nature of their employment.[21]

Despite the fact that stories inhere to the practice of law, very little attention is given to it in legal academy. Legal method classes are no better. Hardly does it remedy the deficiency. Students do not cross the fact-law divide until after graduation. Typical evidence law teaches little about it because it narrowly focuses on the assumption that facts leap from the testimony of witnesses and exhibits tendered in hearing.[22] But that is not so. (show why). In fact, some in the legal academy and profession deride stories as emotive and extra-legal. This is to be expected. Most discourses on transcendentalism associates it with science and its supposed connection with rationality.[23] With the (supposed) decline of the 'natural school' and enthronement of empiricism, the legal academia increasingly creates a felt connection of entailment between science on one hand, and rationality and non-contradiction on the other. From this perspective a state of mind pervades scholarship that implies that rationality conforms to a certain degree of coherence and so propositions not empirically testable are considered improper subjects of meaningful debate, a class to which these scholars would have storytelling classified, a positivism stance to legal scholarship.[24] Flowing from the assumption that empirically testable propositions (science) establishes criteria of universal meaning and validity, matters connected with experience such as

---

[19] Emiri & Eimunjeze, above n 16.

[20] For example, Twining stated that 'the role of narrative in legal discourse. and persuasion are distorted if narrative and stories are only considered in relation to disputed questions of fact in adjudication. Stories and storytelling are also important in investigation, mediation, negotiation, appellate advocacy, sentencing, and predictions of dangerousness. . .. A general theory of narrative in law and legal argumentation needs to encompass all such questions. See William Twining, Taking Facts Seriously (1984) 34 *J. Leg. Educ.* 22; William Twining, Taking Facts Seriously- Again (2005) 55 *J. Leg. Educ.* 360.

[21] Legal employment was traditional thought to fall within two categories: litigation or transactional. We can now add regulatory practice, as an area where lawyers spend time advising client's about and nature and scope of their obligations under various regulatory regimes, ranging from employment, banking, telecommunication, food and drug, health care, immigration, tax, transportation and a host many others. In all of these three categories of legal employment, stories.

[22] Scott W. Howe, Untangling Competing Conception of Evidence (1997) 30 *Loy. L.A. Rev.* 1230.

[23] The scientific posture of law owes its origin to Christopher Columbus Langdell, dean of Harvard Law School, who was reputed to distil principles of law from cases using scientific analysis. See Brian Bix,

[24] Posner, Taking Rights Seriously.

stories are considered meaningless subjects of debate. We respectfully disagree with such a supposition because it simply confuses questioning the *authenticity* of science with the assumption that it establishes universal *criteria* of meaning and consequently universal model of thought and expression as occupying one square.[25] While there certainly will be cases of entailment between both, they do not necessarilly shade into one. It cannot be doubted that there remains merit in humanism even if unexplained in logical terms. There certainly exist transedental truths not unexplained in logical terms. It would therefore be fallacious to ground every claim of truth in empiricism. This is what makes stories transedental in construing knowledge.

Place of Stories in Teaching Pedagogy

The failure of traditional teaching pedagogy to centralize storytelling and legal construction of facts leads to what some have described as 'fact unconsciousness.' Judges and lawyers hardly have any formalised, professional training on legal construction of facts.[26] The reason is not unconnected with the thinking of most lawyers that facts are constant, objective and knowable. In fact, in popular parlance it is said that 'good advocacy cannot change facts.' So, for most lawyers' facts are marginal arsenal requiring formalised, professional attention in pedagogy. While those who subscribe to legal realism would admit of legal indeterminacy, facts are thought not to occupy this square. Such popular thinking is flawed. For while it is plausible to think that facts are determinate in an ontological sense, [27] it is hardly disputable that facts when they arise in the context of disputes are indeterminate in an epistemological sense.[28] The reason for this is

---

[25] See critique on the use of science as the model for thought about human life and society: Richard Rorty, *Philosophy and the Mirror of Nature*, 1979 (for philosophy); C. Geertz, *Local Knowledge: Further Essays in Interpretative Anthropology*, 1983 (for anthropology); Becker, Attunement: An Essay on Philology and Logophilia, in P. Kroskrity (ed.) *On the Ethnography of Communication: The Legacy of Sapir* 100 and Becker, Biography of a Sentence: A Burnesse Proverb, in E. Bruner (ed.) *Text, Play and Story: The Construction and Re-construction of Self and Society* (for linguistics); D. McCloskey, *The Rhetoric of Economics*, 1985 (for economics); S. Fish, *Is There a Test in the Class? The Authority of Interpretative Communities*, 1980; R. Pothier, *The Renewal of Literature: Emersonlan Reflections*, 1987; Edmundson, The Ethics of Reconstruction (1988) 27 *Mich. Q. Rev.* 622 and Baikin, Deconstructive Practice and Legal Theory (1987) 96 *Yale L. J.* 748 (for law and literary studies); L. Havens, *Making Contact: Use of Language in Psychotherapy*, 1986 (for psychiatry); C. Gilligan, *In a Different Voice*, 1982 (for psychology); E. Goffman, *Forms of Tales*, 1981 (for sociology); J. Nelson, A. Megil & D. McCloskey (eds.) *The Rhetoric of Human Sciences: Language and Argument in Scholarship and Public Affairs*,(1981).

[26] There is no faculty of law in Nigeria that teaches storytelling or legal construction of facts as a modular subject or across the curriculum.

[27] Ontology, otherwise known as metaphysics, deals with the theory of reality, dealing with questions such as, what are the fundamental categories and structure of reality and what is the nature of things. (Explain how facts are ontological objective).

[28] Epistemology is a theory of knowledge concerned with what it is to know, the reliability of claims to knowledge, the role that reason and sense experience play in knowledge and the relation among belief, knowledge and truth. See I. Ernst Cassirer, (trans. Ralph Manheim) *Philosophy of Symbolic Forms*, 1953;

the intricate connection between facts, knowledge and cognition. Simplified theory of knowledge using a model of mental activity is divided into three levels: sensation, experience and knowledge. This is what makes storytelling a worthy skill for lawyers.

Even though, early writers approached storytelling more from the standpoint of theory, critical race theory, critical literary and legal theory, feminist theory, and the like,[29] stories now meld with lawyering through the concept of client-representation as narrative.[30] This is to be expected because the connection between storytelling, narrative, communication, understanding and experience is an old one. Nothing better reveals this than the connection between narrative and knowledge. Dictionary meaning of narrative associates it with the process of telling a story. Etymological narrative derives from two Latin words, *narrare* and *gnarus*. *Narrare* mean 'to tell,' and *gnarus* mean 'to have knowledge or experience.'[31] Clearly therefore, narrative constitute a basic form by which we communicate social reality or experience to others with possible view that they acquire insight or knowledge about the object or subject of the story. Deepening the connection, it has been suggested that both Latin words *narrare* and *gnarus* came to the Romans from the Indo-European word *gnd* (to know), a word which is the root of both the Greek *gignoskein* and the Latin *cognoscere*, which yield the English words 'know' and 'cognition.'[32] Therefore, if the essence of lawyering is captured at a level of generality in the descriptiveness of 'representation' as in the case of a lawyer taking stand to present his client's case and interest in court, tribunal, or in negotiating on behalf of a client, then narrative being the means by which it is demonstrated to others would certainly be primary in the legal process.

Steven L. Winter, The Cognitive Dimension of the *Agon* Between Legal Power and Narrative Meaning (1989) 87 *Mich. L. Rev.* 2225; Steven L. Winter, Transcendental Nonsense, Metaphoric Reasoning, the Cognitive Stakes for Law (1989) *U. Pa. L. Rev.* 1105.

[29] Miller, above n. 7. See also Derrick Bell, *And We Are Not Saved*, 1987 (for critical race theory perspective); Katherine Bartlett, Feminist Legal Method (1990) 103 *Harv. L. Rev.* 829 (explaining the dynamic relationship between experience and knowledge in feminist epistemology); Patricia J. Williams, *The Alchemy of Race and Rights*, 1991 (literary and legal theory); Kathryn Abrams, Hearing the Call of Stories (1991) 79 *Cal. L. Rev.* 971 (feminist theory); Clark D. Cunningham, above n. 4 at 1331(ethnography discourse explaining the dynamic relationship between knowledge and experience).

[30] Narrative encompass abstract entities such as the basis for analogizing factual scenarios in some form of reasoning, whereas stories generally refer to specific people and events. See David Herman et al., *Routledge Encyclopedia of Narrative Theory*, Routledge Taylor & Francis Group, 2005, 358-350. While there are certain differences between the stories and narrative, we use both interchangeably in this chapter.

[31] *Oxford Latin Dictionary* 768, 1155 (P. Glare ed. 1985) cited in Steven L. Winter, The Cognitive Dimension of the *Agon*: Between Legal Power and Narrative Meaning (1989) 87 *Mich. L. Rev.* 2223 at 2230, n. 18.

[32] Steven L. Winter, The Cognitive Dimension of the *Agon* Between Legal Power and Narrative Meaning (1989) 87 *Mich. L. Rev.* 2225; Steven L. Winter, Transcendental Nonsense, Metaphoric Reasoning, the Cognitive Stakes for Law (1989) *U. Pa. L. Rev.* 1105

That being so, stories are the very foundation that gives voices to the often voiceless, mute clients, grounding better understanding of their case theory.

Place of Stories across Curriculum

The Carnegie Report and Best Practices for Legal Education describe legal education as deficient in actually producing competent professionals.[33] However by bringing together theory, doctrine, skills and values, narrative theory and storytelling practice can help students develop as fully integrated lawyers that the report envision. It is a perspective that can be used to combines literature, logic, persuasion and morality. Stories are helpful to students develop as competent professionals because it can skilfully be used to bring together theory, doctrine, skills and values in effective teaching and learning. Some teachers for instance, use them to teach specific doctrine or skills, other use works of literature to focus students' attention on particular values like empathy, ethics, justice, cross-cultural competence, and the like.[34]

It is now time to consider how narrative can be taught across the curriculum.[35] Narrative pedagogy can be used across curriculum to teach skills whether the course is doctrinal or clinical. Some teachers use it to help students become keenly aware that as lawyers they are not simply hearers of client's stories, which they tell as in representing the stories, but that they are in fact, the constructors of stories. Teachers however, can better use the pedagogy if they understand the narrative theory which describes the study of constructing stories to enhance effective teaching and learning. Story construction is like the act of building. It requires putting together the elements of the story.[36]

---

[33] Carnegie Report, above n. 2.

[34] For reading on the use of stories to teach specific doctrines, see Stacy Caplow, Putting the "I" in Wr*t*ng: Drafting an A/ Effective Personal Statement to Tell a Winning Refugee Story (2008) 14 *Leg. Writing* 249 (discussion on how to tell a winning refugee case); Paul L. Caron, Back to the Future: Teaching Law Through Stories (2002) 71 *U. Cin. L. Rev.* 405; Stacey A. Tovino, Incorporating Literature into a Health Law Curriculum (2005) 9 *Mich. St. U. J. Med. & L.* 213; Judith G. Greenberg & Robert V. Ward, Teaching Race and the Law Through Narrative (1995) 30 *Wake Forest L. Rev.* 323. Some narrative theory scholars however, suggest that the study of literature should be added to the law school curriculum to help the imagination of students in challenging the apparently objective and machine-like character of the law. See James R. Elkins, Writing Our Lives: Making Introspective Writing a Part of Legal Education (1993) 29 *Willamette L. Rev.* 45; Richard K. Sherwin, Pathologizing Professional Life: Psycho-Literary Case Stories (1994) 18 *Vt. L. Rev.* 681, 686–687.

[35] Carolyn Grose, in Storytelling Across the Curriculum (2010) *7 J. Asso. Legal Writing Directors* 37.

[36] Using the pedagogy of stories across the curriculum requires an appreciation of three reflective considerations: (I) what make stories good-persuasive and compelling, (ii) the substantive elements, the "what" of the story (i.e. the story plot comprising of the various parts: the steady state, the trouble, efforts to redress the trouble, outcome and the coda/moral of the story), (iii) and the technical elements, the "how" of the story-(i.e. in making the legal argument of *what matters* in putting together the case-theory, the consideration of the law, the facts, and the client's goal. See Anthony G. Amsterdam & Jerome S. Bruner, *Minding the Law*, Harv. U. Press, 2000, 1-165.

For example, in teaching evidence through short stories, Blaustone constructs the elements of the rules of evidence around the great evidence law author, John Henry Wigmore.[37] To teach rules of evidence before courts, the commentator tells the class a short story concerning admission of relevant facts, especially how relevant facts are excluded on the basis of prejudice, confusion, unnecessary delay, inadmissibility of character evidence and the policy objective underlying compromises.

The story is so compelling and graphic in teaching the rules. It tells of young Wigmore, eight years old, who attends school on his third day only to be forced out of the class by a teacher because he was placed in the wrong class. The narrative tells that the young boy clung to legs of his desk and would not let go and out of terror, he wrapped himself around his desk. But the teacher will not have any of that. The teacher tugged him out, in the process inflicting bruises on him. So, the parents of Wigmore in outrage sued the school for assault and negligence in operation, that is, a lack of care in admitting new students to wrong class.

The school was however horrified by the extremity of the Wigmores reaction, seeing no connection between the erroneous assignment of a wrong class to young Wigmore and the subsequent wrongful action of the teacher. In their view, it is not logical to infer that the behaviour of the teacher was triggered by the wrong placement, rather than being triggered by the teacher's propensity for force. (Relevance)

To make up, the school fired the teacher. He had shown several propensities of violence before. The school sent out a memo to all teachers warning them to observe school protocol in dealing with hysterical young ones. After taking these steps the school met with the Wigmores to forge an amicable settlement. They apologized to them and offered to settle the claim by paying a small amount of money. The offer was accepted and the suit was dropped. Thereafter, young Wigmore acclimated to his new school environment and subsequently did well in school. (Compromise)

Later in life, Wigmore ponders over the incident as he writes his treatise on evidence. Was the school right in thinking that there is no logical relevance and connection between the classroom placement and the later assault upon him-issue of relevance in evidence. Also, in deliberating on the truth of what happened, truth should not be pressed with unnecessary facts in coming to judgment, for distraction and subjective distortion should be kept at a minimum-exclusion of otherwise relevant evidence on grounds such as undue prejudice, unfair surprise, confusion of issues.

---

[37] Beryl Blaustone, Teaching Evidence: Storytelling in the Classroom (1992) 41 *Amer. U.L. Rev.* 453

Pondering further, he believes that the remedial action by the school is commendable. People should strive to improve on the goods and services they offer-acknowledging legitimacy of policy argument with particular emphasis on potential undue influence on jury of subsequent remedial measure evidence.

Reflecting further about his nightmare with the teacher, he muses how dangerous it would be to judge the teacher's not for what did to him but what he has done before. Yes, the school admitted he had done so before. Judging a man's guilt by previous history increases the chance that the inquiry would change from an examination of what the teacher had done into an examination of the man himself-his character-character evidence.

Wigmore then uses his musings to contribute in writing his learned commentary on why these social values deserve protection-forbearance of considering relevant evidence in coming to judgment where there is valid social policy regarding how individuals should conduct their affairs with one another.[38] The teacher here uses the stories to cover selected rules of law. For instance, the story combines the rule on relevant evidence with the subsequent 'relevant but" rules-its limitations. Like most narrative pedagogy, it starts with a non-legal adventure or journey which is used to draw attention to the topic under discussion without separating the rules from life's experience. This enhances learning in that it creates two levels of interpretation. First, is the telling of the story. Next, is the reflection on the meaning of the facts of the adventure as it relates to the relevant rules of evidence-which reinforces the fact that reasoning is a product of applying a rule to an event.[39]

Let us now discuss how teachers can use the narrative pedagogy across the curriculum, using as connective tissue persuasive stories to teach doctrinal and skill courses. Grose provides a useful insight on how this can be done, using his own examples, which we shall unashamedly employ.[40]

Using Stories in Skills Courses

Students in all courses can be made to work with narrative and storytelling in their class assignments. In her first semester course on Legal Planning Clinic, students break up into pairs and take turns describing to each other a significant personal experience.[41] As is expected their stories range from telling stories about their person, family and friends. Thereafter, they are required to tell the stories

---

[38] Beryl Blaustone, Teaching Evidence: Storytelling in the Classroom (1992) 41 *Amer. U.L. Rev.* 453 at 465.

[39] Blaustone at 483.

[40] Carolyn Grose, in Storytelling Across the Curriculum (2010) *7 J. Asso. Legal Writing Directors* 37.

[41] The course is organized around tools of advocacy broken down to topics on case-theory, timekeeping/billing practices, interviewing and counseling, listening, forms, and closing letters. See Grose, above n. 40 at 54.

they have heard from their partners, making the stories now their own. There is then the debrief session, and students report their feeling of self-consciousness and worry about saying something inaccurate in front of the person whose story they tell. Those hearing their stories being told by their partners report on their discomfort hearing others tell their stories. They discover to their amazement alteration and gap-filing of their original stories. This provides the lesson for the class. They come to recognize (i) empathy-how it feels for clients to describe their legal problems to lawyers they may never have met before and how they may feel to sit in court to her their story told to an audience; (ii) how listening and taking notes are important to lawyering-they see how the exercise might help them think about and perform their lawyering role, whether in recalling clients stories they gap-fill based on assumptions and stereotypes; (iii) they become keenly aware that as lawyers who hear, construct, and retell stories, they must make conscious choices for stories to be persuasive, compelling, and respectful of clients, and that those choices can result in stories that meet or fail to achieve clients goals.

With this arsenal in storytelling, she then assigns her class various assignments in the course of the semester. One such in teaching tools of advocacy in filling forms of persuasion is an assignment to on drafting wills, power of attorney, durable health care proxy forms, and the like. Each student is made to read her story and thereafter discussion starts. The students are made to imagine the context in which the various forms would be read and heard, by whom, and for what purpose. For example, how bank managers would read a power of attorney to decide whether to grant money facility, how durable health care directives could be read by doctors in faraway hospitals, how tax authorities would interpret the documents to determine tax liability or exemption. The real-world scenario helps them to see how they ought to construct stories that can persuade decision-makers to act favorable.

Next, the discussion focuses on how the goals of the particular client for whom the forms are grafted can be advanced. The focus is on the peculiarity of the client. They are made to imagine representing say an elderly homebound individual with diminishing memory and increasing paranoia-a control freak person, who wants her legal planning documents to anticipate and resolve all possible scenario. They find out that for such a client the health care directive they draft is significantly longer and detailed. Why? Simply, this. To satisfy the client goals and also to persuade future doctors to act. The exercise helps the students to connect drafting forms, whether it be power of attorney, will or health directive, to connect with case-theory, contextualizing law and facts to advance the client's goal. They come to see how both the audience and client's goals inform choices lawyers make in telling stories that persuade.

The exercise ultimately teaches and the students learn even in a skills course, that by simply imagining the client's goals and setting where documents would be used in future, they should intentionally tell stories to persuade others to act. Yes, drafting exercises go beyond mere checking boxes and filling blanks.[42]

Using Stories in Doctrinal Courses

It is mistakenly imagined that doctrinal courses being focused in teaching legal analysis is averse to the narrative pedagogy. Stories in doctrinal courses enhances an understanding of both how to persuade a particular decision-maker in the future, and how a particular decision-maker was persuaded in the past. Doctrinal courses can be laced with story exercises that reveal how context and audience ought to change story content and structure. Grose tells us again how she uses the "point of view" in her family law class.[43] After reading say a custody dispute case, the students are asked to identify the elements of the story-the characters, the plot, the genre, the moral, the frame, the setting, the organization, and the point of view. The class is then broken to groups, with each having to retell their story from its character's point of view, filling in any necessary details about any of the elements of the story. They come to see how the elements change depending on who tells the story-father, mother, child, social worker- each telling the story from their point of view. The exercise involves imagining other possible stories, stories that weren't adopted by the decision-maker, deconstruction of the choices the lawyers made in telling those other stories and in telling the story that was ultimately adopted. This teaches them not only an analyse of the law, but also, how it came to be made through the argument of the parties. They can then see how law is comprised of stories that have been constructed by lawyers and adopted by decision-makers. They then can see themselves as future constructors and adopters of stories that shape law and society.

Let me assume that the doctrinal course is say legal methods or legal theory, or even civil procedure, and the teacher wants to teach critical thinking about legal materials so that her students do not overestimate the certainty of law and underestimate the value of critical thinking in law. Let me use the famous Biblical story of Solomon to teach civil procedure.[44] She can proceed this way. Narrate the story leading up to the Solomon's Judgment.[45] Assign the students to read and to

---

[42] For example, on how case-theory can be helpful in filling tax returns, see Festus Emiri & Ayuba Giwa, Akpomiemie Book.

[43] Grose, above n. 39 at 59. Kim Lane Scheppele, Foreword: Telling Stories (1989) 87 *Mich. L. Rev.* 2073 (discussion on "point of viewlessness, positing that there is no such thing as an absolutely neutral description of the facts. See also, David Luban, Paternalism and the Legal Profession [1981] *Wis. L. Rev.* 454, 463.

[44] The story is drawn from the analysis of Hess and Friedland. See Gerald F. Hess & Steven Friedland, *Techniques of Teaching Law,* Durham: Carolina Academic Press, 1999, 42.

[45] Holy Bible, 1 Kings 3: 16-27. At that time two prostitutes came in to the king and stood before him. The first said: "Please, my lord this woman and I live in one house, and I gave birth while she was in the

analyse Solomon's Judgment as a case and prepare a solution. It would appear that this is a simple assignment. In the story King Solomon is asked to decide between two women who is the real mother of the baby. Let see how this can be done.

The students are asked to stand in his place and decide in accordance with the available evidence. They all agree that the baby should be given to the *real* mother- that is a position that better meets with justice of the case. But here is where the skill of critical thinking becomes material. We may ask our students, what was the burden of proof required in the case? Was it satisfied by the evidence which led to the judgment? May be, we should ask them to state the reasoning of King Solomon. What was his major premise about *reality*? Simply this: that the real mother would prefer to have his child alive, even in the hands of a stranger, rather than let it cut in two. That is understandable. A split would be death of the child.

Can our students act as lawyers for the other party- the second woman? Is there any tangible evidence or law they can employ to overcome the orthodox position- that taken by wise King Solomon? Most of them would be reluctant. They cannot think of a better case. This where the teacher should step in. Doesn't the story of the first woman imply that she saw the second woman's baby die? Is that not almost certainly false? Why do we think so? Think for once, if they were in different rooms (but in the same house), she would not have seen the baby die, and even if they were in the same room, she would not have let the other woman crush her own baby. If they were in the same room, and she saw the other woman lay on her baby she probably would using mother's instinct have asked her to correct situation. She would not have let the first woman crush her own baby and then proceed to change the babies.

From this perspective, it is now possible for them to think that Solomon *may* have reached a wrong custody conclusion. All are no longer in agreement that the

---

house. On the third day after I gave birth, this woman also gave birth. We were together, two of us; there was no one else with us in the house. During the night this woman's son died, because she lay on him. So, she got up in the middle of the night and took my son from my side while your slave girl was asleep and laid him in her arms, and laid her dead son in my arms. When I got up in the morning to nurse my son, I saw that he was dead. So, I examined him closely in the morning and saw that it was not my son whom I had given birth to." But the other woman said: "No, my son is the living one, and your son is the dead one." But the first woman was saying: "No, your son is the dead one, and my son is the living one." That is how they argued before the king.

Finally, the king said: "This one says, 'This is my son, the living one, and your son is the dead one' and that one says, 'no your son is the dead one, and my son is the living one." The king said: "Bring me a sword," so they brought him a sword. The king then said: "Cut the living child in two, and give half to one woman and half to the other." At once the woman whose son was the living one pleaded with the king, for her compassions were stirred towards her son. She said: "Please my lord, you should give her the living child. By no means put him to death. But the other woman was saying: "He will be neither mine nor yours. Let them cut him in two. At that the king answered: "Give the living child to the first woman. By no means put him to death, for she is the mother."

judgment is flawless as they initially thought. What is more, is there not a possibility that guilt by the first woman rather than love for the baby would have influenced her to be willing to give up the baby? Some lesson for us. This brings into the burner the importance of procedural rights, for even with a King as wise as Solomon, cross-examination can alter legal conclusion.

Now let us examine a little further the judgment. If we concede (with doubt) that Solomon was (could have been) wrong, in awarding the baby to a mother not the true one, what can be said about it, awarding custody not to the *true* mother, but the *better* mother? Was that what Solomon set out to do? At this point the students come pointedly to see how society would be unsettled if the rule for awarding custody is on the basis of being the *better* parent. The litigation gate would be open for those who want a child more than its parents claiming to be better parents. The possibility of this mean that Solomon followed a different rule from that which he said he was following. He set out to award custody to the *true* mother, but could have ended up doing so to the *better* mother. The possibility of a judge following a different rule from that which he claims to follow can become a further teaching point in legal reasoning, legal fiction and judicial insincerity later in jurisprudence.

We are not done. An ethics angle yet remains. How should lawyers deal with matters related to witness coaching, especially women seeking legal advice within the Solomon Judgment case square? With hindsight of our analysis, we could ask the students, would you coach your witness if she were to appear before Solomon? What ethical dilemma does this present to you in lawyering? Just to move up a step further, we could ask what they as judges would decide if both women have said, "Let her have the baby." This certainly would be a second serious challenge to the *received* wisdom in Solomon's Judgment. Hess and Friedland graphically summaries our conclusion: "The difficulty of using Solomon's approach twice suggests that Solomon was more concerned than our system is with justice in the individual case and less concerned with general rules and procedures."[46] This sort of pedagogy encourages students to read cases carefully in the future. The fact that in deciding Solomon could be wrong emboldens them to challenge court decisions, as they learn the lawyering skills of scrutinizing critically and thinking about how to ask questions and present arguments. The exercise also allows them to see how procedural rules answer the procedural needs of the society in which they are used. For example, it could reveal to them (in a jury-judge setting) how

---

[46] Gerald F. Hess & Steven Friedland, Techniques *of Teaching Law,* Durham: Carolina Academic Press, 1999, 42.

juries function like Solomon, without concern for precedent, while judges must on the other hand, provide reasons consistent with precedent and reason.[47]

The story lesson can encourage our students to read carefully. Deciding, or nearly deciding that Solomon could have reached a wrong conclusion emboldens them to challenge court decisions on appeal. It is hoped that this simple story would have thought them some lawyering skills and values: how to critically analyse facts, how to ask questions, present arguments and avoid some ethical pitfalls. This is how to teach literature in law. Present composition in the NUC benchmark making the study of *pure* literary texts such as reading Wole Soyinka, Chinua Achebe and the like as requirement for law to render it interdisciplinary is therefore the wrong route. What is rather needed is the *application* of that body of knowledge to law.[48] Literature is replete with stories that can teach empathy. Shakespeare's *Merchant of Venice* is one such great work. What legal educators should strive to do for example is not to leave the teaching of literature to our colleagues in the arts and humanities, but to incorporate the gem of these literary texts in applied form to teach critical thinking, skills and professional responsibility.

We can do another story on using the pedagogy as a tool for persuasion without necessarily connecting it to literature, but with constructed fiction in teaching legal methods or theory.[49] Many teachers use the IRAC analysis to teach reasoning in law, despite it perceived deficiencies.[50] IRAC creates a situation where our students come to see law as a special form of reasoning divorced from values. But this is not true. Law develops and is acting in a world of values, and our students would have to recognize the fact. The degree of values that however shape law remains fluid.[51]

Let us consider how the use of the story pedagogy constructed by Singer can be used to teach the complex and flexible nature of say property rights and legal reasoning and analysis.[52] We shall contextualize his story while keeping the thread. It is a story about plant/factory closure. A factory in a city has operated for

---

[47] Ibid at 44.

[48] For example, see Shulamit Almog, Windows and Windows: Reflections on Law and Literature in the Digital Age (2007) 57 *Univ. Toronto L.J.* 755, where the learned writer uses Shakespeare's *Measure for Measure* to teach poetic justice in law and literature.

[49] Joseph W. Singer, Persuasion (1989) 87 *Michigan L. Rev.* 2442.

[50] Festus Emiri, Ayuba Giwa & Jonathan Ehisani, Revisting the Traditional IRAC Organizational Structure for Legal Analysis: Towards a Multidisciplinary Approach (2016) *Nig. L.J.* 1. See also, Laura P. Graham, Why-RAC? Revisiting the Traditional Paradigm for Writing About Legal Analysis (2015) 63 *Kansas L. Rev.* 681 Tracy Turner, Flexible IRAC: A Best Practice Guide (2015) 20 *J. Legal Writing Inst.* 233; Tracy Turner, Finding Consensus in Legal Writing Discourse Regarding Organizational Structure: A Review and Analysis of the Use of IRAC and its Progenies (2012) 9 *Legal Comm. & Rhetoric: JALWD* 351 at 359.

[51] Duncan Kennedy, Freedom and Constraints in Adjudication: A Critical Phenomenology (1986) 36 *J. Legal Educ.* 518.

[52] Joseph W. Singer, Persuasion (1989) 87 *Michigan L. Rev.* 2442.

over fifty years. The city has grown around it, relies on it for employment and most of the city's activities are connected with it. Yet the company appears to be unconcerned about the welfare of the city. Its managers operate on the shareholder maximising philosophy. Ruled by a distant and seemingly unapproachable board of directors, the company closes the factory. The effect of this on the city is enormous. Many suffer financial reverses, drop in their living standard. All its workers are unable to put things, including family life. Can this be a betrayal case, one in which the workers trusted the company and depended on it? Should we think the company lived off the trust, took advantage of it, and abused it?

This no doubt would be nonsensical argument by common count. Most lawyers will think that such an argument is unlikely to persuade a court. It simply would not work. Instead, they may consider the fact of closure regrettable. Those who subscribe to an economic analysis of law can write off the situation as one example of efficiency at work-the efficient restructuring of production through the invisible hand of the market.[53] Yes, market decisions should pay less regard to social expectations.[54] I have no quarrel with these shades of reasoning. After all it is not the business of a company to provide welfare to people. That business rest squarely with government under chapter two of the Constitution.[55]

If this fact scenario were to be a Bar Final examination question, I am sure you know what kind of answer it would generate from the examinees. Four pillars of argument against regulating factory closures would be erected. The first is that which the students' garner from property law. A necessary incident of property right is ability to treat owned *res* the way the owner wishes, subject to a few rules on use and enjoyment. The factory is property. The owners can choose to do what they want with it. Regulating closures would derogate on the right. For this purpose, I shall call such an argument the *property argument*. Two, they apply their learning from company law. Quickly they remember that the general rule is that a company belong to its shareholders for who the managers ought to maximise profit. That being the case, if the investment decision is closure, so be it. Let me refer to this as the *market argument*. Further, they may just wonder why the workers think that the situation raises an abuse of trust argument. The

---

[53] Coase theorem is the most celebrated application of the concept of opportunity cost. See Ronald H. Coase, The Problem of Social Cost, (1960) 3 *Law & Economics* 1, see reprint in Coase, *The Firm, the Market, and the Law*, Chicago Univ. Press, 1988. The theorem posits that under conditions of rational cooperation, full information and zero transactional costs, parties will negotiate around inefficiencies to allocate rights in order to establish optimal level of resource deployment.

[54] But cf. Neva S Makgetla & Robert B Seidman, The Applicability of Law and Economics to Policymaking in the Third World (1989) 23 (1) *J. Econ. Issues* 35.

[55] 1999 Constitution of the Federal Republic of Nigeria.

foundation of contract they learnt in school makes central freedom of contract.[56] The workers should have been smart when they took their job offers. It was a bargain relationship. If they now feel disappointed because their fortune nosedives, that is their fault. Freedom of contract should have propelled them to negotiate severance payments to cushion the challenges. I shall refer to this as the *freedom of contract argument.* They may also question the legitimacy of the breach of trust workers position by arguing that what the workers are demanding in the circumstance is tantamount to asking the court to create and recognise new property rights. That they say should be the business of the legislature rather than the courts. I choose to call this *deference to the legislature argument.*

I am confident that most would be pleased with their arguments. They have shown that they really do *think* like lawyers. But for me here is the real problem. The students take a monolithic, atomistic, abstract and acontextual view of the problem. IRAC is the key to solve the factory closure case. The reasoning and answer are crystal clear. No controversy. But that is exactly where the problem is- their professional competence. They obviously cannot do a good job in representing the miserable workers in a factory closure case. The exact opposite is what is required of a competent and ethical lawyer. Lawyers need to be trained to see the merits and demerits of every argument. Yes, the two sides of the coin.

What the teacher would need to do in a doctrinal class would be to introduce transformative power to the scenario to help the class see that this can indeed be a hard case, requiring interplay of complex rules and principles, all in a state of flux.[57]

Abstract argument to generate thinking that closure is a breach of trust does not convince them. Even so will an argument that marketplace works through a mixture of self-reliance and trust. So to arrive there I simply would tell a story. It goes like this. All the students of the Nigerian Law School six campuses are to be in their campus auditoriums on the Monday, a week to the commencement of the Bar examination. The purpose is to listen to an important satellite talk by the Director-General (DG) of the Nigerian Law School (NLS) on behalf of the Council of Legal Education (CLE). Accordingly, they are gathered. The DG opening speech is revealing. For some time now the profession and the public are concerned about the competence and character of new wigs. Reports of scandals involving lawyers are on the increase. The Legal Practitioners Disciplinary Council (LPDC) is increasingly saddled with malpractice complains. As a result of this the CLE two years ago set up an advisory committee to help address the challenge. The committee members were drawn from the judiciary, inner and outer Bar, and

[56] PS Atiyah, The Rise and Fall of Freedom of Contract, Oxford: Clarendon Press, 1979.
[57] Ronald Dworkin, *Taking Rights* Seriously, London: Duckworth, 1977, 81

the ministries of justice across the country. Their report is now out. In it they attribute the downslide in competence and character to the large number of people seeking to become lawyers in the faculties and the NLS and have recommended a 50% reduction across board and that the pass mark for all law subjects will be 50% no longer 40%. They have also asked the CLE to increase the Bar vocational training from one year to two. It is also their recommendation that it be implemented immediately to prevent further slide.

The CLE at its last meeting a few days ago unanimously approved all the recommendations and have instructed the NLS to commence its implementation with you. So, ladies and gentlemen we have no choice but start with you. Please take a good look at your neighbour. He or she may never become a lawyer. Only 50% of you can be lawyers. The minimum pass mark is 50%. Even if more than 50% of you score above the minimum 50% pass mark in the five Bar vocational subject, we would have no choice but fail them because only half of you can be lawyers. Also, your programme of study with us is no longer one year. It is now two. Your exams will not be next week. It will be one year one week from today. We recognise that implementing this new policy can be disruptive to you, nonetheless these measures are to promote efficient delivery of legal services. Good morning Bar-aspirants. That ends my speech. You may now respond if you have anything to say.

You can imagine how charged all the auditoriums would be like. The students are overwhelmed with anger. You cannot do this. It is totally unfair, a breach and abuse of trust by CLE. They insist the position of CLE is unsustainable. If you do not immediately reverse yourself we shall seek redress in court. You cannot toy with our rights this way and get away with it. I end the story here.

Let me now take the dialogue. I will play the devil's advocate. I now use the four-pillar argument against the students which they erected against the city workers in the closure case. I start with the property argument. I ask them, do you have rights? The NLS is the property of CLE. Consult the Act.[58] An owner of property can do what he wants with it. That is what we have just done by change of policy. Remember the market argument. The board of CLE is charged under the Act with regulating vocational training and continuing legal education for lawyers to improve legal service delivery. We are simply promoting market efficiency for legal services. It is like an investment decision to gravitate resources to most valued person.[59]

---

[58] Legal Education (Consolidation) Act, 1976, Cap L10 LFN 2004.

[59] Efficiency in a legal situation arises if a right is given to a party willing to pay more for it. This explains why if the Coasean market is unavailable courts are urged to imagine what the parties would have agreed to in a hypothetical Coasean market. Since the right to a resource will have been secured by the party

The students may think this most unfair that we have changed the rules in the middle of the game. Here again I resort to the freedom of contract argument. Gentlemen, please take a good look at your students' prospectus. It is clearly written that CLE/NLS can change the rules of engagement at any time. That is exactly what we have done. If you didn't like it you should have bargained out of it. Finally, I take them on the deference to legislature argument. Suppose (without conceding) that you think it is a breach of trust to change the rules in the middle of the game, this still does not ground reason for a court to grant you injunctive or monetary reliefs. By litigating against CLE/NLS you are asking for a right to attend our school, participate in our programme and be to sponsor by us for admission to the Nigerian Bar-all that against the better judgment of the CLE who run the NLS. Is that something we promised you? Did you bargain for it? In the absence of contract giving you the right, your claim would effectively be seeking the creation of a new property right-an entitlement to a qualifying certificate for call to Bar. This is a business more appropriate for the legislature, not the court. The students at this point disagree because they think the court should interpret contracts in the light of new social conditions and values in a way and manner that promotes reasonable reliance on contract.[60] They argue that the court has an obligation to promote justice. In the absence of legislation to their aid, the court should create (new) rights that prevents the CLE from frustrating their reasonable expectations. They trusted the CLE, and that trust is abused.

You agree with me (at a minimum) that this story carries transformational power. They now can see something in the factory closure case they were initially dismissive of. In one swoop, they realise that rights should transcend explicit contracts terms. By creating a felt connection between them and the vulnerable

---

willing to pay most for it, the court is expected to mimic by auctioning entitlements to those who value them most - judged by each litigant's willingness to pay. See Jules Coleman, Economics and the Law: A Critical Review of the Foundations of the Economic Approach to Law (1984) 94 *Ethics* 649, Richard Posner, *Economic Analysis of Law*, 8th ed., 2011. But cf. David Campbell, 'Ayer versus Coase; An Attempt to Recover the Issue of Equality in Law and Economics,' (1994) 21 *J. Law &* Society 434, for critique of law and economics pure materialistic theory of rights. But economists defend its position on the grounds that the term 'efficiency' when used to denote allocation of resources in which value is maximised does not extend to ethical criterion as basis for social decision-making. See Richard Posner, p. 16. Coarse, above n. 35, Steven Shavell, *Economic Analysis of Accident Law,* Cambridge, Mass.: Harvard Univ. Press, 1987.

[60] Fuller & Perdue, The Reliance Interest in Contract Damages (1936-37) 46 *Yale L.J.* the writers argued that remedies for breach of contract respond to the protection of three interests, reliance, expectation and restitutionary interests. Reliance interest seek to put the plaintiff in the position he would have occupied if the defendant had performed the contract, and the restitutionary interest is concerned with the prevention of gain by the defaulting promisor at the expense of the promisee. See Friedman, The Performance Interest in Contract Damages (1995) 111 *LQR* 628, Farnsworth, Legal Remedies for Breach of Contract (1970) 70 *Columbia L. Rev.* 1145, Joseph Raz, Promises in Morality and Law (1982) 95 *Harv. L.* Rev. 916, 937, where the learned commentator stated that: "harm includes institutional harm. Preventing the erosion or debasement of the practice of undertaking voluntary obligation is therefore a fit object for the law to pursue."

factory workers they realise how narrow legal reasoning can be. They graphically see that lawyers may be experts in knowing which arguments are likely to work in particular context, but they are not necessarily experts in knowing which argument *ought* to work. Their atomistic view of legal rules and principles suddenly get converted to energy, expressed in legal creativity and invention. They can now see that the prevailing plant closure rules translated into company law, property law and the like are mere superstructure buildings of law constructed from the perspective of corporate managers who make investment decisions on behalf of shareholders, without outsider perspective. An outsider perspective as told from the CLE/NLS story to connect the factory closure case can be more insightful. The free market argument and its *cousins* assume too much. In real live situations, the relative bargaining power of parties to contracts is often unequal. The factory closure scenario teaches the students to understand and experience both vulnerability and broken trust. They are forced to see what it is for the city workers to be at the absolute mercy of corporate managers in the absence of contract hedging their future. Yes, stories do have power and can be useful in teaching.[61]

We have told the factory closure story not for the sake of telling stories. We have used it to teach tits and bits of contract law, company law, property law, jurisprudence, and very importantly to teach our students that at times received wisdom is susceptible to flaws. We have simply used unconventional reason to draw on empathy in experiential learning.

Stories in Advocacy Courses

One specific idea that skills teachers share is that students need to be taught that lawyering is often more about facts than it is about law. It is facts that often govern the formulation of what constitute the *ratio* of the case. That being so the narrative pedagogy sits well with advocacy courses. It helps teach the indeterminacy of facts-that they are not just out there in the real world. Facts are often laden with patent subtleties that can confuse even the skilled lawyer.[62]

---

[61] See Symposium: Law, Knowledge, and the Academy (2002) 115 *Harv. L. Rev.* 1278. Festus Emiri, Stories in Law Curriculum. Festus Emiri & Ayuba Giwa, above n. 24. Stories can be created using dialogue, narratives or parables. Drucilla Cornell, Two Lectures on the Normative Dimensions of Community in the Law: In Defense of Dialogic Reciprocity (1987) 54 *Tennessee. L. Rev.* 335 (example of dialogue), Robert Williams, Taking Rights Aggressively: The Perils and Promise of Critical Legal Theory for People of Colour (1987) 5 *Law & Inequality* 103 (parable), 1 King David and Bathsheba, Jeremy Paul, A Bedtime Story (1988) 74 *Virginia. L. Rev.* 915 (combines dialogue and parables). Generally, on creating a felt connection to trigger empathy see Toni M. Massaro, Empathy, Legal Storytelling, and the Rule of Law: New Words, Old Wounds ((1989) 87 *Michigan L. Rev.* 2099.

[62] Critique of traditional legal education argue for storytelling to be taught as a skill in law schools. See Brain J. Foley, Applied Legal Storytelling, Politics, and Factual Realism (2008) 14 *J. Legal Writing Inst.* 17 at 18 ("Proponents of legal storytelling may find themselves in the position of criticizing legal education as sometimes falling to get at the human element of the conflicts that become lawsuits.") Id at 20. See

Unfortunately, indeterminacy of law as opposed to indeterminacy of facts characterizes the focus of much traditional law teaching.[63] So lawyers are hardly taught how to construct facts and interpret them. The thinking is that legal construction of facts will be learned on the job of lawyering. Traditional law school pedagogy hardly has a place for teaching indeterminacy of facts because it is reasoned by the academy that when the students begin practice of law they will learn indeterminacy of facts on their own. It is this gap that storytelling curriculum addresses. Since stories bear an intricate connection with legal reasoning and argumentation, teaching students how to tell stories improves legal education.

Stories are told to create imagination, bring to bear clients experience and realities negotiated through law and its institutions. That being so, good lawyering ought to account for the client's theory of the case.[64] It is the theory of the client's the case that makes all the difference. Stories create and recreate consciousness, incorporating the voices of clients, especially the voices of outsiders in negotiating legal reality.

Let us see how stories can be used in an advocacy course, like law of evidence. We shall use the Elmer Davis story, especially in the context of helping our students see that facts are indeterminate, that our students are not just hearers and tellers of stories, but importantly are constructors of stories; and that in constructing stories, why they must make conscious, intentional choices as to how to tell stories. In fact, the case also reveals that where a story start or end can be deliberately chosen for purposes of persuasion.

The Elmer Davis story is one storyline constructed by Kim Lane Schepple.[65] It is a narration of an African-American, Elmer Davis, who confessed to rape of a

---

also, Richard Neumann, *Legal Reasoning and Legal Writing: Structure, Strategy and Style*, 5th ed. Aspen Pub. 2005, 207 ("facts have subtleties that can entangle you if you are not careful. Beginners tend to have difficulties with four fact skills: (i)separating facts from other things; (ii) separating determinate facts from other kinds of facts; (iii) building inferences from facts; and (iv) purging analysis of hidden and unsupportable factual assumptions.")

[63] Lorie M. Graham & Stephen M. McJohn, Cognition, Law and Stories (2009) 10 *Minn. J.L. Sci. & Tech.* 255 ("narrative plays a fundamental role in legal reasoning, in such areas as memory, moral decision-making, reasoning by analogy, explanation, and even organizing of vast amount of information that lawyers contend with. ... A narrative approach provides a more dynamic view of how people think about cases.") Id at 258; Brian J. Foley, Applied Legal Storytelling, Politics, and Factual Realism (2008) 14 *Legal Writing* 17; Brian Foley &Ruth A. Robbins, Fiction 101: A Primer for Lawyers on How to Use Fiction Writing Techniques to Write Persuasive Facts Section (2001) 32 *Rutgers L.J.* 459 ("facts are determinate in an ontological sense, but the facts of a lawsuit as argued by lawyers ... are indeterminate in an epistemological sense.")

[64] See Symposium: Legal Storytelling (1989) 87 *Mich. L. Rev.* 2073; Symposium, Speeches from the Emperor's Old Prose: Reexamining the Language of Law (1992) 77 *Cornell L. Rev.* 1233; Symposium, Lawyers as Storytellers and Storytellers as Lawyers: An Interdisciplinary Symposium Exploring the Use of Storytelling in the Practice of Law (1994) 18 *VT L. Rev.* 565.

[65] Scheppele, above n. 43. For purposes of this chapter we would adopt the scenario played out of the story by Carolyn Grose, in Grose, above n. 40.

white woman in North Carolina. We shall only examine the case from the perspective of the voluntariness or otherwise of his confessional statement. The simulation class can be made to see that the facts of voluntariness are not objective facts out there for capture. Both the prosecution and the defendant would sure have their different case theories all stepped in facts that are true. It is expected that the prosecution will be happy to sustain the charge by showing the voluntariness of the defendant's confessional statement. That being so, its evidence will be as follows:

Prosecutor (P): Who is in charge of overseeing the interrogation of Mr. Davis?

Witness (W): I was.

P: Is there a Department protocol for interrogating prisoners?

W: Yes.

P: Describe that protocol to the judge.

W: We limit interrogation to twice daily, once in the morning and once later in the day.

P: What procedure did you follow for the interrogation of Mr. Davis?

W: We followed the Departmental protocol. I typically interrogated Mr. Davis in the morning, and another officer questioned him later in the day.

P: Did the procedure vary?

W: No, we followed that procedure the entire time Mr. Davis was in custody, up until the time he confessed.

With evidence like this, the simulation teacher could ask the students to identify the state's theory of the case and how it is constructed to tilt in favour of voluntariness of Mr. Davis confession. They can see it revealed in evidence that the Departmental protocol was followed, a policy in place against around-the-clock interrogation. The prosecution kept faith with (what seemed) good police practice, which should ordinarily satisfy the judge.

But this is only side of the coin. Simulation calls for deep reflection. Let us see how the defence can also construct the theory of the client's case to raise involuntariness.

Defence Attorney (DA): Mr. Davis, how long were you in jail before you gave the statement to the police?

Defendant (D): Sixteen days.

DA: Please describe the cell where you were being held?

D: It was a small cell in the back of the jail, with a bed and a chair. There was a little window out into the jail yard.

DA: Was there a clock in the cell?

D: No.

DA: Did you have a wristwatch?

D: No, they took my watch away from me when they put me in jail.

DA: During the sixteen days, how often did the police question you?

D: Pretty much all the time.

DA: When you say "pretty much all the time," what do you mean?

D: After I woke up in the morning, one of them would come and start asking me questions. That would go on all morning and then he'd leave. Then after a little while another one would come in and start up all over again.

DA: Was it light out while you were being questioned?

D: Sometimes it was.

DA: And was it ever dark out while you were being questioned?

D: Sure, it was.

DA: How long did the questioning go on?

D: Every single day until they got me to sign this statement.

The students can identify the client's theory of the case. It is radically different from the state's theory. It is all about the involuntariness of the confessional statement. Yes, the defendant was of the considered view that the interrogation was persistent, constant harassment, especially from the perspective that he didn't know what time it was and the questioning took place during dark hours.

The exercise reveals to the students that two stories are true constructed of the facts, but from different viewpoints. It is true that the prosecution adhered to its protocol on questioning prisoners. It equally true that from the defendant's sense of time based on the changing light from the little window, the interrogation was sporadic. While the prosecution can argue that the circumstances were not sufficient to constitute coerced confession, the defence could argue that the repeated nature of the interrogation created a kind of duress which should vitiate the confession. What the story has done is to encourage the students to learn first-hand how they are themselves constructors of stories and eventual legal reality, and that reality is not fixed, as though cast in steel. What happened is nothing near objective. What position gets vindicated as fact may just turn out to be the story adopted by the decision-maker. They begin to appreciate experimenting with choices about how to use facts, frame examination of witnesses, how to structure facts, choose where a story should start and end, what evidence to highlight and the like.

The exercise can be furthered by moving the hypo somewhat into trial.[66] Assuming the judge disbelieves the defence and admits the confessional statement of Davis, how can you continue to centralize the client in defence? How will the

---

[66] In this respect, we simply follow the plan drawn by Grose by in our simulation class. See Grose, above n. 43 at 52.

centralizing motivation determine when and where to begin direct examination of your client? It is of course expected that the prosecution will frame a story with the simplistic thread like this: description of the murder committed by Davis, his subsequent arrest and his confession to the crime. Readily, the judge sees a bad black-man who enjoys killing. He should be convicted without more. But simulation requires that our students attempt to loosen the tight frame drawn by challenging the apparently objective and machine-like character of law and facts drawn by the prosecution. Some thinking and skills must come to play. The "when" and "where" to begin direct examination could provide the missile.

Grose tells us how he and his colleague do this by engaging in another direct examination of Davis. We unashamedly copy it in our simulation class. It goes like this:

Defence Counsel (DC): Mr. Davis, where did you grow up?

Defendant (D): Here in Alabama in Jefferson, just five miles from here.

DC: Do you remember the first time a policeman ever talked to you?

D: Yes.

DC: Tell the jury (judge) about that, please.

Prosecutor: Objection, relevance?

Ending the role-play here the students are asked why the line of argument by defence counsel will lead to relevant information. They only gain insight to this by visualising how the added construct goes to support the client's case-theory of involuntariness of the confessional statement. Even if the judge rules that the statement is voluntary and eventually convict Davis for murder, at least the defence would have built a structure of (seeming) coercion as ground for appealing the decision of the trial court on the voluntariness of Davis statement.

At this point, we can assign to our student an article by Cunningham as a must read.[67] With the hindsight of the paper, they could be asked, why is the

---

[67] Lucie E. White, *Goldberg v Kelly* on the Paradox of Lawyering for the Poor (1990) 56 *Brook. L. Rev.* 861; Anthony V. Alfieri, Reconciling Poverty Law Practice: Learning Lessons of Clients Narrative (1991) 100 *Yale L.J.* 2107; Cunningham, above n. 4. See also, related literature, John M. Conley & William M. O'Barr, *Rules versus Relationship: The Ethnography of Legal Discourse*, 1990 ("the law has come to define the problems of ordinary people in ways that may have little meaning for them, and to offer remedies that are unresponsive to their needs as they see them.") Id at 177. Generally, ethnographic lawyering brings lawyers into the construal world of those who experience disempowerment and marginalization to attain multiple-consciousness that enables them to imagine other kinds of marginalized viewpoints. Richard Delgado, Storytelling for Oppositionists and Others (1989) 87 *Mich. L. Rev.* 2411, Mari J. Matsuda, When the First Quail Calls: Multiple Consciousness as Jurisprudential Method (1989) 11 *Women's Rts. L. Rep.* 7; Miller, above n. 21 (a case of a black man charged with disorderly conduct, resisting arrest, assault after he was stopped and wrongly accused of shoplifting by three white security guards, thereby raising provocative questions about the defendant's life experience about the various case theories that lawyers construct); White, above n. 8. For reasons, why legal education should go beyond formalism and be expansive to context, see Phillip C. Kissam, The Decline of Law School Professionalism (1986) 134 *U. Pa. L. Rev.* 251 ("the study and practice of law would be improved by a more contextual approach that places a greater emphasis on both the application of law to concrete situations and the understanding of how

defendant's first contact with the police relevant? They know why from reading about legal literature on ethnographic lawyering which creates multiple consciousness. They quick see the picture-story. A poor black kid brought up in Southern America at the dawn of the civil rights movement, afraid of the police known (whether rightly so or otherwise) for intimidating people of colour. This background provides context to the confessional statement of Davis and supports his theory. It supplies the bridge for the judge to link the statement with coercion. The exercise makes pointed that it matters to lawyers their choices about how to use facts, frame examination of witnesses (that examination is not just about not asking leading questions in examination in chief or not asking offensive questions in cross examination and the like stipulated in the sections of Evidence Act), that case theory is a conscious, intentional choice lawyers must make in constructing persuasive and compelling stories. Case theory analysis in the context of storytelling teaches the lawyering skills. When stories are made with choices they are persuasive, compelling, and the choices can result in stories that achieve client's goals in ways they feel comfortable with.

Using stories across the curriculum thus reveal that it is a teaching technique readily applicable all courses whether they are designed to hone skills in negotiation, pre-trial proceedings and transactional lawyering. It is mistaken to think that stories enjoy a lesser place of prominence in transactional lawyering.[68] The reason isn't farfetched. Every transaction is a story. It is the stories that give life to transactions. It is it that metamorphoses to become the basis of agreements, and the ultimate clauses of documents executed by the parties. For example, a conveyance is itself a story of negotiation, title investigation, and the purchase agreement. Therefore, the ability of lawyers to visualise and conceptualise transactions as stories benefits the negotiation, drafting, implementation, interpretation, and the ultimate enforceability of the transaction document.[69] It is all about client-centred lawyering.

Ethical Considerations in Using the Narrative Pedagogy

Integrated legal education demands finding a place for storytelling across curriculum. They are useful tools for teaching professional responsibility, skills and doctrines. Some traditionalists deride stories for introducing too much values

---

law serves or fails to serve conflicting social values. This approach would improve professional education by initiating future practitioners into the uncertainties, complexities and value conflict of the 'practice situation.'") Id at 254; Edward D. Re, The Causes of Popular Dissatisfaction with the Legal Profession (2012) 68 *St. John's L. Rev.* 85 (discussion why the legal profession should re-access itself in the face of growing public dissatisfaction).

[68] Susan M. Chesler & Karen J. Sneddon, Once Upon a Transaction: Narrative Techniques and Drafting (2016) 68 *Okla. L. Rev.* 263

[69] Ibid.

into law, also charging it for possible violation of ethics. They reason that critical lawyering which stories bring to the front-burner is discounted as unethical and a deviation from professional responsibility. Law to them defines the boundaries of stories. Classic, proper practice sees client stories through the law saturated lens. So, in the Davis scenario for example, the frame consists of only 'relevant' stories: 'what happened.' What happened is merely a story of how trouble started; where the defendant met the deceased, murdered her, his arrest, detention and subsequent trial. No more! Interestingly, that is the frame constructed by most criminal legislation and procedure statutes. Section 316 of the Criminal Code Act defines murder as the wilful killing of another. The Criminal Procedure Act makes provision for arrest, detention and trial process. The Evidence Act sets the ambits of what constitute confession, etc. So, for traditionalist, (like the prosecution did in Davis case) once an account of 'what happened' is given, all stories must be those that only fit within the frame constrained by law. No one is allowed to wrestle with the law to fit into their client's lived realities. Client's lived realities must be funnelled into what they understand the law requires. The paradigm gives facts a secondary role to law. Stories are subsumed in law, which is the starting and ending point of case theory. Facts are simply to be fitted to legal theory. They place so high the objectivity about facts and so they can only conceive a limited universe for case theory.

It is all of this that critical lawyering, stepped in the narrative pedagogy explodes. *What* happened is constructed to include the *meaning* of what happened. That is what the defence did by asking Davis "do you remember the first time a policeman ever talked to you?" It is the story's attempt to provide context and meaning to support the case theory of the non-voluntary nature of Davis statement. Meaning of what happened becoming intricate connected with the story of the client as to what happened. In contrast with traditional legal counselling model, which assigns a passive role to clients, case theory located in client-centred lawyering is rooted in the philosophy that lawyers should interact with clients in a way that allows clients to be decision-makers.[70] This demands that together the lawyer and client should consider various alternatives available in a case and the likely consequences in reaching the decision, a perfectly ethical position, which aligns with the concept of client autonomy.[71]

---

[70] Critical lawyering aligns with rule 14 of the RPC which enjoins lawyers to be dedicated and devoted to the cause of their clients.

[71] Rule 14 (2) (a)-(e) of RPC demands lawyers to consult with their clients, keep them informed of important developments and possible strategies. On observation of client's autonomy as a key concept in representation, see, Miller above n. 21 at 503. See also, Mark Spiegel, Lawyering and Client Decision-making: Informed Consent and the Legal Profession (1979) 128 *U. PA. L. Rev.* 41; Marcy Strauss, Towards a Revised Model of Attorney-Client Relationship: The Argument for Autonomy (1987) 65 *N.C. L. Rev.* 315; Robert D. Dinerstein, Client-Centred Counselling: Reappraisal and Refinement (1990) 32

Conclusion

The concluding remark of a commentator tells why law faculties should make storytelling and legal construction of facts part of curriculum. It states "law is made through the telling and the believing of stories. Thus, all lawyering involves some kind of persuasion, and all persuasion involves some kind of storytelling. To be effective professionals, lawyers need to know how to construct and tell stories. That means they need to recognize stories as constructed, and they need to recognize themselves as constructors of stories. Law teachers, therefore, need to help students develop these skills across the curriculum because they are skills that lawyers will need to use in all facets of their practice as responsible and effective professionals."[72]

This summary should be compelling for those who take effective teaching and learning as the primary responsibility of the law teacher. Context supplied by stories enrich an understanding of how law serves or fails to serve conflicting social values.[73]

Ariz. L. Rev. 501; David A. Binder, et al. *Lawyers as Counsellors: A Client-Centred Approach*, 1991. See Robert F. Cochran, Jr., Legal Representation and the Next Steps Toward Client Control: Attorney Malpractice for the Failure to Allow the Client to Control Litigation and Pursue Alternatives to Litigation (1990) 47 *Wash. & Lee L. Rev.* 819 (discussing why client should control important decision-making).

[72] Grose, above n. 40 at 43.

[73] Phillip C. Kissam, The Decline of Law School Professionalism (1986) 134 *U. Pa. L. Rev.* 251.

Chapter 12

Lesson Plan as Instructional Strategy

Introduction

Strategy is important to any endeavour. Learning theories greatly influence the choice and development of designed instructional strategies. The guiding principles applicable to all learning objectives is that a lesson plan should be organized to have an introduction, a body, a conclusion, and assessment. Another principle universally applicable is that it should be learner-centred, active, and meaningful. Even at that, instructional strategy is not an exact science as though a particular design as one-fit-all. Designers can only draw on a range of possible appropriate strategies that would work, reviewing the strategies from time to time in the context of effective teaching and learning outcomes.[1]

Lesson Plan Design

Introduction

The lesson plan introduction should arouse interest in the topic, so should accomplish four goals: get the students to attend class, establish the instructional purpose, arouse interest and attention, and preview the lesson.[2] These are the things that cause the learners to attend class against other competing outside stimuli.

Body of Lesson Plan

The body of the lesson plan should embody five expanded events: (i) recalling relevant prior knowledge, (ii) processing information, (iii) focusing attention, (iv) employing learning strategies, (v) and give feedback.

Recalling prior relevant knowledge involves the retrieval of what is known by the learner from her long memory. Since prior knowledge has been processed as schemata and stored in the long memory, the recall process should be such that makes it easy for it to be now look like single unit knowledge in the working memory so as not to overwhelm its capacity to receive further instruction. This

---

[1] Michael H. Schvartz, Teaching Law by Design: How Learning Theory and Instructional Design Cam Inform and Reform Law Teaching (2001) 38 *San Diego L. Rev.* 347.
[2] Smith & Ragan

can be achieved by having the students restructure prior knowledge into new structures that help them to identify and distinguish similar classes of problem. For example, after studying unjust factors which trigger the remedy of restitution, such as claims for money had and received, duress, mistake, failure of consideration, the interpretive aspects of restitution by subtraction can be studied together to provide the students with necessary knowledge of the organizing thread of restitution founded on principle of reversal of unjust enrichment or unjust benefits. This sort of review of prior knowledge is different from a superficial reference by the teacher to just previous class discussion from a prior class. Rather what is required in the recall process is a much more structured event which seeks to pick the students memory on weeks of prior learning, causing them to review all prerequisite information on the course not just the prior week learning. This way students can assess particular concept patterns that run through the course and can come to appreciate the big picture, and thus acquire skills of legal analysis.

Next is the processing of information and examples event. Two basic options are open to the teacher on how the new instructional material would be presented. She may choose the discovery or expository sequence to present the new material.[3] In discovery sequence, the teacher provides examples and non-examples of the concept to be learned and requires the learners to derive the concept at play. For example, if the topic learned is offers in contract, the teacher using the discovery sequence could ask a pattern like this: "teacher presents different types of offers and scenarios for students to identify offer." If the goal of the instruction is procedure outcome or problem-solving outcome to sharpen skills of legal analysis, such as "at the end of the lesson, the students should be able to: state the different types of offers, explain why an invitation to treat is not an offer, discuss the scope of modern e-offers, draft various offers, identify ethical issues in acting for offerors and offereees, the public etc." then the teacher would have the students work on the multiple task identified as lesson outcomes, guiding the class through their effort at offer-spotting.

The process is somewhat different in the expository sequence. In the expository sequence, the teacher presents the principles governing the topic, defines the various concepts related to the topic, then presents examples and non-examples, and demonstrates the use of the procedure or concept definition to the topic. A typical example of expository processing of information using our offer topic in contract could look like this: "*Activities in Class*: teacher's overview on principles on offer, types of offer, differences between an offer and an invitation to treat, validity test for an offer, electronic advertisement and offers, counter-offer,

---

[3] Smith & Ragan at 117, cited in 412

ethical issues involved in an offer etc. (55 minutes); teacher presents different types of offers and scenarios for students to identify offer (30 minutes); teacher gives an overview of the philosophy in case-law and students present their opinion on offer using Case Study No. 1 (40 minutes)."

The American Socratic teaching technique formulated by Langdell more closely resembles discovery sequence, while the lecture mode resembles the expository technique if student-centred.[4]

The third event is focusing attention. It involves getting students to interrogate the critical features of the principle related to the topic, such as its fundamental elements which trigger the application of the procedure or grounds legal liability. For example, if the class topic in criminal law is stealing, a property offence, the teacher would have to draw attention to the elements of stealing founded in either fraudulent taking or fraudulent conversion of a thing capable of being stolen.

Thereafter the focus would shifts to employing learning strategies. This could involve all or any of following strategies for remembering: helping the students generate alternative ways of representing the information, such as by creating outline, graphic imaging, analogy or mnemonic; supplying students with additional examples; rehearsal; monitoring or teaching students to self-monitor their learning.

Practice/performance and feedback is last event of the body of instruction. While some teachers are of the view that performance and feedback are designed to test for grades, that should not be the purpose. Rather performance and feedback are designed to help the learner perform competently, to develop competent skills.[5]

Thus, performance and feedback in a lesson plan (on activities in class) on say offer in contract should look like this: "students present three applications on counter-offer, invitation to treat, draw up an offer to all the world (20 minutes); short quizzes are given to students on likely issues of ethics and discussions follow on the morality of promise in law (40 minutes). *General Assessment and Debrief:* questions and answers (15 minutes)."

---

[4] One justified criticism of the Langdell's Socratic case-method technique is that while it relies heavily on students' ability to read and understand cases, most bluebook essay law school exams do not test case reading skills at all, thus creating a disjunction between the use of the discovery approach and the American law professors' instructional goals.

[5] See generally discussion on assessment and examinations, chapters respectively.

Conclusion

The goal of conclusion section in the lesson plan is to consolidate students' learning. It therefore consists of three events: the summary and review, the transfer of learning, and the re-motivate and close.[6]

Summary and review is important in ingraining new learning to the memory of the learner. It is very likely that the conclusion is often remembered the longest. It should therefore say something that moves the learner to take action on what is learned. That being so, it should directly relate to the things learned.

Transfer of learning involves the application of learning to new context relatively similar to the contexts in which the learner learned the information. For example, transfer enables the learner in transactional subjects to transfer principles of law from cases and legislation into drafting with new legal implication.

Finally, re-motivate and close event enables the students to explore how the information can be used in future either in connection with exam or practice by linking the information to other issues.

Sample Lesson Plan

A model lesson plan for teaching say offer in the law of contract can follow a simple design like this:[7]

Content

Types of offer, differences between an offer and an invitation to treat, validity test for an offer, electronic advertisement and offers, counter-offer, ethical issues involved in an offer etc.

Outcomes/Instructional Objective

At the end of the lesson, the students should be able to: state the different types of offers, explain why an invitation to treat is not an offer, discuss the scope of modern e-offers, draft various offers, identify ethical issues in acting for offerors and offereees, the public etc.

Overview of Lesson

To develop the skills and underlying knowledge required to deploy the skill, we will begin by reviewing the ideas you already know that are relevant to your understanding of offer. We will refer to the two hypotheticals in Case Study No. 1 and 2 to learn why the first is an illusory offer and the second is not. In the course of the discussion of the two hypotheticals, you will be introduced to the rules used

---

[6] Smith & Ragan at 120, cited in 418
[7] Michael H. Schvartz, Teaching Law by Design: How Learning Theory and Instructional Design Cam Inform and Reform Law Teaching (2001) 38 *San Diego L. Rev.* 347 at 439.

by the courts to determine whether an offer is conditional or unconditional and to see how this shades into the principle of acceptance. We shall then look at six matched sets of examples and non-examples, using the analysed rules to identify why certain offers stated in our hypotheticals are examples or non-examples.

Note, to prepare for the classroom portion of the lesson, you will read and respond in writing through the course webpage to specific questions regarding four short court opinions. It would be helpful to prepare your own paraphrase of the rules and to develop a flowchart or mnemonic device (in accordance with our last discussion on self-encoding of information) to help you encode the rules.

Also, you will be required to analysis, in writing, whether the attached list of undertaking or promise made by the (supposed) offeree are made with the intention to bind on the other party making it as soon as it is accepted.

To prepare for class discussion of the hypotheticals, consider what questions you have regarding the topic, and then identify the broad and narrow sets of recurring facts patterns in which offer cases arise.

As part of class activity, we will begin with a review of the rules on offer, your paraphrase of the rules, your flowcharts and mnemonics, and then we shall discuss the four cases, focusing on the courts' reasoning. Thereafter, you will exchange your answers to the problem set, and the class will discuss the two hypotheticals.

It is after this that we shall break into small groups to develop our examples and non-examples of offers, each group reporting on their work. The class will then discuss and review the critical attributes that make an offer binding, and if possible attempt to rewrite some of the promises deemed illusory to make them non-illusory.

After class, on your own time, you will take a quiz. Those who do not score at least eighty percent will be expected to review these materials, read the suggested hornbook section and their lecture notes, and then explain why their incorrect answers were incorrect and why the correct answers are correct.

Activities Before Class
Students are required to read *Carlil* v. *Carbolic Smoke Ball Co* [1893] 1 QB 256; *Akinyemi* v. *Odu'a Investment* [2012] 1 SC (pt. IV) 1, (2012) 17 NWLR (pt. 1329) 290; PS Atiyah, *An Introduction to the Law of Contract* 44 (3d ed. 1981); Itse Sagay, *Nigerian Law of Contract*, Ibadan: Spectrum Books, 2009, 8-58, prepare a list of counter-offers, prepare list of likely issues of values that may arise from the subject of offer etc.

Activities in Class
Teacher's overview on principles on offer, types of offer, differences between an offer and an invitation to treat, validity test for an offer, electronic advertisement

and offers, counter-offer, ethical issues involved in an offer etc. (55 minutes); teacher presents different types of offers and scenarios for students to identify offer (30 minutes); teacher gives an overview of the philosophy in case-law and students present their opinion on offer using Case Study No. 1 (40 minutes); intermission of 15 minutes for break; students present three applications on counter-offer, invitation to treat, draw up an offer to all the world (20 minutes); short quizzes are given to students on likely issues of ethics and discussions follow on the morality of promise in law (40 minutes).

General Assessment and Debrief
Questions and answers (15 minutes).

Questions
State your answer in the space provided below before reading on.
Why are courts concerned about the illusory nature of offer and acceptance? ------
----

How does this concern tie with the nature of promise in law? ----------------------
----

Why is the promise in hypothetical Case No.1 illusory? ----------------------------
----

Why is it non-illusory in Case No. 2? ---

In your view is there real fundamental differences in the promise in Case No. 1 from Case No. 2? ---
----

If so, state why? ---

Case Analysis of *Carlill* v. *Carbolic Smoke Ball Co*
Write out your answers to the following questions.
What did the plaintiff promise? -------------------------------------
What did the defendant promise? --------------------
Does an understanding of modern contracts as agreements fit easily in a unilateral contract case, as where A promises to do something if B does something else? -----
----

Should the performance by B of the condition be sufficient to bind A? ------------
----

How is the bilateral offer in the case similar and different from one for advertisement? ---------

Are adverts intended for further bargain and so illusory offers? --------------------
---

If so, why is it different from Carlill's case? ----------------------------
Does the fact that the defendant stated that they have had deposited 1,000 Pounds with their bankers for anyone who uses a carbolic smoke ball made by them and then catches influenza, change the nature of the promise from an illusory to a non-illusory offer? --
Does this make common sense? ----------------------------
Would the Carlill holding be applicable to advertisement for rewards for return of lost or stolen property or for information leading to capture of criminals? ---------
----
What if the information is given by several persons in succession, would one only or all of them be entitled to reward? ------------------------
Should this also depend on the construction of the promise or the conduct of the parties? --------------
What of a case where the person who knows of the offer does the act required for acceptance with some motive other than that of accepting the offer? ---------------
----
In Carlill, the predominate motive of the plaintiff in using the product was to avoid catching influenza, so should it not matter to the success of the claim? ------
----
If an offer requires acceptance to bind, is the requirement satisfied by performance of the required act or abstention without any previous intimation of acceptance? --------------
In deciding contractual intention, is the operating test objective or subjective? ----
----
What is the difference, if any, between the Carlill case and "mere puff" statement inducing contract? -----------------------------
How does unilateral offers shade into the concept of consideration? ---------------
----
Should performance rendered by the promisee by legal consideration? ------------
----
What if any, is the difference between consideration (as in the case of performance rendered by the promisee) and condition for consideration? ----------------------
--
In Carlill, was the consideration furnished by the plaintiff using the product? -----
----
Was the condition for entitlement "catching influenza"? ----------------------------
---
How do both relate to ground legal remedy?

What ethical issues are here interrogated? ------------------------------

Paraphrase or Flowchart or Mnemonic
Please paraphrase the rules of law you have learned regarding offer in the space provide below.

Please read and reread the cases and materials regarding flowcharts and mnemonic. Attach your flowchart for offer to this page or describe your mnemonic device you have created to enhance your learning of the doctrine of offer.

Questions on Offer
In the space provided below, please write down the questions you have about illusory and non-illusory offers. --
----

List of Recurring Illusory and Non-Illusory Fact Patterns
In the space provided below, list the recurring illusory and non-illusory fact patterns you have observed from reading case-law. --------------------------------
----

Case Study No. 1
Case Study No. 2

LESSON PLAN FOR GENERAL COURSE USING LAW OF RESTITUTION

Teacher: Festus Emiri
Email: festus.emiri@dfandco.com.ng
Venue: Classroom 1
Time: As per time-table

Overview and purpose
Law of Restitution is an elective course in the final year of LLB. Restitution is a part of the law of obligations (like the Law of Contract and the Law of Torts). The course should prepare you to understand much of what has been described as Quasi-Contract. This course commences by examining the historical development, revealing why its explicit recognition as the third category of

obligations remained obscure until recently. Importantly, it examines why every civilized system of law must provide remedies for cases of unjust enrichment or unjust benefit. Thus, the course combines both the theory of the law of obligations and the concept of gain-based recovery and loss-based recovery. This structure attempts to speak to the three divisions of restitution, restitution for the reversal of unjust enrichment, restitution for the reversal of gains from acquisitive wrongs, and restitution for the vindication of proprietary rights.

For 2017, I have chosen the theme 'towards an explicit recognition of restitution' since we are on the precipice of interesting times in our private law jurisprudence in Nigeria, suffering from palpable, preventable errors, that can be simply corrected by an explicit remedy for reversing unjust benefit or enrichment. The first three weeks of the course will be reserved for the discussion of this important aspect. I believe that – as students – you have much to offer to the legal profession in making a real difference as to how the law of obligations should be shaped in Nigeria to explicitly recognize like all civilized systems of law have done, the rightful place of restitution in our private law jurisprudence. I hope you find the course both interesting and fulfilling. Most importantly, I hope that you are able to implement some of the principles learnt into your professional practice to shape new ways of thinking about law, especially obligations related remedies.

Assumptions of prior learning
In order to successfully complete this course, students should:

. be grounded in equity and trust, especially the resulting and constructive trust concepts

. be capable of communicating competently in written and spoken English

. be capable of critically analyzing and extracting relevant legal information from case   law, legislation and other source materials

. be aware of the influence of contract and tort principles on source material

. be capable of independent learning and use of technology in learning.

Outcomes
In addition to those outcomes included under the overview and purpose above:
Knowledge Outcomes: It is intended that students know and understand:

• Why Restitution Law took so long a time to be recognized in Anglo-American jurisprudence.

- The three main heads of Restitution Law.

- The sources of legal ethical rules.

- The kinds of ethical dilemmas which are presented in gain-based and loss-based recoveries.

- Some of the fundamental rules and principles of Restitution Law.

- Typical restitution professional scenarios. [SEP]

Skills Outcomes: It is intended that students should be able to:
- Debate current unjust benefit or enrichment issues and think critically about existing remedial regimes and practices which provide limited relief. [SEP]

- Apply restitution rules to practical scenarios. [SEP]

- Research and write an essay on a restatement or civil code for restitution for the country. [SEP]

- Present the results of the above essay to the class, and in so doing demonstrate presentation skills. [SEP]

Values Outcomes: It is intended that students should be able to:
Reflected under 'Overview and Purpose' heading above.

Teaching Method

This elective course for the LLB degree is taught in two semesters by Prof. O. F. Emiri and runs for 25 weeks. The course will take the form of a seminar on a Tuesday afternoon (1.00 am-12.30 pm). The course is divided into 5 sections which will be covered in the two semesters in the form of *vive voce* lectures, seminar discussions, role play, simulation, clinic, and presentations by students.

Students are expected to read ahead of the next lecture so that they may participate in the lecture and consider practical scenarios either individually or in groups. There is no comprehensive handout for the course and as such, students are expected to take their own notes during lectures and to supplement these with readings provided in the course outline. Students are expected to assume responsibility for their own learning by independent study according to guidance provided by the reading list. Throughout the course and in test and exam evaluation, problem-solving scenarios will be put before students on a regular basis.

In line with the 2017 theme of 'towards an explicit recognition of restitution,' students are required to write up and present a research project on why Nigeria should recognize restitution as a fundamental category of law of obligations. You will also be required to draw up a restatement or code for restitution, using the American model of Restitution Restatement or the Dutch Civil Code, justifying their preference and how the this can positively impact legal development in the country. The writing up of this project must be completed in the second semester of the course. Details of the content and structure of the research project is contained in appendix III. Presentation of the project will take place in weeks 20-21 of the course.

Students are referred to the Faculty's Brochure on registration requirements for attendance of lectures. Students are welcome to discuss problems with the teacher.

Course content:
. A Development and contemporary issues on Restitution Law.
. B Restitution for the reversal of unjust enrichment.
. C Restitution for wrongs.
. D Restitution for vindication of proprietary rights.
. E Restitutionary defence

Source reference
You need not purchase any book(s) for this course. Useful material will be made available for you to read on short loan from the library and other materials will be available in the course webpage.

Unfortunately, there is very little written in Nigeria on the subject apart from the few learned articles on quasi-contract you will find to read in Journal of Legal Science, published by the Centre for Legal Science, DF LLP, Lagos.

However, the following international and local texts may be useful:

George Palmer, *The Law of Restitution*, Toronto, 1978.

Peter Birks, *An Introduction to the Law of Restitution*, Oxford: Clarendon Press, 1985.

Robert Goff & Gareth Jones, *The Law of Restitution*, 5th ed. 1998.

Andrew Burrows, *Understanding the Law of Obligations: Essays in Contract, Tort and Restitution*, 1998.

Graham Virgo, *The Principles of the Law of Restitution*, Oxford: Clarendon Press, 1998.

Festus Emiri, *The Law of Restitution in Nigeria*, Lagos: Malthouse Press, 2015.

You are advised to consult the *Restitution Law Journal*. Other required readings not listed above are accessible through Hein-on-Line or the course teacher will make his private copies available.

Student assessment

The final mark for the course is comprised of the following components:

- Class work: out of 40 marks
- Examination: out of 60marks
- Total: 100 marks

Class work

In a semester, students are assessed for the class work component on the basis of four pieces of work (assignment, presentation and test). The assignment and presentation will count 20% (10% for each part) and the two tests will count 20% (10% for each test) of the final class mark.

Please note that no late assignments or failure to present assignment on the due date will be accepted for purposes of the class mark. Late assignments or late presentations will receive 0% unless the student has a valid leave of absence.

The test (date to be announced) may contain:

- Hypothetical problem questions which require the application of theory, skills and values law to solve practical issues;
- Case notes;
- Theory-type questions, in which students are required to describe, explain and critically evaluate the current law.
- Multiple choice questions
- Note, the failure to complete the class work on time will be considered a failure to perform the work of the class. This may result in the taking away of a student's registration for the course by the Dean or appropriate authority.

Examination

The semester examination for this course will comprise a three-hour examination paper (comprising of 20 MCQ questions and long essay exams) out of 60 marks. The doctrinal component of this course will comprise of +-50 marks while +-10 marks will be allocated to the professional liability component.

General

Note, all assessments and evaluation (examinations) shall be open book. Feel free to bring along any of your book. You may also come in with your class notes. No university library books are not allowed.

All class notices, assignments, inquiries, and many more shall be available via the course webpage, **www.reslaw.edu.ng**. Please interact through the webpage save in exceptional cases where you have a specific query or question not congruent with the technology.

My consultation time is Tuesdays 2.00-5.00 pm. I will be available for you as my priority first-line preference for consultations.

I hope that you will find this an interesting and worthwhile course.

Festus Emiri, 2015.

Restitution Law, 2017

Date	Topic	Source material
Week 1	1. Historical development of restitution 2. Scope and nature; 3. Contemporary issues	*Fibrosa Spolka Akeyjina* v. *Fairbairn, Lawson, Combe Barbour Ltd* [1943] AC 32. *Lipkin Gorman* v. *Karpnale* [1991] AC 548. Peter Birks, Misnomer in Restitution, in W.R. Cornish, et. al. eds. *Restitution: Past, Present and Future*, Oxford: Hart Pub. 1998. Festus Emiri, *Law of Restitution in Nigeria*, Lagos: Malthouse Press, 2015, chapter 1-3.
Week 2	General principles underlying restitution for unjust enrichment	Robert Feenstra, Grotius Doctrine of Unjust Enrichment as a Source of Obligation: Its Origin and Its Influence in Roman-Dutch Law, in Eltjo Schrage, ed. *Unjust Enrichment: The Comparative History of the Law of Restitution*, 1995, 197. S.J. Stoljar, *The Law of Quasi-Contract*, Sydney, 2nd ed. 1989, 9. G.B. Klippert, The Nature of Unjust Enrichment (1980) 30 *U. Toronto L.J.* 356. Beatson, *The Use and Abuse of Unjust*

		Enrichment, Oxford: Clarendon Press, 1998. Sue Arrowsmith, Ineffective Transactions and Unjust Enrichment: A Framework for Analysis (1989) 9 *O.J.L.S.* 121.
Week 3	1.The unjust factors (plaintiff-oriented, defendant-oriented and policy-oriented factors) 2. Ignorance 3. Incapacity 4. Compulsion	Graham Virgo, *The Principles of the Law of Restitution,* Oxford: Clarendon Press, 1998, chapter 7. Illiterate Protection Law, 1994, Lagos State. *Otitoju* v. *Gov. Ondo State* (1994) 4 NWLR (pt. 340) 518. *Westdeutsche Landesbank Girosentrale* v. *Islington BC* [1994] 4 All ER 890. Smith, Contracting Under Pressure: A Theory of Duress (1997) 56 *CLJ* 343.
Week 4	Restitution from public authority	Beatson, Mistake of Law and Ultra Vires Public Authority Receipts (1995) 3 *R.L.R.* 280. *Kleinwort Benson Ltd* v. *Lincoln City Council* [1998] 4 All ER 513.
Week 5	Restitution for mistaken payment	Needham, Mistaken Payments: A New Look at an Old Theme (1979) 12 *U. Brit. Col. L. Rev.* 159.
Week 6	Failure of consideration	*FATB* v. *Basil Ezegbu* (1984) 9 NWLR (pt. 367) 249. *Kleinwort Benson Ltd* v. *Lincoln City Council* [1998] 4 All ER 513. *Westdeutsche Landesbank Girosentrale* v. *Islington BC* [1994] 4 All ER 890. Peter Birks, Failure of Consideration, in Rose, ed. *Consensus Ad Idem,* London, 1999.

		Law Reform Contract Law, 1961, Lagos State. Itse Sagay, *Nigerian Law of Contract,* 2nd ed. Ibadan: Spectrum Books, 2000, 610-613. A.M. Haycroft & D.M. Waksman, Frustration and Restitution [1984] *JBL* 207.
Week 7	1.Exploitation	David Capper, Undue Influence and Unconsciousability: A Rationalization (1998) 114 *LQR* 479. Tiplady, The Limits of Undue Influence (1985) 48 *MLR* 579. Cretney, Mere Puppets, Folly and Imprudence: Undue Influence for the Twenty First Century (1994) 2 *RLR* 3. *Barclays Bank Plc* v. *O'Brien* [1994] 1 AC 180. Festus Emiri, *Law of Restitution in Nigeria,* Lagos: Malthouse Press, 2012, chapter 13.
Week 8	Free acceptance	Andrew Burrows, Free Acceptance and the Law of Restitution (1998) 104 *LQR* 576. Mead, Free Acceptance: Some Further Consideration (1989) 105 *LQR* 460. *Falcke* v. *Scottish Imperial Insurance* (1886) 34 Ch. D. 234.
Week 9	Necessity	Samuel Stoljar, Unjust Enrichment and Unjust Sacrifice (1987) 50 *MLR* 603. Peter Birks, *Negotiorum Gestio* and the Common Law (1971) 24 *CLP* 110. Wade, Restitution for Benefits Conferred Without Request (1966) *Van. L. Rev.*

		1183.
		Falcke v. *Scottish Imperial Insurance* (1886) 34 Ch. D. 234.
Week 10	Resulting trusts	Graham Moffat, *Trust Law,* 2nd ed. London: Butterworths, 1994, 578.
		Festus Emiri & Ayuba Giwa, *Law of Trust in Nigeria,* Lagos: Malthouse Press, 2012, chapter.
		Robert Chambers, *Resulting Trust,* 1997.
		P.J. Millett, Restitution and Constructive Trusts (1998) 114 *LQR* 399.
		Westdeutsche Landesbank Girosentrale v. *Islington BC* [1994] 4 All ER 890.
		FATB v. *Basil Ezegbu* (1984) 9 NWLR (pt. 367) 249.
		Lipkin Gorman v. *Karpnale* [1991] AC 548.
Week 11 & 12	1. Write up of research 2. Student presentation 3. Revision/Final Discussion/Test	Developing Restitution Restatement or Civil Code. *Lipkin Gorman* v. *Karpnale* [1991] AC 548. Dutch Civil Code American Law Institute- Restatement (Third) of Restitution & Unjust Enrichment, 2011.

Second semester

Week 13	General principles governing restitution for wrongs	Peter Birks, Equity, Conscience and Unjust Enrichment (1999) 23 *Mel. U. l. Rev.* I.

		Friedman, Restitution for Wrongs: The Basis of Liability, in W.R. Cornish, et. al. eds. *Restitution: Past, Present and Future*, Oxford: Hart Pub. 1998, 133.
		I.M. Jackman, Restitution for Wrongs (1989) 48 *CLJ* 302.
		A-G v. *Guardian Newspapers Ltd* (No. 2) [1990] 1 AC 109.
		Boardman v. *Phipps* [1967] 2 AC 46.
Week 14	Restitution for torts	Graham Virgo, *The Principles of the Law of Restitution*, Oxford: Clarendon Press, 1998, 477.
		United Australia Ltd v. *Barclays Bank Ltd* [1941]AC 1.
		J. Beatson, The Nature of Waiver of Tort (1979) 17 *U. W. Ont. L. Rev. 1.*
		Sharpe & Waddams, Damages nor Lost Opportunity to Bargain (1982) 2 *OJLS* 290.
Week 15	Restitution for breach of contract	Fuller & Perdue, The Reliance Interest in Contract Damages (1936-37) 46 *Yale L.J.* 52.
		Gareth Jones, The

		Recovery of Benefits Gained from a Breach of Contract (1983) 99 *LQR* 443.Chen-Wishart, Restitutonary Damages for Breach of Contract (1998) 114 *LQR* 363.
		Peter Birks, Restitutionary Damages for Breach of Contract: Snap and the Fusion of Contract Law in Equity (1987) *LMCLQ* 421.
		Tito v. *Waddell* (No.2) 1977] Ch 106.
		Federal Sugar Refining Co v. *United States Sugar Equalization Board* (1920) 268 F. 575 (SDNY)
Week 16	Restitution for equitable wrongs	*Keech* v. *Sandford* (1726) Sel. Cas. Ch. 61.
		Boardman v. *Phipps* [1967] 2 AC 46.
		Tito v. *Waddell* (No.2) 1977] Ch 106.
		Graham Moffat, *Trust Law,* 2nd ed. London: Butterworths, 1994, 578.
		Festus Emiri & Ayuba Giwa, *Law of Trust in Nigeria,* Lagos: Malthouse Press, 2012, chapter 20.
		Robert Chambers, *Resulting Trust,* 1997.
		P.J. Millett, Restitution and Constructive Trusts (1998)

		114 *LQR* 399. J.C. Shepherd, Towards a Unified Concept of Fiduciary Relationship (1981) 97 *LQR* 51. C. Harpum, The Stranger as Constructive Trustee (1986) 102 *LQR* 114. *Westdeutsche Landesbank Girosentrale* v. *Islington BC* [1994] 4 All ER 890. *FATB* v. *Basil Ezegbu* (1984) 9 NWLR (pt. 367) 249. *Lipkin Gorman* v. *Karpnale* [1991] AC 548.
Week 17	Restitution for criminal offences	*A-G* v. *Guardian Newspapers Ltd* (No. 2) [1990] 1 AC 109. Peter Birks, The Proceeds of Mortgage Fraud (1996) 10 *TLJ* 1. T.G. Youdon, Acquisition of Property by Killing (1978) 89 *LQR* 235. Money Laundering Act, 1992.
Week 18	General principles for restitution vindicating proprietary rights	*Lipkin Gorman* v. *Karpnale* [1991] AC 548. *Westdeutsche Landesbank Girosentrale* v. *Islington BC* [1994] 4 All ER 890. *FATB* v. *Basil Ezegbu* (1984) 9 NWLR (pt. 367)

		249.
		Gerald McCormack, Proprietary Claims in the Wake of Westdeutsche ([1997] *JBL* 48.
		P.J. Millett, Restitution and Constructive Trusts (1998) 114 *LQR* 399.
		Goode, *Proprietary Rights and Insolvency in Sales Transactions,* 2nd ed. 1989.
		Williston, The Right to Follow Trust Property When Confused with Other Property (1980) 2 *Harv. L.J.* 29.
		Peter Birks, Property and Unjust Enrichment: Categorical Truths (1997) *N.Z.L. Rev.* 623.
		Grantham, Doctrinal Basis for the Recognition of Proprietary Rights (1996) 11 *OJLS* 574.
Week 19	Restitutionary remedies to vindicate property rights	*Lipkin Gorman* v. *Karpnale* [1991] AC 548.
		Foskett v. *Mckeown* [2000] 2 WLR 1299.
		Virgo, What is the Law of Restitution About? in W.R. Cornish, et. al. eds. *Restitution: Past, Present and Future*, Oxford: Hart Pub. 1998, 314.
		Lord Nichols, Knowing

		Receipt: The Need for a New Landmark in W.R. Cornish, et. al. eds. *Restitution: Past, Present and Future*, Oxford: Hart Pub. 1998, chapter 15.
Week 20	Defences to restitution for the vindication of property rights	*Tinsley* v. *Milligan* [1994] 1 AC 340. William Swaddling, The Role of Illegality in the English Law of Unjust Enrichment [2000] *Oxford U. Comp. L. Forum* 5. Fox, Bona Fide Purchase and the Currency of Money (1996) 55 *CLJ* 547. Graham Virgo, *The Principles of the Law of Restitution*, Oxford: Clarendon Press, 1998, 639.
Week 21	1.General Restitutionary defences and bars 2. Estoppel 3. Change of position	*Woolwich Equitable Building Society* v. *IRC* [1993] AC 70. *Lipkin Gorman* v. *Karpnale* [1991] AC 548. Halson, Rescission for Misrepresentation (1997) 5 *RLR* 89. Andrews, Mistaken Settlement of Disputable Claims [1989] *LMCLQ* 431. Key, Excising Estoppel by Representation as a

		Defence to Restitution (1995) 54 *CLJ* 525.
		Nolan, Change of Position in Anticipation of Enrichment [1995] *LMLQR* 313.
		Peter Birks, Change of Position: The Nature of the Defence and its Relationship to Other Restitutionary Defences in McInnes, ed. *Restitution: Developments in Unjust Enrichment,* Sydney: LBN Info. Serv. 1996, 49.
Week 22	1. Limitation 2. Laches 3. Illegality 4. Incapacity 5. Passing on and mitigation of loss	H.M. McLean, Limitation of Actions in Restitution (1989) 48 *CLJ* 472. Limitation Law, 1974, Lagos State. *Adekeye* v. *Akin-Olugbade* [1987] 6 SC 268. *Tinsley* v. *Milligan* [1994] 1 AC 340. William Swaddling, The Role of Illegality in the English Law of Unjust Enrichment [2000] *Oxford U. Comp. L. Forum* 5. *Woolwich Equitable Building Society* v. *IRC* [1993] AC 70. *Air Canada* v. *British Columbia* (1989) 59 DLR

		(4th) 161. McInnes, Passing On in *The Law of Restitution: A Reconsideration*, Sydney, 1997.
Week 23	Round up/critical analysis	*Lipkin Gorman* v. *Karpnale* [1991] AC 548. R. Zimmermann, *The Law of Obligations: Roman Foundation of the Civilian Tradition*, Cape Town, 1990. Festus Emiri, The Place of Equity in the Modern Law of Restitution: An Exercise in Taxonomy, in E. Chianu, ed. *Legal Principles and Policies-Essays in Honour of Justice Idigbe, JSC,* Benin: U. Benin Press, 2003. S. Hedley, The Taxonomical Approach to Restitution in A. Hudson, ed. *New Perspectives on Property Law, Obligations and Restitution,* Oxford, 2004. R. Sutton, We Just Mislaid It: The Great Project and the Problem of Order in Private Law (2005) 11 *Otago L. Rev.* 97.
Week 24	1.Write up of research 2. Student presentation	Rewrite and Further Development of a Restitution Roadmap for

	3. Revision/Final Discussion/Test	Nigeria, exploring the options of (i) Case development, (ii) Restitution Restatement (iii) a Civil Code.
Week 25	Skills component	
Week 26	Value components	
Week 27		
Week 28		

Hypothetical Case No. 1 (see course webpage)

Hypothetical Case No. 2 (see course webpage)

Hypothetical Case No. 3 (see course webpage)

Hypothetical Case No. 4 (see course webpage)

Assessment Criteria for Research Project (see course webpage)

www.ingramcontent.com/pod-product-compliance
Lightning Source LLC
Chambersburg PA
CBHW061244220326
41599CB00028B/5533